Culture and Creativity in Organizations and Societies

Published by
Adonis & Abbey Publishers Ltd
P. O. Box 43418
London
SE11 4XZ
http://www.adonis-abbey.com
Email: editor@adonis-abbey.com

First Edition, 2010

Copyright 2010 © John Kuada, Olav Jull Sørensen

British Library Cataloguing-in-Publication Data
A catalogue record for this book is available from the British Library

ISBN: 9781906704728 (HB)/9781906704735(PB)

Layout Artist/Technical Editor, Jan B. Mwesigwa

Culture and Creativity in Organizations and Societies

Edited By

John Kuada and Olav Jull Sørensen

Adonis & Abbey
Publishers Ltd

CONTENTS

OTHER BOOKS PUBLISHED BY THE AUTHORS

Kuada, John (2008) International Market Analysis – Theories and Methods (Adonis & Abbey Publishers) 160 pages

Kuada, John (2007) Internationalisation and Economic Growth Strategies in Ghana: A Business Perspective (London, Adonis & Abbey Publishers)

Kuada, John (Ed.) (2005) Internationalisation and Enterprise Development in Ghana (London, Adonis & Abbey Publishers) 324 pages

Kuada, John (Ed.) (2003) Culture and Technological Transformation in the South: Transfer or Local Innovation? (Copenhagen, Samfundslitteratur) 2003, 262 pages

Kuada, John and Olav Jull Sørensen (2000) Internationalisation of Companies from Developing Countries (New York: Haworth International Business Press) 225 pages

Kuada, John (1999) Ghana: Understanding the People and their Culture (Accra, Woeli Publishers) (With Yao Chachah)

Kuada, John (1994) Managerial Behaviour in Ghana and Kenya – A Cultural Perspective (Aalborg, Denmark: Aalborg University Press, 1994) 247 pages

PREFACE

This book is devoted to a great scholar and colleague of many years, Professor Hans Gullestrup from Aalborg University, Denmark. Hans Gullestrup earned his Master's degree in Organization and Sociology of Work from Copenhagen Business School in 1965. He then started his doctoral work at the Department of Organisation, Copenhagen Business School doing research on a project entitled: "Community Development in Western Samoa – Survey of a Project Form and its Implementation". Hans Gullestrup became Professor of Social and Economic Planning at the newly established Aalborg University in 1976. Before joining the university as a faculty member, he played an important role in building a new BSc programme in Business Administration in Aalborg from 1972-1974 (as an affiliate of the Copenhagen Business School).

Since 1976, Hans Gullestrup has worked with great engagement and devotion to develop the pedagogical foundation of Aalborg University. He has taught students at both bachelor and Master degree levels, and was an active researcher who contributed immensely in building a research culture at the new university. He was also active in university administration both as head of department for Development and Planning and Dean of the Faculty of Social Sciences. As a member of the International Business Research Group (now the Centre of International Business), Hans Gullestrup has been instrumental in developing our intercultural management research programme.

Devotion and engagement are the basic prerequisites for becoming a great scholar. Hans Gullestrup has always been and is still devoted and engaged in the development of innovative thinking. A fascination for seeing things from many angles seems to be what drives him. He is not the scholar who takes the easy road in developing the interpretation of a phenomenon. No, he always brings a variety of novel perspectives on board in all discussions, including odd ones. It is this approach to research that enables him to see a phenomenon more clearly. And he enjoys challenging – perhaps the right word is teasing – his colleagues by looking at their research from various perspectives.

There is, however, another aspect of Hans Gullestrup's engagement and devotion. He sides with the "weak ones" in society. Both his research and his long-time membership on the board of the Red Cross shows that he favours a society with equal opportunities, a society that protects the weak ones. Whenever he senses social injustice of any kind, he readily reacts with articles and comments in news papers. Some of the issues also receive his sharp analytical attention in academic articles. His chapter contribution in the present volume is an evidence of his social engagement.

But nobody becomes a great scholar without knowing the tools and having the skills of an eminent researcher. Apart from the adoption of multiple perspectives on a social phenomenon, Hans Gullestrup is a keen observer. Leaving the stories of his observations from his hen-house apart, this skill to observe fits well with his academic interests in culture and this skill has been well developed in his studies of the cultures of Greenland and Samoa, where he spent almost two years.

For Hans Gullestrup, the analysis of culture is a core discipline in our understanding of human society, as it brings together all aspects of life, so widely scattered in multiple scientific disciplines. He combines his observations with reflections on the deeper values underlying all human behaviour and actions. These multiple reflections have been very well presented in his latest book: *Cultural Analysis – towards cross-cultural understanding* published by Aalborg University Press. Statistics and quantitative methods are not Hans Gullestrup's cup of tea – except of cause, when he can challenge the figures and find alternative perspectives to what they measure and mean.

To become a great scholar also requires social capabilities and to engage in dialogues and discourses. Hans Gullestrup finds dialogue and intensive discussions more important than elegant speeches. His discussions with people are always seasoned with his solid Danish humour, inviting smiles, and the sincere wish that the dialogue will lead to progression in thoughts and attitudes. Hans Gullestrup is a good communicator and a very popular as member of dissertation committees where the focus is on constructing dialogue with young scholars.

Personally, I have had the pleasure of working closely with him for almost 25 years. This has been a period rich with new initiatives, devoted work, exciting scientific debates, all in an atmosphere of collaboration, trust, and a good sense of humour. "Fighting" has never been Hans Gullestrup's style. He cherishes the view that science and academic life provides a platform for scholarly debate and can therefore accommodate people with divergent perspectives.

Apart from honouring Hans Gullestrup, this book also marks the 25th anniversary and, therefore, an important era in the history of the Centre of International Business. A big thanks goes to Hans Gullestrup for being part of our group. Fortunately, he is still a great scholar and now professor emeritus with us. We will continue to enjoy his thought-provoking dialogue and sense of humour for many years.

Olav Jull Sørensen
Professor of International Business
Aalborg, Denmark
February, 2010

Chapter 1

CREATIVE LEADERSHIP AND MANAGEMENT: AN OVERVIEW OF THEORIES, CONCEPTS AND PERSPECTIVES

John Kuada

Introduction

"Take the road less taken, as it will lead you to new discoveries", goes a popular saying. Pablo Picasso has been quoted as saying: "I am always doing things I can't do; that's how I get to do them". In a similar vein, jazz pianist Keith Jarrett has been quoted: "I think the fear of failure is why I try things ... if I see that there is some value in something and I'm not sure whether I deserve to attempt it, I want to find out.". All these statements carry useful messages for high achieving business managers who seek to sustain the competitive advantages of their companies through creativity.

Commenting on the quote from the jazz pianist, Barrett (1998) informs that jazz players constitute a group of diverse specialists living in a chaotic, turbulent environment; making fast, irreversible decisions; highly interdependent on one another to interpret equivocal information; dedicated to innovation and the creation of novelty. But jazz bands improvise coherently and maximise social innovation in a coordinated fashion. This is why they nearly succeed each time to produce something new, charting new territories and creating new values. While they do so, they nevertheless have discipline at the heart of these activities.

Most business managers have realized that achieving the desired levels of creativity in their companies is nearly impossible with conventional approaches. There is, therefore, a continuous search for novel approaches to speed up processes of creativity and innovation of individuals and organizations both within and across nations. At societal levels, policy makers have also realized that they cannot solve the challenges that their citizens face in today's world by adopting approaches that create the problems in the first place.

Concepts such as "value innovation", "creative intelligence", and "collective creativity" have now surfaced in the management literature as new strategic orientations. The jazz analogy captures these concepts quite vividly. Just 40 years ago many of the multi-billion dollar industries of today did not exist. Google, Yahoo, Microsoft, Starbuck were not established. What brought them into existence? In simple terms, the answer may be found in the innovative capabilities of groups of individuals. Scholars have been advising organizations (small and large) to develop cultures that allow their employees to engage in creative endeavours individually and jointly – i.e. to think "outside the box, challenging deeply held assumptions, and combining different, often seemingly unrelated, kinds of expertise and knowledge" (Watts, 2004).

The importance of thinking differently and daring to take chances in business has been part of entrepreneurial wisdom since the days of Max Weber, Schumpter and David McClelland. But the strength of this message has been lost to many business managers. Business strategies are most often decided by a small, coherent group of individuals (top management) with the belief that everyone else would efficiently and effectively execute them.

The focus on creativity by business managers in recent years has led to the emergence of a new platform for academic research into how businesses develop creativity-enhancing strategies and how they ought to do so in different cultural contexts. The present volume contributes to the creativity debate in business economics and management by recasting the concept of creativity into a broader societal context and discourses. It brings together the works of scholars from diverse backgrounds and professional interests who share the common ambition of understanding the creativity process in organizations and societies and the implications that they carry for human civilization.

Creativity as a Business Concept

Creativity is generally understood in the business literature simply as an ability to take risks, and ask new questions and thereby generate novel, original and valuable ideas, products and processes that enhance corporate excellence (Sadi and Al-Dubaisi, 2008). In that sense, all humans with normal capacities are able to exhibit at least moderate levels of creativity in their work life. It is also believed that the social environment can influence both the level and the frequency of creative behavior. In addition to this, creativity can be nurtured and developed at both individual and organizational levels (Amabile, 1996).

People, processes, organizational structures and the right cultural orientation must be in place for creativity to occur in organizations. Organizations that have those conditions tend to motivate individual employees to go beyond the call of duty, exerting energy and initiative to the best of their abilities and assume ownership of the value innovation processes in their organizations.

Leadership and Creativity

This understanding forms the bedrock of the papers in this book. It introduces the reader to some of the main factors that influence creativity. The first building block of the book is the concept of leadership as it is applied in management studies. Following Napier and Nilsson (2008) positive leadership behaviours help develop employees' expertise and enhance their intrinsic motivators. Again Amabile *et al.*, (2004:25) shows that through the results of their study "a leader who interacts daily with subordinates may, through certain behaviours directed at those subordinates, influence their daily perceptions, feelings, and performance, ultimately influencing the overall creativity of the work that they do." Similarly, Oke *et al.*, (2009) argue that leaders serve as important means for enhancing innovative behaviours and modifying attitudes that are beneficial to innovative activities. They cited Akio Morita, the late Chairman of Sony Corporation, who challenged the company's R&D unit to develop Betamax, the first successful consumer videocassette recorder, as an example of executive influence on creative talent development in organizations.

The discussions in this volume have therefore been initiated in chapter 2 with Kuada's discussion of leadership qualities that can ensure expatriate success in building creative cultures within foreign subsidiaries. The chapter draws on studies in leadership, intercultural management, creativity and innovation to address these issues. It starts with a discussion of the differences between transactional and transformational leaderships and draws attention to how they relate to creativity and innovation. Leaning on Oke et al., (2009) he argues that transactional leaders tend to think more about specific goals, work skills and knowledge needed to accomplish those goals. Conversely, transformational leaders place greater emphasis upon intellectual capability and creativity by providing the emotional glue that causes employees to excel. In his view, the complex nature of organizations and the environments in which they operate make both styles of leadership indispensable to positive organizational performance. But they serve organisations in fundamentally different ways and are, therefore, not substitutable. For example, whereas transactional leadership is likely to be effective in stable and predictable environments, transformational leadership is more likely to focus on change and actions that challenge the status quo and may, therefore, thrive in a relatively uncertain and unstable environment.

The chapter also discusses the expatriate personality as a factor that moderates the impact of culture on creativity. To him, cultures can be seen as homogenising, differentiating and fragmentary. Employees therefore belong to multiple cultures and this multiplicity poses serious challenges to expatriates that seek to develop creative organizational cultures in subsidiaries located in national cultures with which they are not very familiar. Building on studies in intercultural competence, he advises expatriates to be mindful of the culturally prescribed comfort zones of their local staff and communicates with them in a manner that both respects and challenges their comfort zones.

Creative talents are developed through knowledge generation and dissemination. There is a strong link between learning and creativity. This understanding forms the foundation of chapter 3 in which Kuada and

Sørensen introduce the concept of *culture-in-action* and relate it to learning and creativity in R&D teams. Building on Brown and Duguid (1991) they see knowledge as a *"situated action"*, with learning taking place through peoples' interactions with each other within a context. The main thrust of their argument is that people produce experiences through their day-to-day actions ("practices") and interactions. They then reflect on these experiences and learn through their reflections. They describe this process as *reflection-in-action,* in which people shift attention from doing the action to examining how the action is done. When employees interact, they do so within both organizational and national cultural environments. Culture provides them with a meeting place and rules that guide their interactive behaviours. As they interact they re-define these rules, maintaining some and replacing others with rules that the team members consider appropriate for their task accomplishment and the management of their social lifeworld. That is, new cultural values and norms emerge through the interactive processes. For this to be effective, team leaders must develop good communicative competencies that enable them to function as transformational leaders – providing their followers with inspirational motivation, intellectual stimulation, and individualized consideration (Bass, 1985, 1990; Bass and Avolio, 1989).

Kuada and Serles present the concept of human and organizational energy in chapter 4, building again on the theme of transformational leadership and its impact on creativity. They argue that concepts such as vision, values, service, empowerment, intrinsic transformation, authentic leadership and stewardship of leaders have now surfaced in the management literature. This development is a reflection of the inadequacy of existing models to sufficiently explain the bewildering range of challenges that organizations face today and their, apparent, limited capacity to address them using existing models and guidelines. As people are increasingly searching for meaning from their workplace they are turning to their inner resources to supplement their cognitive capabilities. Some successful leaders tend to believe that they can tap hidden resources of power, allowing them to live in harmony with some greater, more universal purpose or intention in the world (James, 2004). These types of leaders see organizations in terms of networks, relationships and interconnections through which human and organizational energies flow. They see their role as lubricating these relationships and facilitating the energy flows. They do so through listening to the voices of their employees, providing them with emotional support and empowerment – i.e. making them free to take decisions, to develop their potentials and to work creatively with others. These perspectives are consistent with recent perspectives of leadership presented by such management gurus as Stephen Covey (see Covey, 2004).

Chapter 5 revisits the concept of leadership with a focus on transactional leadership and a leaders' use of reward systems to motivate their followers. In this chapter, Andrałojć compares compensation packages, pay structure and pay inequalities in six EU countries. She built her study on theories of motivation at work, drawing distinction between extrinsic motivators, and intrinsic motivators. As she explains, extrinsic motivators are concerned with the external factors affecting employees, such as salary, working conditions, and job security. Intrinsic motivators are factors such as opportunities for creativity, opportunities to use ones' initiative, and employees' perception of meaning in their work. Seen from this perspective, the discussions in chapter 7 deal with extrinsic motivators.

The also chapter examines whether culture impacts the preferred compensation packages of organisations located in the six EU countries. The investigations suggests that the more individualistic a country, the more likely it is that management would vary the pay packages of employees as a motivational instrument. Furthermore, the larger the power distance, the bigger the gap between pay packets of different categories of employees on the organisational hierarchy.

The issue of creativity and communication is taken up by Gram in chapter 8. She examines how a number of Danish companies deal with language and culture on their websites aiming at a cross-cultural audience and invites to reflection on companies' need to localize their websites. She argues that websites are cultural zones like any other behavioural zones in human societies. Although Internet users – both in B2B and B2C contexts – are more used to seeing web communication from various contexts, different cultural values, traditions and communication styles play a role in the effectiveness of web-based advertisements and publicity. It is therefore relevant for website designers to gain substantial cultural insights from their target markets in order to design creative websites that ensure that a company's public relations campaigns are unique and outstanding.

The last three chapters of the book shift the creativity debate from an organizational level to a macro level. This discourse is initiated in chapter 7 by Gullestrup's contribution. He argues that individuals as well as societies make choices all the time. Successful societies appear to be those whose people and leaders choose deliberately and carefully. This means, for the most part, as human beings, we are in control of our actions. However we are also a function of factors which we can learn to control for our purposes. He discusses some of the common characteristics in the European culture and their significance to the social debate in Europe and Denmark. In his view, the European cultural characteristics offer powerful guidelines to politicians and the citizenry as to how Europeans should select the social issues that require research focus and creative solutions. They also impose some limitation on the possible solutions that Europeans seek for the problems that their citizens face. He also offered suggestions for reducing the constraints inherent in the culture and ways in which the social debate in Denmark and the rest of Europe can be broadened.

The moral plane for decisions in organizations does affect creativity. Yet the issue of morality is largely ignored in creativity research. In business organizations, managers are likely to bracket the moralities they hold outside the workplace, doing what is expedient for short term organizational goal attainment. The moral fabrics of their societies appear not to cover their economic calculations and decisions. This awareness has motivated Petersen's contribution in chapter 8. He discusses the moral fabric of society in general. He argues that individuals and groups in any given society seldom perceive and discuss the moral fabrics that constitute the foundations of their social habits, conventions and norms. That is, moral fabrics act as an anchor on attempts to move values beyond certain limits. The chapter provides a penetrating insight into how societies create their unique moral fabrics and the challenges that these unique fabrics face in this increasingly uncertain, dynamic and shrinking globalised world.

Burmester initiates the discussions in chapter 9 by asking the question "Why is China doing so much better than Egypt in its economic development?" The suggestion is that cultural considerations provide some insight into the developmental opportunities, actions and challenges in these two countries, and, by extension, other countries in those two regions of the world. In his view the glaring incompetence of the administrative system in Egypt combine with discrimination against women, and poor quality of education to constrain the country's economic growth. These weaknesses may be traced to the interpretations of Islam endorsed by the religious leaders in the country. On the other hand, China is the shining example for the rest of the developing world. With appropriate policies, good governance, and intense investment in human resources and science and technology, China is well on its way to joining the First World.

Looking Ahead

Put together, the contributions in this book provide insightful and provocative considerations in our enquiry into creativity at individual, organizational and societal levels. The discussions echo thoughts presented via the jazz analogy in the introduction. Let us go back to the jazz musicians while we ponder on the way forward.

Barret (1998) describes the process as follows:

> "Within a split second musicians must project images and goals gleaned from some musical model. Some musicians seem to be deciding which notes to play within shorter time spans. One jazz player describes the process as a subtle interplay between pre-heating, responding, and following an idea ... Others speak of going on automatic pilot while they think of something – repeating a phrase in order to buy time while their imagination wakes up. ....This no doubt, is one characteristic that distinguishes great soloists: how far ahead they are thinking and strategizing about possible phrases, how to shape the contour of their ideas, how and when to resolve harmonic and rhythmic tension. This points to a delicate paradox that musicians face. On the one hand, too much reliance on

learned patterns (habitual or automatic thinking) and/or regulation tends to limit the risk-taking necessary for creative improvisation; on the other hand too much free-will restricts the interplay and coordination of musical ideas."

The quotation above supports the view that creative thinking does not mean an absence of judgement. Rather it requires a disciplined and dynamic flow between imaginative generation of ideas, solutions and actions – and critical evaluation in each of those phases. Napier and Nilsson (2008) suggests that organizational creativity-enhancing strategies include having a cadre of leaders that inspire the right people with the right values and attitudes to do the right things on time within an enabling organizational framework. This is the art of disciplined creativity.

The contributions in this volume also suggest that creativity is a group endeavour in most organizations. Without denying the role of individual contributions, it is important for leaders to strive to increase moments when the creative insight emerges not within single individuals, but rather across the interactions of multiple participants in the process. The contributors have argued strongly that a combination of transformational and transactional leadership styles is important for nurturing creative organizational cultures. The right combinations may vary from one cultural environment to another and also vary with industry types as well as positions of individual organizations in their life cycle. All these considerations create fertile grounds for further research into the link between culture, creativity, leadership and talent development.

References

Amabile, T.M. (1996), Creativity in Context, Westview Press, Boulder, CO.

Amabile, T.M., Schatzel, E.A., Moneta, G.B., and Kramer, S.J. (2004), "Leader behaviors and the work environment for creativity: perceived leader support", *Leadership Quarterly* 15 pp. 5-32

Barrett, Frank, J., (1998) "Creativity and Improvisation in Jazz and Organizations: Implications" Organization Science Vol 9, No.5.

Bass, B.M. (1985). Leadership and Performance beyond Exceptions, New York: Free Press.

Bass, B.M. (1990) "From Transactional to Transformational Leadership: Learning to Share the Vision". *Organizational Dynamics*, Vol. 18 No.3 pp: 19-31.

Bass, B.M., and Avolio, B.J. (1989) "Potential biases in leadership measures: How prototypes, leniency, and general satisfaction relate to ratings and rankings of transformational and transactional leadership constructs" *Educational and Psychological Measurement*, Vol. 49 No.3 pp: 509-526.

Brown, John Seely, Duguid, Paul (1991) "Organizational learning and communities-of-practice: Toward a unified view of working, learning and innovation" http://www2.parc.com/ops/members/brown/papers/org learning.html. Sourced on 31-10-2003.

Covey, Stephen (2004) *The Eighth Habit – From Effectiveness to Greatness* (London, A viacom company)

James, Rick (2004) Reflections on current thinking on spirituality in organisations" Svenska missionsrådets skriftserie No. 1

House, R.J. (1977). "A theory of charismatic leadership". in Hunt, J.G. and Larson, L.L. (Eds.). *Leadership: The cutting edge*, Carbondale: Southern Illinois University Press.

Napier, Nancy K. and Nilsson, Mikael (2008) *The Creative Discipline-Mastering the Art and Science of Innovation* (Praeger, Westport Connecticut)

Oke, Adegoke, Munshi, Natasha and Walumba, Fred O., (2009) "The Influence of Leadership on Innovation Processes and Activities" *Organizational Dynamics*, Vol. 38, No. 1, Pp. 64-72

Sadi, Muhammad Asad and Al-Dubaisi, Ali H. (2008) "Barriers to organizational creativity: The marketing executives' perspective in Saudi Arabia" *Journal of Management Development* Vol. 27 Iss. 6 pp: 574-599

Watts, Duncan (2004) "Decentralized Intelligence"Originally posted on the Slate website on Aug. 5, 2004 Available at: http://www.leader-values. com/Content/detail.asp?ContentDetailID=952. Sourced on April 20, 2009

Chapter 2

CREATIVITY AND LEADERSHIP IN A CROSS-CULTURAL CONTEXT: THE ROLE OF EXPATRIATES

John Kuada

Introduction

One of the recent developments in international business management has been the establishment of new knowledge and innovative centres outside the developed countries to help companies to speed up the pace of their new product development. Expatriates are frequently sent out to manage these knowledge centres with the mandate to recruit and nurture the creative talents of the local staff. This development has brought the challenges of cross-cultural leadership again to the fore of international business management. Scholars such as Harvey and Novicevic (2002) argue that the complexity and dynamism of global business environments today mean that successful expatriates must possess multiple competencies that are both relational and functional in nature. Finding the combination of leadership qualities that improve expatriate performance in different cultural contexts has therefore become an eminent challenge for scholars and practitioners.

The questions that researchers have been concerned with include the following:

1. What leadership qualities can ensure expatriate success in building creative cultures within foreign subsidiaries (Oke *et al.*, 2009)?
2. What are the cultural challenges in undertaking such assignments and how can expatriates prepare themselves to meet these challenges (Andriopoulos, 2001)?

Addressing these issues requires knowledge from three principal fields of management – leadership, intercultural management and creativity studies. The present paper seeks to pull together perspectives in the three areas and to offer some research propositions that can guide future work in expatriation studies.

The paper is structured as follows: This introduction is immediately followed by an overview of leadership theories and a discussion of the link between leadership and creativity. I then introduce the concept of culture, discussing differences between macro and organizational cultures and how the different cultures influence expatriate leadership behaviours. I also discuss expatriate personality as a factor moderating the impact of culture on creativity. The final section of the paper discusses the implications of the existing literature for the development of creative organizational cultures in foreign subsidiaries.

An Overview of Leadership Theories

The first question to guide our discussions is whether one can find universal leadership characteristics that can help build creative cultures in different organizations located in different societies. This requires a quick overview of the leadership literature and a discussion of how leadership impacts creativity.

Bolden and Kirk (2009) group theories of leadership into four main categories; (1) *essentialist theories*, (2) *relational theories*, (3) *critical theories*, and (4) *constructionist theories*. The essentialist theorists rely on objectivist paradigm and seek to identify and define what "leadership" is in universal terms – i.e. focusing on predictable leadership traits and behaviours. Bolden and Kirk cite the works of most leading leadership scholars in management (Blake and Mouton, 1964; Fiedler, 1967; Stogdill, 1974; Hersey and Blanchard, 1977; and Bass, 1985) as examples of this theoretical perspective. Relational theorists on the other hand, argue that leadership resides not within leaders themselves but in their relationship with others. These theorists therefore call for recognition of the emergent nature of leadership processes and the distributed nature of expertise and influence. Critical theorists focus their attention on the underlying dynamics of power and politics within organizations and therefore emphasise the social and psychological processes that characterise the performance of leadership functions in organizations. Finally the constructionist theorists draw attention to the manner in which the notion of 'leadership' is utilized to construct shared meanings that enable people to make sense of their predicaments. This perspective relies on the works of such scholars as Weick (1995) to analyse leadership in organizations with a sensemaking conceptualization.

It is evident from this brief presentation that the ontological and epistemological positions of scholars inform their understanding and application of leadership theories. Together, the studies have greatly enhanced academic and practitioner understandings of leadership during the last century. But although the categorizations are highly useful in academic studies, they are admittedly simplistic and one can observe substantial areas of overlap between them in practice.

Since my concern in this paper is to explore the extent to which the management literature can inform our understanding of leadership challenges in managing creative businesses in foreign countries, I will rely largely on the managerial theoretical perspectives that fall under the first category of theories identified by Bolden and Kirk (2009) as essentialist theories. I will however be guided in the discussions by my awareness of the substantial overlap between the four theoretical positions.

Trait Theories

One of the influential leadership theories of the 1920s and 1930s was the *trait theory* which posits that successful leaders adopt a combination of such key physical attributes as energetic, tall, and handsomeness with such personality traits as drive, desire to lead, integrity, self-confidence, intelligence, adaptability, assertiveness and emotional stability to mould their leadership behaviours. Social characteristics such as being educated at the "right" schools and being socially prominent or upwardly mobile feature also prominently on the list of traits that successful leaders are expected to possess (Nahavandi, 2009; Yukl, 2010). Some proponents of this theory actually believed that people were born with these leadership attributes, and as such leadership talents cannot be acquired through training. Extensive empirical studies have, however, failed to establish the generalizability of these traits. The traits theory came into quick competition with a wide range of other leadership theories during the mid 1950s.

Situational/Contingency Theories

One of the competing theories at that time was the situational (or contingency) leadership theory, with roots in studies by (Fiedler, 1967), as well as Hershey and Blanchard (1969, 1977). The main thrust of these studies is that there is no one best way to influence people – i.e. different situations call for different types of leadership orientation and action. Scholars subscribing to the contingency theory placed the dominant leadership behaviours on a continuum with task-centred behaviour at one end and employee (relationship) centred behaviour at the other end. *Task-centred leaders* consider it their responsibility to supervise their subordinates closely – telling them what to do, how, when, and where to do what should be done. They were also very much concerned with what was described as generic leadership functions, including planning, and organizing. *Relationship-centred leaders* were expected to address the social and emotional needs of their peers and subordinates with emphasis on recognition, work satisfaction and self-esteem. These two dimensions were also described in the literature by such terms as effectiveness and efficiency (Barnard, 1938), goal achievement and group maintenance (Cartwright and Zander, 1960), instrumental and expressive needs (Etzioni, 1961), and system- or person-oriented behaviours (Stogdill, 1963).

Contingency scholars maintained, however, that the extent to which a leader is task-centred or employee (relationship) centred in his behaviour would depend on the nature of the task, the degree of urgency with which the task was to be completed and the level of maturity of the employees carrying out the task. Maturity is defined in this context as the willingness and ability of a person to take responsibility for directing his or her own behaviour. People tend to have varying degrees of maturity, depending on the specific task, function, or objectives that are to be fulfilled.

Transactional and Transformational Leadership

The task and relationship perspectives of leadership have evolved in the 1980s into two new perspectives – transactional and transformational perspectives of leadership. *Transactional leadership* focuses on exchanges of favours that occur between leaders and followers and on reward or punishment for good or poor performance. Fiedler's path-goal model (Fiedler, 1967) is an earlier development of the transactional leadership perspective. He argued that leaders motivate their subordinates in the direction of established goals by clarifying the role and task requirements and by dispensing rewards and punishments as appropriate. The model takes its roots in the *expectancy theory* which holds that an individual employee's motivation to achieve success is a product of the individual's perceived probability of success and the incentive value (reward) of that success (Atkinson, 1957). Similarly, his motivation to avoid failure would be a product of perceived probability of failure and the negative incentive value (punishment) of failure. A manager can therefore present rewards as *goals* which his subordinates should aim at. He then specifies what subordinates should do (i.e. show the *path*) to earn the rewards. Rewards can take the form of increased pay and/or promotion with increased productivity or training being the presented path. This implies that task-centred managers would simply present company policies on pay and promotion to their subordinates with the understanding that employees will take the required steps to earn them.

In general, transformational leadership involves binding people around a common purpose through self-reinforcing behaviours that followers gain from successfully achieving a task and from a reliance on intrinsic rewards. Following Oke *et al.*, (2009) transformational leaders act as role models and are able to motivate and inspire their followers by identifying new opportunities, providing meaning and challenge, and articulating a strong vision for the future. They are also enthusiastic and optimistic, communicate clear and realistic expectations and demonstrate commitment to shared visions. Subordinates are encouraged by such leaders to share in the organizational vision, seeing deeper purpose in their work and exceeding their own self-interests for the good of the organisation. They also consider the needs of others over their own, are consistent, share risks with others, and conduct themselves ethically. Transformational leaders also provide their followers with individualized consideration – i.e. they focus on followers' individual needs for achievement, development, growth and support. Such leaders also engage in coaching and mentoring, create new learning opportunities and value diversity in their followers. For all these reasons they are admired, respected and trusted by their followers (Nahavandi, 2009).

Complexity and Authentic theories of Leadership

Two other leadership theories have emerged in the 1980s: – complexity theory of leadership and authentic theory of leadership. Complexity theory of leadership focuses on the idea that leadership is part of a dynamic and evolving pattern of behaviours and complex interactions among various organizational players, producing power structures and networks of relationships (Schneider and Somers, 2006). In effect, no single leader can shape the trajectory of organizations; the power of each leader depends on his/her position within the complex network of relationships within the focal organization and ability to distribute resources and emotional support (Ardichvili and Manderscheid, 2008).

Authentic leadership theory draws from both positive psychology and organizational theories. It focuses attention on self-awareness and self-regulated positive behaviours of leaders. Such behaviours encourage openness and employees' desire to share information with each other and with their leaders. A derivative of the authentic leadership is the servant and coach leadership theories. Servant leadership is based on the devolution of power to follower. That is, leaders see themselves as stewards, serving their followers in a manner that allows them to contribute their very best to fulfilling organizational objectives.

In sum, leadership theories have matured through an intellectual journey starting with an emphasis on the unique traits of individuals to an emphasis on the uniqueness of individual employees who must be transformed through serving and coaching in order for their potentials to blossom for the great good of their organizations. Transformational leadership theory – and its derivatives, the complexity and authentic theories – is seen by some as a new leadership paradigm. Leaders must actively engage themselves not only in creating an environment in which employees grow, they must also concern themselves with the inner feelings of the employees and see them as human beings that they are rather than sheer resources whose talents and physical capacities should be exploited by work organizations.

Put together, the overarching conclusion from the existing leadership theories is that there is no universal leadership model for enhancing individual and organizational level creativity in different societies. This awareness has provided legitimacy to intercultural management studies in international business literature during the past three decades and provides a justification of the focus of the present paper – i.e. to provide some insight into the different roles that culture plays in building creative business organisations and how the divergent cultural practices can challenge the leadership behaviour of expatriate managers. To answer this question, we first turn to the existing literature on culture at societal and organizational levels. It is also important to explore the existing literature on expatriate managers' intercultural competencies.

Culture and Behaviour of Expatriate Managers

The increasing internationalization of companies during the last half a century has encouraged the introduction of cultural dimensions into the leadership literature, drawing attention to the cultural consequences of leadership behaviours and practices. But in spite of the vast volume of publications on the subject there are wide divergences in scholars' perspectives on the impact of culture on leadership behaviour in different societies. There are currently two dominant and competing perspectives – the divergence and convergence perspectives. The *divergence perspective* maintains that management concepts and practices are products of specific cultures – i.e. they are culture-bound. That is, as long as nations maintain their cultural identities the development of their organisations and management practices would vary. It is further argued that the greater the cultural distance, the bigger are the differences in the organizational and administrative practices found in them. Employees' expectations and their interpretation of organizational environment will correspondingly be different. Consequently, many of the difficulties associated with cross-border business operations may be traced to differences in culture (Schein, 1994). Major contributors to this perspective include Hofstede (1980), and Trompenaars and Hampden-Turner (1997).

The convergence perspective entered the literature in the late 1970s when a number of scholars argued that global interdependence is producing a convergence of cultures within and across borders (Levitt, 1983). The revolution in information technology, the use of English as an international language, and the decreasing power of national states have been presented as distinctive examples of this convergence (Neghandi, 1978). Even if differences in organisational characteristics and leadership practices do exist at present in some societies, this would rapidly decline (if not disappear completely) in the near future.

Other scholars suggest that convergence and divergence of cultures and management practices are occurring simultaneously between national and regional cultures throughout the world and must therefore not be seen as alternative routes to effective management in international business. Leaders must instead pay attention to the duality of these processes, noting areas in which management practices converge and areas in which they diverge and tailor their behaviours accordingly. The next section of the paper draws attention to the central perspectives in the cultural debate and relates them to the transfer of management practices across borders.

Perspectives on Macro Cultures

One of the dominant strands of cultural research subscribe to the view that culture represents the shared values and norms that bind members of a society or organization together as a homogenous entity (Roberts, 1970).

Culture therefore sustains and reproduces social relations. It is also instrumental in the transformation of these relations through history. Viewed from this perspective, the cultural contexts of individuals' behaviour can be construed to be homogenizing. Chaharbaghi and Cripps, (2007) argue that homogenizing cultures tend to isolate and often punish or even demonise individuals that have the potential to break free from the mould and think differently. Failures are not cheered but rather jeered at in such cultures. Given the risk factor involved in being creative within such contexts, individuals have to make a choice about the level of risk they are prepared to undertake at any given point in time.

Another strand of cultural studies subscribe to the view that culture can differentiate one group of people from another (Sackmann, 1992, 1997). The fact that the members of a given group share a common frame of understanding and interpretation (i.e. culturally prescribed mental models) means that they perceive themselves as different from other groups of people. The sense of belongingness generated by the commonalities of behaviour and perception is jealously guarded and can be a source of conflict during inter-group interactions (Martin, 1992).

This understanding derives from theories of social identity, which are based on studies of inter-group relations in social psychology. The core concept in the social identity theory is ethnocentrism, which embraces both positive feelings towards one's own group (the in-group) and negative feelings towards outsiders (the out-group). The foundational argument here is that cultural groups normally engage in mutual stereotyping, reflecting real, noticed but simplistic observations of each other's behaviour or hearsays from others.

A third perspective challenges both the homogenizing and differentiating notions of culture. It argues that cultures are complex, pluralistic, diverse, fragmentary, and some times paradoxical (Sackmann, 1997; Gullestrup, 2006). That is, individuals are better seen as having fragmented, fluctuating self-concepts derived from multiplex of cultures. Viewed from this perspective culture may be considered a metaphor that makes sense of this complexity.

This perspective has encouraged Kuada and Gullestrup (2000) to argue that enculturation processes introduce individuals to a wide variety of cultures. As such, individuals do not consistently identify themselves with any one dominant culture. Each given situation activates a set of cultural properties that fit the situation. Since individuals have different role identities in the various situations, their behaviours are accordingly fluid and context specific.

Perspectives on Organisational Culture

The understandings of cultures presented above have also guided studies in organisational culture and management. In management, the concept of culture is generally used as a metaphor for understanding how organizations differ and how their members cohere and interact. One of the most cited definitions of organizational culture is that offered by Schein (1984:3) which presents organizational culture as "the pattern of basic assumptions that a given group has invented, discovered or developed in learning to cope with its problems of external adaptation and internal integration which have worked well enough to be considered valid, and therefore, to be taught to new members as the correct way to perceive, think and feel in relation to those problems".

Organisations may be viewed as sub-cultures of the surrounding society's macro-cultures. As such, organisational cultures contain elements of work, hierarchy, class, race, ethnic, and sex-based identifications which can produce a high degree of diversity in and among the individual organisations (Meyerson and Martin, 1987). However, organisations are not exclusively dependent on the surrounding macro-culture when establishing their 'own' cultural values. They tend to create boundaries which in part delineate them from the surrounding macro-culture. This prevents them from losing their own more specific characteristics.

Organizational boundaries however encourage the development of routines and standardized behaviour that, over time, act as competency traps (Levitt and March, 1988), defensive routines (Argyris and Schön, 1978) or rigidities in organizational behaviour and therefore tend to constrain creativity and innovation in organizations (Hacklin, 2009). That is, managers and employees tend to over-exploit what has proved to be successful operational recipes at certain points in their organisations' operational history although such approaches have proved invalid in new operational situations.

The Ethnocentric-Polycentric Dispositions of Organisations

How do organizations manage their relationships with other organizations located within and/or outside their macro cultural domains? The available literature offers a variety of answers to this question. One of the answers takes its point of reference in the ethnocentric-polycentric continuum of organizational dispositions suggested by Heenan and Perlmutter (1979). Ethnocentrism reflects the understanding conveyed in social identity theory. It is a belief in the inherent superiority of ones own group and culture accompanied by a feeling of contempt of other groups and cultures. Polycentrism is the opposite. It describes a group or an individual's belief in terms of values and wisdom in other peoples' accepted ways of behaviour and perception. The two concepts have been applied in management and strategy literature to describe how international companies relate to business partners and affiliates.

To the extent that organisations are seen as products of their society's culture, and are rooted in its deeper patterns, ethnocentric organizations tend

16

to emphasize the superiority of their cultures in their interactions with members from other organisations. In effect, the assumptions that govern the behaviour of the organizational members are very rarely questioned. They therefore inevitably block new learning and cut down on the variety of perspectives brought to bear on management issues – a situation captured in the organizational literature by the concept of "core rigidities" (Leonard – Barton, 1992). Organizations adopting this disposition experience serious difficulties in relating to organizations outside their cultures since they fail to appreciate and accept the different patterns of behaviour that are exhibited in the other cultures.

Polycentric-oriented organisations assume that host-country cultures and organisations have mindsets that are very different from theirs but equally valid in their unique contexts. A polycentric company is, therefore, primarily concerned with legitimacy in every country in which it operates and gives its subsidiaries wider degree of latitude to respond to changes in their environments. Consequently, strategic decisions are tailored to suit the cultures of the various countries. This disposition encourages mutual respect of the opinions emanating from employees at the Headquarters just as those from employees in the various subsidiaries. In relations with other organisations, polycentrism encourages cross-fertilization of new ideas and joint knowledge generation. Furthermore, managers trained in polycentric-oriented organisations would be more willing to adapt to the cultures of their co-partners or host organisations and would be supported by the management of their home organisations to do so. They are also empowered to question norms, values and rules of behaviour in their own organisations.

In-between the ethnocentric-polycentric continuum are wide variations of organisational mindsets. Since organisations are composed of a dynamic and multiplex set of cultures, one should expect certain groups in the organisation to have more or less ethnocentric dispositions at various points in time in the organisation's history. It is also conceivable that the dominant dispositions of organisations (and groups within them) would be context-specific. The farther away they are from the home culture the more or less ethnocentric they may behave.

Personality and Expatriate Behaviour

Various typologies have appeared in the literature over the past four decades to describe the adaptation potentials of individual managers abroad. While some people are described as predominantly conservative, others are seen as flexible and therefore more capable of intercultural adaptation. Going back to the traits theory of leadership introduced briefly above, it may be argued that a person with flexible personality has a wide variety of coping repertoires and exhibits emotional shifts that make him comfortable in bridging cultures (Miller and Toulouse, 1986). He also displays an element of tact in minimising conflict in social relations and therefore relatively free of conflict-induced anxiety. Based on this reasoning, Mendenhall and Oddou (1986) have classified managers in foreign countries in terms of the following three personality orientations.

- Self-Orientation (SO), referring to the degree to which an individual expresses an adaptive concern for self-preservation, self-enjoyment and mental hygiene.
- Others-Orientation (00), referring to the degree to which an individual is concerned about other peoples' well being and desires to affiliate with them.
- Perceptual-Orientation (PO), reflecting an individual's ability to gain rich understanding of other cultures, or to show empathy in general.

The debatable question is how these personality traits influence expatriates' ability to facilitate the development of creative cultures in foreign subsidiaries. Mendenhall and Oddou (1986) suggest that the best results are achieved by the well-adjusted expatriate managers who score high on all the three dimensions – Self-Orientation, Others-Orientation, and Perceptual-Orientation. These three dimensions are the personality traits of a transformational leader. As we noted earlier, these types of leaders are extremely hopeful, optimistic, and resilient. Leaders who are high in hope also have a high degree of confidence in their ability to effect change, devise more and better solutions to work-related problems and to attain organizational goals. They are also able to encourage employees to take risks, transcend the limits of their immediate comfort zones and to pursue innovative and creative activities. Furthermore, hopeful leaders interpret failure differently and seek new pathways to change calamities into opportunities.

Samad (2007) argues that a leader's personality will influence his choice of leadership style. Such attributes as thoughtfulness, originality, imagination, and need for variety will promote transformational leadership style. Further, Peterson *et al.*, (2009) suggest that these attributes also convey the willingness and readiness of leaders to entertain novelty and a sense of divergent and creative thinking. Thus, expatriate leaders who possess these personality types are more likely to be flexible and to understand others' point of views. They are also likely to listen to employees and to empower them to view impediments as opportunities for creativity.

Implications

What are the implications of these discussions for expatriate's efforts to build and manage creative cultures in foreign subsidiaries? Scholars of creativity argue that creative people are celebrated as unique rule-breakers, because they are not like us and neither are they like each other. It is impossible to categorise them as a group or identify particular traits. An expatriate's limited knowledge of the cultural backgrounds of the creative individuals aggravates the difficulties of relating to them or bringing them together and managing them as members of creative teams.

The above discussions suggest that expatriates with transformational leadership styles appear to have the greatest opportunity to succeed in working with such creative individuals. As Gumusluoghu and Ilsev (2009) argue, transformational leaders promote empowerment in local organizations and heighten personal development while taking due cognizance to the local culture within which the subsidiary is located. They also stimulate the intrinsic motivation of the local employees through the articulation of compelling vision and thereby facilitate the establishment of organizational climate where employees feel challenged and energized to seek innovative approaches to their jobs.

Furthermore, the awareness that all cultures are constantly subjected to pressure for change from both internal and external factors (Gullestrup, 2006), provides expatriates with opportunities to facilitate cultural change processes in organizations to which they are posted. But a leader's ability to work with diversity depends on his familiarity with diverse cultural maps of local employees and to see culture as a learned and adaptive response to contextual needs (Collard, 2007). The challenge an expatriate faces is how to facilitate the cultural change that he desires. To do so, expatriates must be reflective learners who can read and respond to the changes they perceive.

Concluding Remarks

I have argued in this paper that the macro cultures within which organisations are embedded greatly influence the organisations' mindset. At the same time the personalities of leaders contribute significantly to the definition of the rules of behaviour that employees endorse in any given organisation. But since individuals belong to multiple set of groups in modern organisations, no single culture could be said to dominate their behaviours. It is the dynamic interactions of individuals in given situations that determine which repertoires of cultural rules they accept as useful guides for their actions. Organizations can therefore be described as "sites of cultural production". These observations carry important implications for expatriate leaders who seek to stimulate the engagement necessary for creativity in foreign subsidiaries. Firstly, expatriates must make deliberate attempts to understand as much as possible the cultural values and motivations that guide behaviours of employees. They should, however, not underestimate the challenge of constructing a bridge between the cultural values that they bring with them from the head office and the values deeply enshrined in the local organizations. Secondly, they must adopt a transformational leadership style in their engagement with the local staff. These types of leaders act as "creativity enhancing forces": paying greater degree of attention to each individual local employee as a person and being mindful about his feelings, goals and determination. They also provide them with recognition and intellectual stimulation and thereby energize them to work towards the organization's vision.

References

Andriopoulos, Constantine (2001) "Determinants of organisational creativity: A literature review" *Management Decision;* 2001; Vol. 39 No.10 pp: 834-842

Ardichvili, Alexandre and Manderscheid, Steven V., (2008) "Emerging Practices in Leadership Development – An Introduction" *Advances in Developing Human Resources* Vol. 10, No. 5 pp: 619-631 Downloaded on April 5, 2009 http://adh.sagepub.com

Argyris, C., and Schön, D., (1978). Organizational Learning: A Theory of Action Perspective. Reading, MA: Addison Wesley.

Atkinson J. W. (1957) "Motivational determinants of risk-taking behaviour" *Psychological Review,* 64 pp: 359 12

Barnard, Chester I. (1938) *The Functions of the Executive* Cambridge, Massachusetts: Harvard University Press.

Bass, B.M. (1985) Leadership and performance beyond expectation New York: Free Press.

Blake, R.; Mouton, J. (1964) *The Managerial Grid: The Key to Leadership Excellence.* Houston: Gulf Publishing Co.

Bolden, Richard and Philip Kirk (2009) "Cultural Perspectives: African Leadership Surfacing New Understandings through Leadership Development" *International Journal of Cross Cultural Management* Vol. 9(1): 69-86 Downloaded on April 24, 2009 from http://ccm.sagepub.com

Cartwright, D., Zander, A. (1960) Group Dynamics: Research and Theory, 2nd ed., Row Peterson, Evanston, IL.

Chaharbaghi, Kazem and Cripps, Sandy (2007) "Collective creativity: wisdom or oxymoron?" Journal of European Industrial Training Vol. 31 No.8 pp: 626-638

Collard, John (2007) "Constructing theory for leadership in intercultural contexts" *Journal of Educational Administration* Vol. 45 No. 6 pp: 740-755

Dorfman, P.W. (2003), "International and cross-cultural leadership research" In: B.J. Punnett and O. Shenkar, (Eds.) Handbook for international management research (2nd ed.), University of Michigan, Ann Arbor, MI

Etzioni, A., (1961) A Comparative Analysis of Complex Organizations on Power, Involvement, and their Correlates (Free Press, New York)

Fiedler, F.E. (1967) *A Theory of Leadership Effectiveness* (New York: McGraw-Hill)

Gullestrup, Hans (2006) *Cultural Analysis – Towards Cross-cultural Understanding* (Denmark, Aalborg University Press and Copenhagen Business School Press)

Gumusluoghu, Lale and Ilsev, Arzu (2009) "Transformational leadership, creativity and organizational innovation" *Journal of Business Research* 62 pp: 461-473

Hacklin, Fredrik, Inganas, Martin, Marxt, Christian and Pluss, Adrian (2009) "Core rigidities in the innovation process: a structured benchmark on knowledge management challenges" *International Journal of Technology Management* Vol. 45 No. 3/4 pp: 244-266

Harvey, Michael and Novicevic Milorad M. (2002) "The hypercompetitive global marketplace: the importance of intuition and creativity in expatriate managers" *Journal of World Business* Vol. 37 Iss. 2 pp: 127-138

Heenan, D.A., and Perlmutter, H. V., (1979) Multinational Organization Development: A Social Architectural Perspective. Reading, MA: Addison-Wesley.

Hersey, P., Blanchard, K.H. (1969), "Lifecycle theory of leadership", *Training and Development Journal*, Vol. 32 No.2, pp.6-34

Hersey, P. and Blanchard, K. H. (1977) *The Management of Organizational Behaviour* 3e, Upper Saddle River N. J.: Prentice Hall.

Hofstede, G. (1980) Culture's Consequences: International Differences in Work-Related Values. (CA Sage Publications, Beverly Hills,)

Kuada, John and Gullestrup, Hans (2000) "Organisationskultur og interkulturel kommunikation i et internationalt perspektiv" in Petersen Helle and Lund, Anne Katrine (Eds.) *Den Kommunikerende Organisation* (Denmark, Samfundslitteratur) pp: 25-58

Leonard – Barton, Dorothy, (1992) "Core Capabilities and Core Rigidities: A Paradox in Managing New Products" *Strategic Management Journal* Vol. 13 pp. 111-125

Levitt, T. (1983) "The globalization of markets" *Harvard Business Review*, Vol. 61 No. 3 pp: 92-102

Levitt, B., March, J.G., (1988) "Organisational Learning" *Annual Review of Sociology*, Vol. 14 pp: 318-340

Martin, Joanne (1992) *Cultures in Organizations: Three Perspectives:* (Oxford, Oxford University Press)

Mendenhall, M. and Oddou (1986) "Acculturation Profiles of Expatriate Managers: Implications for Cross-Cultural Training Programs" *Columbia Journal of World Business* Vol. No. 4 pp 73-79

Meyerson, D., and Martin, J., (1987) "Cultural Change", *Journal of Management Studies* Vol. 24 No. 6 pp 623-47

Miller, Danny and Toulouse, Jean-Marie (1986) "Strategy, Structure and EEO Personality and Performance in Small Organizations", *American Journal of Small Business* Vol. 10 No.3 pp. 47-62

Negandhi, A.R., (1987) *International Management* (Boston, Allyn and Bacon Inc.)

Oke, Adegoke, Munshi, Natasha and Walumba, Fred O., (2009) "The Influence of Leadership on Innovation Processes and Activities" *Organizational Dynamics*, Vol. 38, No. 1, pp. 64-72

Peterson, Suzanne J., Walumbwa, Fred O., Byron, Kristin and Myrowitz, Jason (2009) "CEO Positive Psychological Traits, Transformational Leadership, and Organization "Performance in High-Technology Start-up and Established Organizations" *Journal of Management*, Vol. 35 No. 2, pp: 348-368

Roberts, Karlene H. (1970) "On looking at an elephant: an evaluation of cross-cultural research related to organizations", *Psychological Bulletin*, 74: 327-350.

Samad, Sarminah (2007) "Social Structure Characteristics and Psychological Empowerment: Exploring the Effect of Openness Personality" *Journal of American Academy of Business* Cambridge. Hollywood Vol. 12, Iss. 1; pp: 70-77

Sackmann, Sonja A. (1992) "Culture and subcultures: An analysis of organizational knowledge". Administrative Science Quarterly, 37: 140-161.

Sackmann, Sonja A. (1997) *Cultural Complexity in Organizations* (California Sage Publications, Inc.).

Schein, E. H. (1984): "Coming to a New Awareness of Organizational Culture" *Sloan Management Review*, Vol. 25 No. 2pp: 3-16

Schein, E.H. (1994a): Organizational and Managerial Culture as Facilitator or Inhibitor of Organizational Learning. Organizational and Managerial Culture (available as SoL Working Paper 10.004)

Schein, E.H. (1994b) "Innovative Cultures and Organizations" in Thomas J. Allen, and Scott, Michael S. Morton (Eds.) *Information Technology and the Corporation of the 1990's: Research Studies* (Oxford University Press, New York) pp: 125-146

Stogdill, R. M. (1963) *Manual for the Leader Behavior Description Questionnaire* (Columbus: Ohio State University)

Stogdill, R.M. (1974) Handbook of Leadership: A Survey of Theory and Research. New York: Free Press.

Trompenaars, F and Hampden-Turner, C (1997) *Riding the Waves of Culture* (Nicholas Brealey Publishing, London,)

Weick, K. E. (1995) Sensemaking in organizations (Thousand Oaks, CA: Sage)

Chapter 3

CULTURE-IN-ACTION AND CREATIVE LEARNING IN CROSS-BORDER R&D TEAMS

John Kuada and Olav Jull Sørensen

Introduction

The concept of "creative capability" has emerged as one of the decisive sources of competitive advantage in today's dynamic, knowledge-based economies. The creativity literature has matured from the time when creativity was perceived as rare and novel activities performed by few talented individuals to the current understanding that it is multidimensional and can be just as collective and incremental as it can be individual and rare (Amabile, 1983 and 1996). Some scholars even argue that the creative potentials of organizations tend to be magnified when employees work in concert and approach creativity in a systematic manner (Amabile *et al.*, 2004). Managers are therefore encouraged to build teams of employees with divergent knowledge bases and provide them with internal working conditions that can enhance their joint creative efforts. As Hargadon and Bechky (2006) observe, creative teams look at organizational problems in different ways, making unexpected links among apparently discrepant elements of information, developing new solutions to problems as and when they appear rather than mastering and constantly reapplying standard methods. In their view, organizations must promote creativity in the daily interactions of organizational members and see the process as a learning and knowledge application endeavour of employees.

Cross-border talent identification and development has become a common approach adopted by international firms to enhance the creativity of their employees and to speed up the pace of innovative solutions to their customers. Companies, therefore, design structures that promote links between learning, knowledge management and the development of creative organizational cultures.

Previous studies have indicated that cross-border knowledge management processes through multi-cultural teams encounter two major challenges: (a) the comprehensibility of knowledge embedded in other cultures; (b) the cultural sensitivity which organizations and their managers require to manage the interaction processes (Kuada, 2008). The challenges may include understanding differences and discovering similarities, surfacing differing expectations about leadership styles and modes of working together, as well as creating cross-cultural norms and rules of accepted behaviour.

The aim of the present paper is to explore the joint processes of learning, knowledge management and creativity within multiple cultural contexts. Our focus is on situations in which cross-border R&D teams are purpose-fully formed and mandated to engage in creative undertakings. The paper introduces the concept of "culture-in-action" as a construct that helps schol-ars and practitioners to make sense of the multiple interactive processes of organizations, groups and individuals in cross-border business operations. We argue that action-based creativity is more effectively harnessed when employees are encouraged to exhibit higher degrees of *mindfulness* in their interactions with other employees, as well as stakeholders (customers, suppliers etc.). By being mindful – i.e. paying intense attention to and re-flecting on the details of their interactions – team members build on each other's ideas and experiences cumulatively to produce new insights and take new actions in emerging situations. This is what produces learning and knowledge sharing within and between organizations and units.

We initiate the discussions after this brief introduction with a review of dominant perspectives in the learning and knowledge management litera-ture and articulate our own understanding of how employees learn. The concept of culture is then discussed with a specific focus on the concept of "culture-in-action" and how the culture construct constitutes the context and foundation of learning in cross-border functional engagements. The third component of our framework – creativity – is then introduced and the link between creativity, culture and learning highlighted. Finally, we argue that leadership behaviour plays an important role in coordinating and promot-ing the interactions that happen in teams. We introduce the concept of *3Vs* – Vision, Values and Voices – to underscore the roles of leadership in building and nurturing creative teams.

A Review of the Learning and Knowledge Management Literature

Structure and Process Views of Learning

Two separate streams of research can be identified in the existing learn-ing literature: one is based on *structure* view of knowledge generation and transfer, while the other adopts the *process* view of knowledge. The structure view is predicated on the assumption that knowledge can be seen as a commodity in the sense that there is some universal and absolute truth existing outside the knower. Knowledge can be stocked and accessed by individual knowledge seekers as well as transferred from one unit of a company to another (Spender, 1994). Scholars subscribing to this view lean on metaphors such as drilling, mining, and harvesting to describe how knowledge is managed. The literature further relies on a distinction between codified or explicit knowledge and tacit (implicit) knowledge to explain the difficulties of knowledge management. This classification draws on Po-lanyi's (1966) perspectives on knowledge that sees tacit knowledge as a backdrop against which all human actions are understood. That is, all articulated knowledge is based on an unarticulated and tacitly accepted background of social practices.

But subsequent usage of the term, particularly by scholars such as Nonaka and Takeuchi (1995), tends to see tacit knowledge as knowledge that is difficult to articulate and therefore difficult to transfer and share. Nonaka argues that is because such knowledge is so deeply rooted in action and experiences of individuals as well as in individuals' involvement within a specific context (Nonaka, 1994). Codified knowledge, on the other hand, is more easily articulated, captured, transferred and shared (Kogut and Zander, 1992).

In contrast to the structural perspective on knowledge and learning, the process view builds on the social constructivist perspective in social science which argues that reality (and successful management practices) should be understood as socially constructed. According to this tradition, it is impossible to define knowledge universally; it can only be defined in practice, – i.e. in the activities of and interactions between individuals. Our ability to perceive, interpret and evaluate phenomena is an individual ability, one which is enhanced by the sustained and intensive interactions that we have with other people in a given community or context. Knowledge may, therefore, be viewed as a '*situated action*'. This implies that knowledge and the meaning of words are not independent of context. They lie partly in the context of use, and they shift from one context to another, especially if the contexts are across cultures. Furthermore, these intensive interactions help us to create shared mental models of schemata (Weick, 1979) and enable us to make sense of our environment and to learn.

The social constructivist perspective on learning and knowledge transfer has been popularised in the organisational learning literature by scholars who have studied learning within "communities of practice" (Brown and Duguid 1991, 1996). In general terms, these scholars argue against the implicit distinction between learning and working found in mainstream organisational learning literature. They see working and learning as rather compatible – both being part of the normal flow of organisational life. Building on both Orr (1987) and Lave and Wenger's (1991) research, Brown and Duguid (1991) argue that to understand working and learning, it is necessary to focus on the formation and change of the communities in which work takes place. The argument that knowledge and learning are contextually embedded led these scholars to coin the term "communities of practice" to describe the locus of knowledge stock and learning processes. Community in this regard may refer to members of an organisation or a group that interact on a continuous basis in the execution of an assigned task. Practitioners are immersed in dynamic practices, which are socially, culturally and politically located. Their studies have produced useful insights into how innovative teams in Silicon Valley have generated and shared knowledge through interactions in the course of their daily work processes.

We endorse the "communities of practice" perspective on learning. It ties neatly with the *culture-in-action* construct that we will introduce later in the paper. We hold the view that it is through the day-to-day actions and inter-actions that people learn. The unit of analysis in learning within and be-tween organizations must be their *interactions* and *actions*. But actions themselves do not produce learning. People must reflect on their own ac-tions and the actions of other people. Said differently, it is not the specific actions *per se*, but the ability to reflect on the actions (i.e. interpret the experi-ences) that produces learning at both individual and organizational levels. In order to reflect effectively, employees must mentally "step back" from their actions and consciously observe the actions – thinking them through individually or with others. *Reflection-in-action* requires a certain level of experience that enables the practitioner to shift attention from doing the action to examining how the action is done. An important tool for reflection is dialogue – i.e. articulating and making tacit understanding explicit to self and to others. Building on the discussions above, we submit that employees and their organizations act and purposefully learn from their actions.

Modes of Learning

We have discussed the types of knowledge and the processes of learning in the previous section. This section of the paper provides an overview of specific modes of learning that individuals and organizations adopt to share and/or transfer knowledge between and within organizations. Table 1 provides an overview of six modes of learning spanning a continuum of doing things in practice at one extreme to learning via theoretical studies in formalised settings at the other. In between, we have various degrees of interaction of formal knowledge/theory and practice.

Practical Work: by acting or doing things, employees get experience that they can use to do the things they are employed to do more efficiently and effectively – i.e. with fewer mistakes and/or with a better quality. This approach is usually adopted in manufacturing companies in training skilled and semi-skilled staff members.

On-the-Job-Training: on-the-job training is the most popular mode of transferring knowledge in cross-border inter-organizational relations. This mode may be found highly useful particularly in situations where employ-ees are to be exposed to unfamiliar pieces of technology or instruments required for performing specific tasks. It has a limited relevance in R&D training processes since staff members are expected to be highly skilled and are usually selected on the basis of their expertise. But in some cases junior R&D staff can be trained by asking them to understudy the more experi-enced staff members.

Table 1:   Learning Modes

Learning Mode	Description	General Examples	Relevance for Learning in R&D Teams	Interaction and learning
Practical work	Encourages repeated task performance that results in dexterity and increased productivity.	A factory worker engaged in a routinised production activity.	Not usually adopted in R&D staff development process.	Individuals learn through interaction.
On-the-job training	Entails placing junior employee task performance under the direction and supervision of a more experienced employee.	Useful in training skilled and semi-skilled employees and in transfer of tacit knowledge.	May be considered useful in training R&D staff in the use of new and specialized instruments.	Intensive and personal interaction with the knowledge provider defining the learning frame.
Observing	Focus on learning-by-observation. Requires high level of employee *mindfulness* - i.e. ability to pay attention to details.	Applied in a similar manner as in on-the-job training.	Critical in transfer of knowledge in R&D teams where team members cumulatively build on each other's activities.	Intensive training with knowledge receiver in a relative passive position.
Coaching	Employees are highly proactive in the learning process – using the trainer as a sparring partner.	Useful in management training with senior providing guidance to their junior managers.	Very useful in R&D team learning processes. Each team member may serve as a coach for others.	Knowledge receiver interact with knowledge provider, who may or may not know what is observed.

Table 1: **Learning Modes (continued)**

Learning Mode	Description	General Examples	Relevance for Learning in R&D Teams	Interaction and learning
Problem-based learning	Learning through finding solutions to specific problems. Learners gains new insights through application of existing knowledge.	Typically used when companies form teams or task forces to solve immediate problems.	Mostly relevant for R&D teams. Characterizes the nature of company-based creativity.	Intensive and personal interaction with the knowledge receiver defining the learning frame.
Studying	Formal learning; usually off-the-job. Knowledge presented in books manuals etc.	Typical of university/college level training academies.	Can be used to upgrade knowledge levels of R&D team members in specialized fields.	Intensive and personal interaction among members with a diversity of knowledge.

Observation: the learning impact from observation is less easy to pin down because every astute employee observes things around him continuously and adopts ideas and practices that can enhance his work process. For example, a diligent salesperson would observe competitors' products and sales gimmicks during exhibitions, learn from them and improve his practices elsewhere. By the same token an R&D staff may also observe things from a completely different world or area of competence and through association use what he has observed in his own work practices.

Coaching: while on-the-job-training normally involves the direct transfer of a specific skill, coaching is broader and has a different approach. The knowledge recipient has the lead and can consult the coach whenever needed. The coach, on the other hand, provides guidance on different ways of looking at issues or problems brought to his attention by the learner. His role in the learning process is not that of providing solutions. Those who rely on coaches to learn must have substantial absorptive capacities themselves (Sørensen, 2007).

Studying: studying, in most cases, involves the acquisition of documented or explicit knowledge, often with a certain degree of abstraction. Documented or formal knowledge is not necessarily that it is the truth, but it is consistent and logically rational. From here we use the concept of studying in this paper to imply learning to think in the abstract, logically consistent manner, and to be an expert in a certain field. R&D staff members can be required to study specific subjects in order to broaden and/or deepen their understanding of specific issues of relevance to the organization.

Problem-Based Learning: problem-based learning is a proactive learning mode, where the learner gains knowledge by solving actual problems faced by his company. It may, for example, take the form of an R&D task force challenged with finding a solution to a severe problem. This would normally involve a lot of search work and creative and innovative behaviour leading to discovery of many alternative ways of solving the problem on hand. In the end, the individual employee or task force would come up with a solution to the problem. But along the long road to this solution, numerous alternatives chanced upon would be dropped. These unused ideas become a knowledge stock that the employee could tap into in other situations.

Employees can adopt a combination of these six different modes of learning to acquire their desired knowledge. Their selection of learning modes may depend on the nature of knowledge they seek to acquire, their individual knowledge absorptive capacities, the learning traditions within their organizations and the capacities of the knowledge providers that have been assigned to facilitate their learning. We have also noted that knowledge acquisition may sometimes occur in non-deliberate manner. Individuals may arrive at their new understanding by sheer mindfulness – i.e. alertness and keen observation of things happening around them. The level of dynamism of a learning environment is, therefore, a critical factor in a learning process, particularly so for R&D teams.

The Cultural Factor

We remarked in the introductory section of this paper that culture impacts learning and creativity in business organizations (and, by extension, in all other modern work organizations). We also argued that it is through interactions that employees shape organizational cultures – replacing existing values, norms and rules with those they consider appropriate in their particular operational situations. We believe that the dynamics of cultural change are particularly significant in cross-border R&D units of business organizations. This section of the paper focuses attention on the culture construct. It first reviews three dominant perspectives on culture in the extant literature and relates the discussions to our concept of *culture-in-action*.

Culture as a Homogenizer

The dominant perspective of culture adopted by management scholars is that culture constitutes the social glue that binds members of a society or organization. It is what people share and therefore provides them with a common frame of reference, defining the rules of accepted behaviour. That is, people living within a particular culture have their conduct regulated through a collection of consensual aspirations (i.e. central values) and universal orientations (i.e. patterns of behaviour). This enables them to live their lives with a sense of uniformity and singularity. Viewed from this perspective, culture is a homogenizer and has a powerful influence on the behaviour of people who have been socialized in a given group, organization or community.

At the level of business organisation, scholars of organizational culture argue that organizations function as miniature societies. They are equipped with socialization processes, social norms and structures; they breed meanings, values and beliefs; they nurture legends, myths and stories and are engaged in rites, ritual and ceremonies (Allair and Firsirotu, 1984). Like human beings, organizations are seen as having personality, needs and character. Although organizations do not have brains, they have memories and "cognitive processes" for reflecting on their experiences, learning from them and storing knowledge, just like human beings (Selznick, 1957; Hedberg, 1981). In this sense, employees can be partly perceived as actors with organizational scripts. They become socialized into organizational norms, beliefs, and regulated roles and therefore adopt standardized (taken-for-granted) patterns of action (Schein, 1984). These standardized behaviours (routines) are passed on to new generations long after the rationale underlying them have disappeared from memory and are perhaps no longer valid. This is the organizational culture.

Culture as a Differentiator

The homogenizing perspective of culture competes with the view that different societies, organisations and groups approve of different values, norms and practices. Seen from this perspective, culture is a differentiating phenomenon, drawing a wedge between societies, organizations and groups. This perspective has been popularised in the research works of such scholars as Hofstede, (1980), Redding (1980), Adler (1991), Martin (1992), and Sackmann (1992, 1997). Most of these scholars have found it purposeful to describe national (macro) cultures in dichotomies such as *individualism-collectivism* (Hofstede, 1980; Triandis, 1994), *vertical-horizontal* (Triandis, 1994), *masculine-feminine* (Hofstede, 1980), *active-passive*, (Triandis, 1994), and *universalism-particularism* (Trompenaars and Hampden-Turner, 1997). Other typologies are *emotional expression or suppression* (Triandis, 1994; Trompenaars and Hampden-Turner, 1997), *instrumental-expressive* (Triandis, 1994), *ascription-achievement* (Triandis, 1994; Trompenaars and Hampden-Turner, 1997), and *sequential-synchronic* with respect to time (Trompenaars and Hampden-Turner, 1997). The central argument in many of these studies is that the greater the cultural distance, the bigger are the differences in the organizational and administrative practices found in them. Employees' expectations and their interpretation of their organizational environment will correspondingly be different. Consequently, many of the difficulties associated with cross-border learning may be traced to differences in organizational culture (Schein, 1984). These differences invariably shape the patterns of inclusion and exclusion in the organisations in the sense that those who play according to the rules remain within organisation and those who elect to disobey the rules opt out voluntarily or are required to exit.

Students of national culture who subscribe to the differentiating perspective on culture remind us that each society and organization endorses particular approaches to learning and these are culturally sanctioned. To illustrate this point Hofstede (2001) compares the learning preferences of organizations located in collectivist and individualist societies. He argues that adults in collectivist societies are more reluctant to learn formally (equating formal learning with schooling) than those in individualist societies. While people emphasise skills (know-how) in collectivist societies and strive to maintain harmony in learning situations, people in individualist societies are more inclined to learn how to learn and, therefore, enjoy theoretical and abstract discussions. They are also likely to tolerate confrontational dialogues in learning situations between trainers and trainees. Thus the differentiation perspective has significant implications for managing learning processes in cross-border R&D teams in the sense that team members carry their culturally embedded learning traditions with them into the team. If a team is dominated by people with a particular learning tradition it may be difficult for the team leader to facilitate a change in that tradition, even if he considers that tradition to be dysfunctional in relation to the new knowledge to be acquired and the task to be accomplished. Taking Hofstede's observations on learning in individualist and collectivist organizations as an example, one can expect leaders wishing to introduce some degree of independent thinking in a team dominated by members from a collectivist society to experience such a change process as an uphill task.

Fragmented Multiple Cultures

A third perspective challenges both the homogenizing and differentiating notions of culture. The central argument advanced in the third perspective is that cultures neither produce clear patterns of harmony nor clear dichotomous conflicts. Societies are best seen as characterized by complexity, pluralism, diversity, fragmentation and paradoxes (Martin, 1992; Sackmann, 1997; Kuada and Gullestrup, 1999, 2000; Gullestrup, 2006). That is, societies change their configurations unceasingly and can hardly be viewed as anything but stable. There are also multiplicities of social, occupational and professional groups to which people are attracted (Kuada and Gullestrup, 1999). It is, therefore, erroneous to assume that a given individual's behaviour is influenced by a set of stable cultural properties such as shared norms and values. Individuals are better seen as having fragmented, fluctuating self-concepts derived from multiplex of cultures. Viewed from this perspective, culture may be considered a metaphor that makes sense of this complexity. The literature labels these arguments as constituting *fragmentation* perspective on culture.

We see the three perspectives of culture outlined above as not mutually exclusive. That is, any given culture – national, organizational, professional – has elements of homogeneity, differentiation and fragmentation. It is the presence of the three characteristics at the same time that underscores the dynamism of culture – ensuring an unending process of cultural change. This understanding of culture is important for an analysis of how culture impacts actions of employees working as cross-border project teams and how the actions of the team members, in turn, shape the emerging cultures in the R&D units. When team members enter the team, they bring with them their previously acquired and practised cultural values, norms and rules of behaviour. Initially, they may feel thrown out of their comfort zones, since their previous rules may cease to apply in the new team. In other words, the culture of the team may appear initially to be characterized by a higher degree of fragmentation (i.e. a lower degree of homogeneity). But over time new rules are defined. Those who find themselves as working closely together and socially attached to each other may experience some degree of differentiation from the others. But where the tasks assigned to the team are clearly defined and professionally inspiring enough for most of the team members, the team as a whole will experience the emergence of a new homogenizing team culture, centred on core professional activities. The degree of homogenization may be strong enough to cushion the potential negative effects of differentiation.

Culture-in-Action

The discussions above form the backdrop for our *culture-in-action* construct. The relevance of this construct to an analysis of cross-border team dynamics is based on the understanding that culture is not innate; it is learned and can therefore be unlearned. Furthermore, employees are not blank sheets of paper on which culture writes its scripts; they have personalities and can reach beyond the limits imposed by existing cultural prescriptions and proscriptions and can therefore explore new possibilities and approaches to attaining organisational objectives. Depending on their positions within the organisational structure and decision systems, they can bring their personal convictions to bear on decisions in which they are involved and are actively engaged in implementing. It is this individual free-will and the interaction between people with this free-will (although in different degrees depending on the culture) that drives change and innovation in most organisations. In a culture-in-action perspective, culture is, to a certain extent, seen as an action parameter that participants can manipulate.

As a construct, culture-in-action has the following constituents:

- The *dynamics of culture* – both in the sense of long-lasting changes in values and practices, but especially in the sense of culture as a situational construct with individuals adapting their culture schema to specific situations.
- The *levels of culture*, distinguishing primarily between core cultural values and cultural practices.
- The *cultural meeting place* – e.g. the national and/or organizational locations of the interacting employees.
- *Personality* of interacting parties.
- *Intercultural communicative competences* – i.e. ability to understand and be understood.
- *Leadership behaviours* that guide the responsibilities of the employees in the interactive process
- The *emerging new culture*, i.e. the culture emerging from the situational interaction in, for example, a subsidiary of a multinational company.

The culture of the ambient society and/or organization provides an organising framework for the interaction processes of individuals and the background habits of socialization that they bring into the interaction processes. We have discussed these elaborately above and so will devote the rest of the section to the other constituents of the *culture-in-action* construct.

The Dynamics of Culture

We acknowledge that culture, at any given time, is constituted as a collective programme for a set of people (Hofstede, 1980). At the same time we argue that culture is in a continuous state of change and becoming. This change can be registered as a change in the overall collective programme from one period to another. We will, however, not focus on the changes in the cultural programmes themselves, but on the processes underlying them.

The basic process leading to cultural changes is the interactions of people. In a modern and global world, these interactions are multiple and take place in a number of contexts (Gullestrup, 2006), each with a specific purpose and rationale. The main contexts are the private life, work life, and public life of individuals. In this study, we focus on the work life context and the sub-cultures that emerge from work place interactions, especially those that emerge within multinational companies with their intensive cross-border interactions.

Basically, the dynamics can take a combination of three forms: *adaptation*, where one partner accepts the culture of another; *compromise*, where cultural diversity is settled by meeting each other halfway; and *creation*, where parties interact and resolve cultural conflicts through the symbiosis of the two cultures or the creation of a third culture.

Levels of Culture

The distinction between macro, organisational and group culture is a useful one. However, for our focus on dynamics and interaction, we need to augment this distinction in two ways. First of all, our study is focused on the organisational level in an inter-cultural context. This includes how the macro culture impinges on the organisational culture or rather, how the organisational members deal with and interpret their macro culture when they act as managers or employees of an organisation in an inter-cultural context.

Secondly, and more importantly, we distinguish between the values and the practices of a culture. Both constituents are part of the definition of culture and most definitions state that it is the values that direct or guide the behaviour of individuals. Business is, however, not basically about values, but about very practical matters – e.g. how to move goods and services from producers to the consumers. Managers and employees do not talk about values in the course of their business interactions but focus on how to do things and how to act. For example, when a subsidiary of a multinational company gets the task of developing a new product, its employees do not start by discussing cultural values. They discuss technology, the target markets, the costs and other practical matters. This means that interactions in organisations are around practices, with cultural values serving as background knowledge that unconsciously influence the manner in which the practical issues are addressed. The outcome of the discussions and their subsequent implementation will, over time, form patterns of behaviour because the best practices will eventually become rules and routines.

Table 2 elaborates the distinction between the value and the practice dimension at the macro, organisational and individual levels of culture. In an intercultural context, the focus on practice has two implications: Firstly, the practice of a multinational company may be in conflict with certain values in the host country. Secondly, the practice that is considered the best practice by the multinational company may not be compatible with the way things are done in the host country. In the first case, it may be possible to interpret and slightly alter the practice so that it is culturally acceptable; in the second case, there might be resistance to change from learned routines.

Table 2:   Cultural Values and Practices at Three Levels of Analysis.

	Values	**Practices**
National Culture	Core values of the society.	Rules of accepted behaviour.
Organisational Culture	Designed set of values that underpin behaviours.	Business routines or situational behaviour.
Individuals	Value interpretation (situational values).	Situational actions.

The Cultural Meeting Place

In international business, as a contextual issue, the cultural meeting place is of great importance. When an expatriate works in a subsidiary abroad his situation is different from working at home. As shown in Table 3, in case of a subsidiary of an MNC, the organisational culture of the MNC meets the national culture in the host country. In case of a joint venture, two organisational cultures meet in the national culture of one of the joint venture partners.

Table 3:   Inter-cultural Management in an Interactive Context.

	Meeting in Home Country	**Meeting in Host Country**
Meeting in a JV	Two organisational cultures meet in the same national culture.	Two organisational cultures meet within a national culture of one of the JV partners.
Meeting in a Subsidiary	One organisational culture meets in its own national culture.	One organisational culture meets a new national culture.

The outcome of these meetings depends on the mandate of the expatriates. Three situations will be discussed:

1. Few bindings on the expatriates. In this situation, the expatriates still have their collective macro culture programming from the home country and good knowledge about the values of the organisation, but they are free to interpret them taking into account their present cultural context. Furthermore, they may accept new practices without violating their cultural values. As business is mostly about practices, this possibility to interpret values and adopt new practices makes life easier for an expatriate. The local managers do not have the same freedom as they are embedded in their own macro culture.

2   Organisational values to be transferred and adopted by the subsidiary: Value statements are popular with many organizations, in particular with multinationals. These values are meant to guide practices. In this case, the expatriates are free to choose practices as long as they do not violate the values. That is, expatriates and local managers can discuss what the best practice might be and then in the end give them a value check to make sure that they do not violate the general value statement of the organisation.

3   Organisational practices to be transferred. As business is about practices, subsidiaries are often controlled by a set of best practices that has to be transferred from headquarters and implemented abroad. Here the interpretation space for expatriates and local managers is very narrow.

In all these perspectives, the source of potential conflicts is first of all the practices that headquarters want to transfer to the subsidiaries as such practices leave little room for interpretations compared to values.

Personality and Team Composition

The view that individuals have their own personalities fit well into the concept of culture-in-action. Individuals constitute the starting point of all cross-cultural interactions. Their continuous interactions influence their mindset and their personalities. In turn, the unique personalities of individuals tend to influence the rules of engagement in their cultures. Stevens and Swogger (2009a) identified two main personality types in R&D teams: *Starters* and *Finishers*. They use the *starter* personality types to describe those individuals who are creative, intuitive, visionary, and curious. These people continually challenge the status-quo, and are usually difficult to manage as well as difficult to follow when in leadership roles. They also tend to be unfocused, bubbling over with ideas, with a dislike for details, rigid structures and agendas. But when properly directed, they can create new breakthrough processes. In contrast, *finisher* personality types are far more pragmatic, better focused, more respectful of authority and more task-oriented. They like details, agendas, and are far steadier, consistent workers.

Individuals with strong personalities are instrumental in defining team cultures. The resultant culture may be radically different from the culture of the ambient society and organization. Stevens and Swogger (2009) argue that organizations are typically established by innovative starters. But as they grow beyond the chaos of the start-up phase, other personality types and skills are required to guide them through their growth process. Therefore, the leadership of most organizations typically shifts over a period of 20-30 years toward becoming a culture of finishers. R&D teams, therefore, need a relatively large proportion of members with starter-type personalities.

Emergent Cultures

In addition to the constituents described above, the culture-in-action construct emphasizes the understanding that R&D cultures emerge out of social and task-based interactions. The process of interactions determines the level of creativity that the emergent culture exhibits. In fragmented cultures, team members are likely to move in and out of different project units and work across functional areas (this is particularly pronounced in matrix organisations). This form of organizational structure allows team cultures to be in symbiotic relationships with each other and therefore facilitate the flow of values, norms, methods and work behaviours across teams – i.e. producing highly dynamic overall organizational cultures. Where R&D teams are highly creative, aspects of their creative culture will, over time, influence practices in other parts of the organisation. But deliberate leadership and management activities are required to facilitate such a cultural transformation process.

Inter-cultural Communication

Interaction is a core construct in the concept of culture-in-action. An important instrument for interaction is communication. In line with the discussions in this paper we can argue that new knowledge can only be created when existing bases of knowledge are disseminated through interaction between team members. Similarly, Kratzer *et al.*, (2008) argues that creativity is couched in communication networks. Communication is the means through which a team stores and disseminates information and more frequent communication may make the cross-fertilization of ideas increasingly likely. Previous studies have, however, shown that cultural differences may cause initial discomforts in cross-cultural communications and may result in serious conflicts that can sometimes derail efforts to achieve organisational goals of creativity.

As scholars of cross-cultural communication argue, the shared values within a given culture enable people to interpret both the spoken and unspoken messages conveyed in an interactive process between people (Holden, 2002). In other words, parts of the messages exchanged by communicators are implicit and embedded in the cultural spheres of the communicators. For example, varying degrees of loudness, pauses, intonations and inflections in oral-aural communications add meaning to the denotations and connotations of words spoken and heard. Where the communicants do not have common frames of interpreting these variations in speech, they are likely to hear them differently and impute different meanings to them. Just as these variations in speech produce inferences that may reinforce or distort the messages conveyed, signals received through other sensory organs (sight, scent, touch etc.) can alter the literal meaning of any utterance as well as lend significance to the unspoken (Haworth *et al.*, 1989). It is most likely that communicators in cross-border team communication contexts may lack shared grounds of understanding and may therefore find messages rather confusing.

To be effective, cross-border team members and their leaders must have substantial degrees of intercultural competence. The concept of intercultural competence may be conceived at an individual level in terms through the following three dimensions: 1) the ability to develop and maintain relationships, i.e. have social capital; 2) the ability to communicate effectively and appropriately, including ability to chose the appropriate learning modes suitable for both knowledge provider and knowledge receiver; and 3) the ability to attain compliance and obtain cooperation with others (Kuada, 2008).

Leadership and Organization

Like all other organizational endeavours, leadership efforts are required to manage R&D teams and help team members to overcome the hurdles of collaboration. We have noted earlier that the composition of the team is important for success. One of the important roles of leaders is to identify and recruit the right people with the right values and attitudes to do the things required and to do them with required level of promptitude. Additionally, leaders must provide vision, shape values and listen to the voices of members of their teams in order to manage the teams effectively. We label these roles as the *3Vs* of leadership. Scholars of leadership argue that leadership has to do with purposeful direction – i.e. having a destination. Without vision team members are faced with multiple priorities and end up duplicating their efforts, wasting their energy and resources in engaging in repeated false starts. "A vision builds trust, collaboration, motivation and mutual responsibility for success", declares Blanchard (2007:22). Visions allow leaders to set appropriate goals, support the project teams, and facilitate communication and interaction within the group. Support has to do with motivation of team members. Leaders that explicitly value individual contributions towards a project and provide constructive feedback, showing confidence in the work group, and being open to new ideas are held in high esteem by team members (Amabile, 1988, 1997).

The leadership role is best summarized by the conclusions that Amabile *et al.*, (2004: 30) drew from their study of the impact of leadership behaviour on creativity. They write:

"Several behaviors deserve particular emphasis in the leader's repertoire, behaviors requiring the following: skill in communication and other aspects of interpersonal interaction; an ability to obtain useful ongoing information about the progress of projects; an openness to and appreciation of subordinates' ideas; empathy for subordinates' feelings (including their need for recognition); and facility for using interpersonal networks to both give and receive information relevant to the project. Perhaps just as importantly, there are also several behaviors for leaders to avoid or reduce, including giving assignments without sufficient regard to the capability or other responsibilities of the subordinate receiving them; micromanaging the details of high-level subordinates' work; and dealing inadequately with difficult technical or interpersonal problems (whether due to technical incompetence, interpersonal incompetence, inattention, or sloth).

An essential function of leaders in work organizations is to design structures and procedures that facilitate work processes. Different organizational cultures emerge from different organizational forms or structures.

We will briefly discuss the culture-in-action concept based on three organizational forms: the hierarchy, the matrix organization and the network organization.

In *hierarchical organizations*, with its clear division of labour and decision making, employees work in distinct units or isolated cells. Within the units, intensive interaction takes place and "communities of practice" emerge. In case the unit is comprised of different cultures, inclusion or exclusion processes may take place, depending on the inter-cultural competence of the unit.

In the *matrix organization* with its blurred power structures, employees work and are members of a number of distinct units, some of which are permanent, while others are temporarily established. Matrix organizations are used when complexity increases in an organization and there is a need to combine resources across units. Each unit has its own agenda and when the units meet in the matrix, frictions are inevitable. If the matrix stretches across cultures, we may speak of a frictional organizational culture.

Finally, in the *network organization*, the organization is fluid and employees become members of many "units", even units with both external and internal members. Each network develops its own "network culture" and the members tend to develop as many cultures as there are members of networks. If the network organization includes people from other cultures, the mechanisms are the same: the network develops its own culture through the interaction with its members.

The degrees of homogeneity vary with the three organizational structures. Hierarchical structures exhibit the highest degree of homogeneity (less friction), matrix forms are characterized by moderate forms of homogeneity, while network organizations are highly heterogeneous.

An Integrated Model

The discussions above can be pulled together into an integrated model as shown in Figure 1. The model presents the three set of factors – learning, culture-in-action, and leadership – that jointly shape knowledge generation and sharing processes within organizations. The three factors also impact an organization – or team's – capabilities to reinforce the psychological dispositions of individual team members to work together and manage the anxieties and stress conditions that creative endeavours such as group-based project works entail. They also enhance individual and team capabilities to remain focused and disciplined throughout the project duration Granting that the conditions work together positively, the outcome should be an enhanced creativity at group and individual levels.

We have earlier endorsed the concept of "communities of practice" as a useful metaphor for explaining how learning contexts and interactive structures impact the learning processes of individuals. As Mariotti and Delbridge (2001) explain it, interacting within close-knit communities of practice produce shared metaphors and language or "shared mental models" through which people communicate their feelings, emotions and experience with each other and create enabling conditions for learning. Effective communication is therefore a key requirement for learning and knowledge transfer. The concepts of "collective mind" (Weick and Roberts, 1993), and "collective cognition" (Hargadon, and Bechky, 2006) have also been introduced into the literature to underscore this understanding of learning within teams and organizations. This explains our inclusion of context as an important parameter of learning in the model.

We have also argued earlier that employees use a combination of six different learning modes in their knowledge development process. One of these is experiential learning – i.e. they acquire knowledge through actions and experiences. This process may not always be intentional, but simply require extra vigilance and mindfulness on the part of team members.

Our concept of culture-in-action is closely linked to the different modes of learning. The preferred methods of learning of knowledge seekers and their absorptive capacity are all determined by their comfort zones. The dictionary defines comfort zone as a type of mental conditioning that allows individuals to enjoy a sense of security in their lives and interactions with their environment. The sense of security the individual perceives could be attributed to the mental conditioning formed through an acceptance of culturally prescribed attitudes and beliefs. Any disturbance of an individual's comfort zone may generate cognitive dissonance in the individual – a state of uncertainty and confusion that fills individuals with discomfort because their experienced reality is at variance with what they are used to. This is what happens when new teams are formed and known rules of behaviour are challenged and replaced by new ones. The *culture-in-action* construct aptly captures this process.

The cognitive process that the creation of a new culture initiates allows team members to reorganize their world-views in fundamental ways. It is this change in individuals' world-view that opens up new windows for creativity in their thinking and actions, thereby extending their comfort zones. A team leader that shows awareness of the comfort zones of the members of his team, as well as the anxieties that the transition process generates, should take deliberate steps to guide them, managing the transition with minimum anxiety. To do this, team leaders must have substantial knowledge of the learning culture of individual team members and combine this with intercultural communication skills and a set of psychological toolkit.

Learning also requires reflection over daily experiences either in dialogues with self (personal cognitive reflections) or together with others (i.e. socio-cognitive reflection). Scholars who subscribe to learning through communities of practice argue that story telling and conversations about daily work practices trigger joint reflective processes among team members (Brown and Duguid, 1991). Others suggest that unlearning current knowledge is the first step in a learning process. As Hedberg (1981) argues, unlearning is a process through which learners discard obsolete and misleading knowledge, replacing them with new knowledge.

Figure 1: **A Conceptual and Analytical Model for Studying Creativity in Cross-cultural Teams**

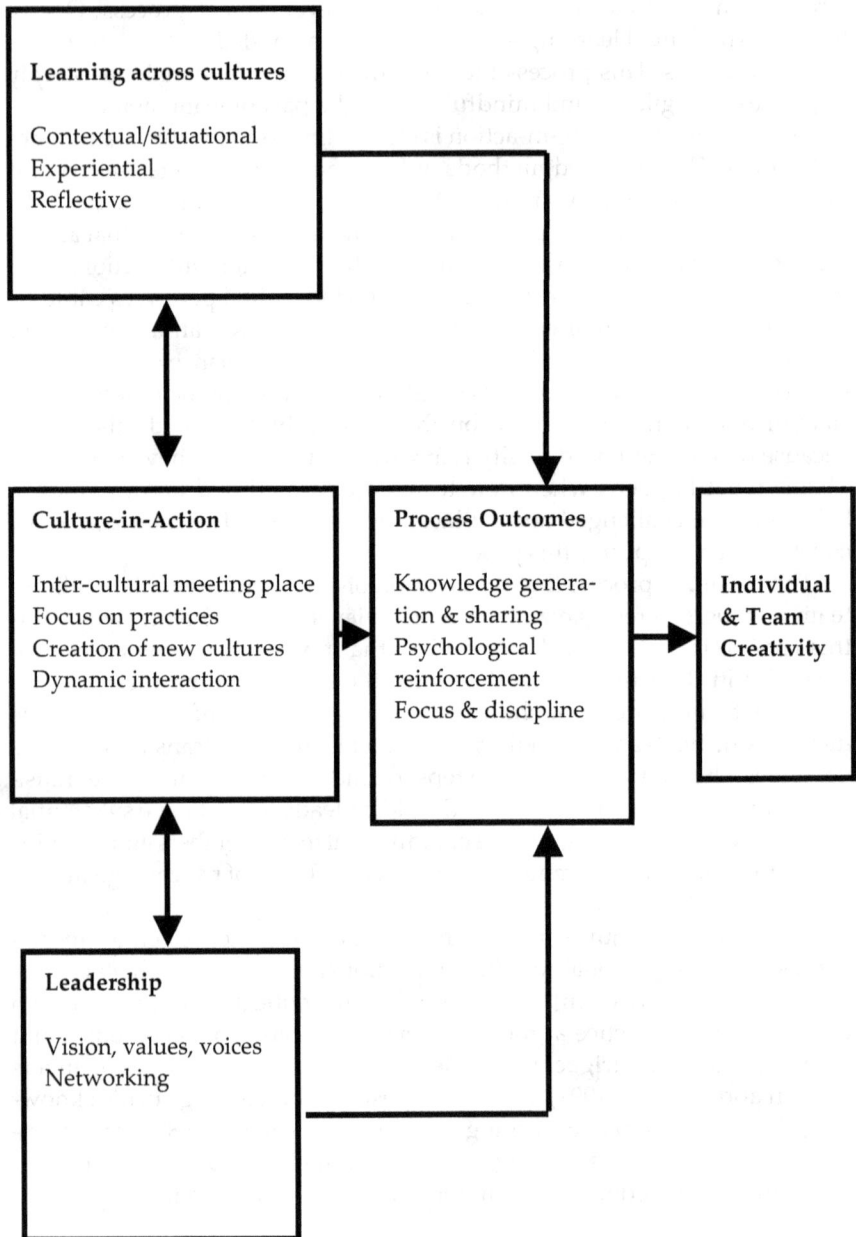

Learning across cultures

Contextual/situational
Experiential
Reflective

Culture-in-Action

Inter-cultural meeting place
Focus on practices
Creation of new cultures
Dynamic interaction

Process Outcomes

Knowledge generation & sharing
Psychological reinforcement
Focus & discipline

Individual & Team Creativity

Leadership

Vision, values, voices
Networking

The leadership component of the model emphasises the importance of *3Vs* (Vision, Values and Voices) and organizational structures to an understanding of leadership behaviours and styles that can promote creativity in teams. Just as societal values inform members of society about what they should see as "right" and "wrong", organizational and leadership values serve as the guideposts in organizations. They provide guidelines on how employees should go about their work. They remind them of the inherent meaning of the job. Voice here relates to the concept of employee empowerment. Since realities on the ground change over time it is important to listen to the voices around oneself and within oneself in order to navigate through the turbulence of organizational realities. Our focus on support, as leadership behaviour derives its theoretical roots from the *transformational leadership* literature. Scholars subscribing to this perspective argue that transformational leaders inspire their followers to exceed their own self-interests for the good of the organisation. To do so effectively, transformational leaders must tailor their leadership styles to the personalities and individual needs of the team members – i.e. by taking due cognizance of their expectations and capabilities.

The model suggests that these factors will positively influence knowledge generation and sharing within R&D teams, psychological reinforcement of team members, strengthen their ability to be focused and disciplined and, thereby, enhance their individual and team level creativities.

Conclusions and Research Implications

Organizations both large and small are interested in the ways in which learning processes at individual, group, and organizational levels can be captured, created, or implemented in order to create value and share new knowledge, or to underpin creativity and positive change. This paper provides a discussion of these parameters of creativity and shows the conceptual linkages among them. We have also argued that teams create knowledge mutually through reflective integrations of divergent perspective and the creation of shared world views and meaning schemes. Through that process, each individual contributes to the team's knowledge. Where co-ordinating structures and mechanisms allow intensive knowledge spreading within an organization, it is possible for creative R&D teams to influence an organizational culture to the extent that they stimulate creativity in a greater part of the organization. Stated differently, organizations must have a combination of people, processes, organizational structures and the right cultural orientation for the desired innovation to happen. This understanding has informed the conceptual and analytical model that we have proposed.

We believe that there is a substantial promise in this field of research and we add our voice to those scholars who advocate increased research into the area. Further research is needed to provide empirical validation for our conceptual framework. The culture-in-action construct that we introduce requires special research attention to establish its validity in cross-border business research in general and the study of international R&D teams' interactive processes in particular. The questions that future research must address are whether our operational definition of the construct is good enough and empirically valid (i.e. pre-operational validity), and whether the construct is fairly generalizable or restricted to specific cross-border interactive situations and contexts.

References

Adler, Nancy J., (1991). *International Dimensions of Organizational Behaviour* (2nd Ed). PWS-Kent Publishing Co. Boston, Mass.

Allaire, Yvan and Firsirotu, Mihaela E., (1984) "Theories of organizational culture" *Organization Studies*, Vol. 5 No.3 pp: 183-226

Amabile, T.M. (1983). *The Social Psychology of Creativity* Springer-Verlag, New York

Amabile, T.M. (1988) "A model of creativity and innovation in organizations" In Staw B.M. and Cummings, L.L., (Eds.) *Research in Organizational Behavior* Vol. 10, JAI Press, Greenwich pp. 123-167.

Amabile, T.M. (1996) *Creativity in Context*, Westview Press, Boulder, Colorado

Amabile, T. M. (1997). "Motivating creativity in organizations: On doing what you love and loving what you do". *California Management Review*, 40, 39-58.

Amabile, T.M., Schatzel, E.A., Moneta, G.B., and Kramer, S.J. (2004), "Leader behaviors and the work environment for creativity: perceived leader support", *Leadership Quarterly* 15 pp. 5-32

Blanchard, Ken (2007) *Leading at a Higher Level* New Jersey FT Press

Brown, John Seely, Duguid, Paul (1991) "Organizational learning and communities-of-practice: Toward a unified view of working, learning and innovation" http://www2.parc.com/ops/members/brown/papers/org learning.html. 31-10-2003 Assessed on 11 May 2009

Brown, John Seely, Duguid, Paul (1996). "Organizational Learning and Communities-of-Practice" in M.D. Cohen and L.S. Sproull (Eds.) Organizational Learning, Thousand Oaks, CA: Sage pp.124-162

Gullestrup, Hans (2006) *Cultural Analysis – Towards Cross-cultural Understanding* (Denmark, Aalborg University Press and Copenhagen Business School Press)

Hargadon, Andrew B. and Bechky, Beth A., (2006) "When collections of creatives become creative collectives: A field study of problem solving at work" *Organization Science Linthicum* Vol. 17 Iss.4 pp: 484-501

Haworth, Dwight A. and Savage, G.T (1989) "A Channel-Ratio Model of Intercultural Communication" *Journal of Business Communication* Vol. 26 No. 3 pp 231-254

Hedberg, B (1981) "How organizations lean and unlearn" in Nystrom, P.C. and Starbuck, W.J. (Eds.), *Handbook of organizational design.* London, U.K.: Oxford University Press pp: 3-27

Hofstede, G. (1980) Culture's Consequences: International Differences in Work-Related Values (CA Sage Publications, Beverly Hills,)

Hofstede, Geert (2001), *Culture's Consequences,* Second edition, (Sage Publication, Thousand Oaks, London, New Delhi)

Holden, Higel J. (2002) *Cross-Cultural Management: A Knowledge Management Perspective* (London, Prentice Hall Financial Times)

Kogut, B. and Zander, U. (1992) "Knowledge of the organization, combinative capabilities, and the replication of technology" *Organization Science,* 3 (3): 383-397.

Kratzer, Jan, Leenders, Roger Th.A.J., Engelen, Jo M.L. Van (2008) "The social structure of leadership and creativity in engineering design teams: An empirical analysis" *Journal of Engineering and Technology Management* Vol. 25 Issue 4, pp: 269-286

Kuada, John and Hans Gullestrup (1999) "Cultural Categories and Profiles: A Framework for Studying Individuals' Behaviour in Organizations" in Lauristin, M and Rahnu,L (Eds.) *Intercultural Communication and Changing National Identities* (Tartu, Estonia Tartu University Press) pp: 155-174

Kuada, John and Gullestrup, Hans (2000) "Organisationskultur og interkulturel kommunikation i et internationalt perspektiv" in Petersen Helle and Lund, Anne Katrine (Eds.) *Den Kommunikerende Organisation* (Denmark, Samfundslitteratur) pp: 25-58

Kuada, John (2008). "Leadership, Culture and Management in an International Context" (Centre for International Business Working Paper Series No. 46, Denmark, Aalborg University)

Lave, J.; Wenger, E. (1991). Situated Learning, Legitimate Peripheral Participation (Cambridge, UK: Cambridge University Press)

Mariotti, Francesca and Delbridge, Rick (2001) "Managing portfolios of ties in inter-organization networks" Paper presented at the Nelson and Winter Conference, Aalborg, Denmark June 12-15

Martin, Joanne (1992) *Cultures in Organizations: Three Perspectives:* Oxford, Oxford University Press

Nonaka, Ikujiro (1994) "A dynamic theory of organizational knowledge creation" *Organization Science,* 5: 14-37

Nonaka, Ikujiro and Takeuchi, Hirotake (1995) *The knowledge-creating company.* New York: Oxford University Press.

Orr, J. (1987). "Narratives at Work: Story Telling as Cooperative Diagnostic Activity" *Field Service Manager* pp: 47-60.

Prahalad C.K. and G. Hamel (1990) "The Core Competence of Corporations" *Harvard Business Review* Vol. 66 May/June pp: 79-91

Polanyi, M., (1966) *The Tacit Dimension London.* Routledge and Kegan Paul

Redding S.G. (1980) "Cognition as an Aspect of Culture and Its Relation to Management Processes: An Exploratory View of the Chinese Case" *Journal of Management Studies* May, pp: 127-148

Sackmann, Sonja A. (1992) "Culture and subcultures: An analysis of organizational knowledge". *Administrative Science Quarterly,* 37: 140-161.

Sackmann, Sonja A. (1997) *Cultural Complexity in Organizations* (California Sage Publications, Inc.)

Schein, E. H. (1984): "Coming to a New Awareness of Organizational Culture" *Sloan Management Review,* Vol. 25 No. 2 pp: 3-16

Spender, J.-C., (1994) "Organizational Knowledge, Collective Practice and Penrose Rents" *International Business Review* Vol. 3 No. 4 pp. 353-367

Stevens, Greg A., and Swogger, Kurt (2009a) "Creating a Winning R&D Culture – II" *Research Technology Management* Vol. 52 No. 2 pp: 22-28

Stevens, Greg A., and Swogger, Kurt (2009b) "Creating a Winning R&D Culture – II" *Research Technology Management* Vol. 52 No. 1 pp: 35-51

Sørensen, Olav Jull (2007) The Management Dimension of FDIs in a Culture and Learning Perspective (Centre for International Business Working Paper Series No. 44, Denmark, Aalborg University)

Triandis, H. C. (1994) *Culture and Social Behavior* (New York: McGraw-Hill, Inc.)

Trompenaars, F and Hampden-Turner, C (1997) *Riding the Waves of Culture* (Nicholas Brealey Publishing, London,)

Weick KE, Roberts KH. (1993) "Collective mind in organizations: heedful interrelating on flight decks" *Administrative Science Quarterly* Vol. 38 pp: 357-381

Weick, Karl E., (1979) *The Social Psychology of Organizing* (University of Michigan Ann Arbor)

Chapter 4

CREATIVE HUMAN AND ORGANIZATIONAL ENERGY

John Kuada and Dorthe Serles

The last two decades have witnessed burgeoning academic and management interest in the inner development of employees as a means of addressing three distinct challenges in modern corporate entities: (1) stimulating creativity and innovation; (2) maintaining ethical probity; and (3) reducing the incidence of employee burnout. Creative problem solving and the development of cultures of creative imagination are now buzz words in academic and consultancy literature. It has been argued that although creative breakthroughs may occur by chance, the development of the inner powers of people can help harness their creative talents and speed up the pace of creativity and innovations in work organizations. Probity relates to moral integrity – i.e. what organizations do when no one is watching. This defines the spirit or soul of a given organization. Burnout is reflected in situations where stress beats employees down long enough that the fight goes out of them and they show visible signs of dislike for their jobs and senior managers.

The need to address the three challenges has encouraged renewed search for alternative perspectives on organisational reality. The searchlight has been directed at the inner constituents of human beings and organizations – i.e. the soft side of organizations, and the concept of *energy* has emerged in recent years as a useful metaphor and construct for capturing these "soft" constituents of organisations (Cleveland and Jacobs, 1999; Luthans, 2003). It has been argued that organizational energy may manifest itself in either negative or positive forms (Cameron *et. al.*, 2003). Negative energy manifestations are most frequently reflected in behaviours that promote greed, selfishness, manipulation, secrecy, distrust, anxiety, self-absorption, fear, burnout and feelings of abuse that tend to derail organisational efforts. In contrast, the behaviours of employees in an organization in which energy flows positively tend to be characterised by appreciation, collaboration, virtuousness, vitality, trustworthiness, resilience, compassion, loyalty, honesty, respect, and forgiveness.

In its current usage the concepts of human and organizational energy lack clarity and this reduces their potentials as conceptual frameworks for rigorous empirical analyses. They have, therefore, not been fully integrated into the mainstream organisational studies and their implications for creativity and innovation have not been explored. There is a need for serious academic attention to be paid to concepts since their importance in organizational practices is growing rapidly.

The purpose of this paper is to contribute to their conceptualisation and to help position them at the centre stage of research. We argue that energy is best seen in the relationships between people and organisations and therefore an important concept in understanding talent and creativity development initiatives in modern work organizations.

In order to position the human energy construct within the contemporary discourses in organisational development and to affirm its connection with business operations we initiate the discussion in the next section by reviewing the resource based perspective (RBP) of organisations. We argue that the RBP provides a powerful and rich conceptual framework for understanding the internal mechanisms of organisations. But it is woefully inadequate in defining the characteristics of the intangible components of these resources. These discussions lead on to a more elaborate introduction of the concepts of human and organizational energy. The sections that follow highlight the limits of our current understanding of the composition of human/organizational energy. They also suggest a list of research themes that could improve our understanding of the field.

Organizations as Bundles of Resources

There is a long tradition in the economic literature for seeking a comprehensive understanding as to why organizations are established, how their boundaries are defined and how their activities are internally organised and co-ordinated to ensure their existence and growth. Consequently, various theories of the organization have emerged in contemporary literature. Most studies of organization over the past decade have drawn extensively on the seminal works of Coase (1937) and Penrose (1959). While Coase's work emphasises the contractual characteristics of organizations and thereby places ownership, property rights and contractual obligations at the centre stage, Penrose places a greater emphasis on organizations' resources, thereby giving birth to the resource-based perspective (RBP) of the organization.

The resource-based perspective (RBP) of organizations has been popularised in more recent years through the seminal works of Teece (1980), Wernerfelt (1984), as well as Prahalad and Hamel (1990). In brief terms, it holds that each organization consists of a bundle of resource. The RBP scholars redefine resources not merely as inputs that an organization may use, but as constituting the organization as a whole. Organizational resources are therefore generally defined to include all assets, capabilities, organisational processes, information, knowledge and other attributes they control and are considered necessary for the implementation of their strategies. The governing logic of RBP is that those components of an organization's resources that are valuable, rare, inimitable and non-substitutable enable the organization to bundle the other resources together and to implement value-creating strategies that cannot be readily duplicated by other organizations (Barney, 1991). Such resources combine to form what Eisenhardt and Martin (2000) describe as "dynamic capabilities". They are manifested in the ability of key actors of the organization to demonstrate exceptional alertness in identifying changes within the operational environment and to take actions sooner than competitors in order to take advantages of the opportunities and avert the threats (Barney, 1991). They also determine the organization's ability to transform its other resources into sustainable competitive advantages (Eisenhardt and Martin, 2000). Organizations are therefore required to deliberately protect their "core resources" or dynamic capabilities so as to keep a step ahead of their key competitors.

The ability of an organization to develop a sustainable competitive advantage depends also in part on the degree of stability of its operational environment. When the operational environment is relatively stable, a lesser degree of attention is required to align a organization's efforts with changes within the environment and to deploy its resources either to create or take advantage of new opportunities. But where the environment is dynamic, organizations are required to show a higher degree of nimbleness in order to create and maintain their competitive advantages. Furthermore, the value of tangible, i.e. "non-core resources" or static efficiency producing resources, is expected to decline rapidly in dynamic environments.

How do organizations then deploy their dynamic capabilities? That is, how are resources actually "bundled" together to make individual organizations highly competitive and how can the competitiveness be sustained? In recent years, scholars have suggested that the ability of a organization to bundle its resources in a unique manner will depend on its knowledge base as well as its capacity to continuously learn (Prahalad and Hammel, 1990; Spender, 1994; Grant, 1996). In other words, knowledge has been identified as the "core" resource on which dynamic capabilities are based. This assertion is a strong one and has significant implications for the creation and sustenance of the competitive advantages of organizations. If the knowledge base of the organization is weak, its other resources will remain fragmented and their rich potentials remain untapped. Conversely, as the organization's knowledge increases, its dynamic capabilities increase correspondingly, thereby raising its competitive advantages.

Organisations learn only through their members.[1] They do so either by benefiting from the knowledge acquired by the existing members or by recruiting new members who bring with them knowledge that the organisation did not previously have. In other words, knowledge actually exists in individuals' thoughts and it is communicated, transformed and used through thought processes. Since thoughts feed on memory, it can be argued that the knowledge creation process is underpinned by the manner in which memory responds to new and emerging issues in the operational environment of organizations. The premise of this argument is that individuals create mental models of the world they have experienced in their active life, and this shapes the way they perceive and interpret events in their lives. In the words of Kim (1993: 39) "mental models provide the context in which to view and interpret new materials and they determine how stored information is relevant to a given situation". Learning is seen as a process of creating knowledge. This process entails integrating the experiences that individuals acquire into their existing mental models or concepts. This integration involves reflections and interpretations that may produce modifications in the mental models. This process invariably affects individuals' behaviour and actions. The more varied interpretations are given to information, the greater the probability that they will result in changes in organisational behaviour as a whole. Knowledge creation may therefore be said to have twin dimensions: *conceptualisation* and *action*.

Having said this, it must be noted that knowledge is not absolute, static, timeless and entirely objective or non-human. Its validity changes with context and time. Knowledge may therefore be said to "decay" over time and with changes within the internal and external situations of organizations. For this reason, a continuous process of knowledge creation and dissemination is necessary if managers are to forestall situations where organizations are managed by a dominant logic that is out of tune with the environmental changes.

The Concept of Human Energy

The theoretical viewpoints sketched above indicate that RBP offers a useful conceptual framework for analysing and understanding the internal configurations of organizations. Furthermore, there have been recent attempts to give prominence to the role that intangible resources play in creating superior competitive position for some organizations within a given industry. The emphasis on intangibility of resources is a powerful one. But most RBP scholars shy away from accepting psychic and metaphysical considerations within their conceptual domain. We submit that learning is not just a simple biological process. It also entails the deployment of spiritual energy. This suggests that the existing RBP literature is woefully inadequate in providing a comprehensive understanding of sustainable competitive advantages of organizations.

Managed as resources people do what other resources do: they become depleted or absent – they burn out or move to another organization. Many organisations experience high attrition levels when work environments become too turbulent and the demands placed on employees are more than they can bear. This results in substantial investment losses (including knowledge leakages). The concept of "human assets" has, therefore, been introduced into the literature to emphasize the inherent positive characteristics of employees. Managed as "assets" employees are expected to flourish, growing in value for themselves and adding value to their organizations. We prefer the concept of human energy or fundamental life condition since this concept takes us beyond *who* we are as humans as reflected in our rational being and belief systems and gets us closer to an understanding of that aspect of our being that makes us uniquely and typically human. Religious scholars describe this aspect of human life as the human spirit or soul (Arbaugh, 2001).

In physics, energy is the ability or capacity to do work or to produce change. It is common for energy to be converted from one form to another. However, the law of conservation of energy (a fundamental law of physics) states that although energy can be changed in form, it can neither be created nor destroyed. Therefore, understanding psychic energy is not only a matter of assessing the conditions of the energy as such, but also the circumstances that determine, inhibit, and generate certain conditions of energy. It also requires an understanding of the consequences of particular energy conditions and the kind of transformation processes that energy can potentially undergo in order to produce change.

Energy generally exists in a *latent* form and is as such not visible to people. That is, human beings are not aware of their energy until some external causes trigger it into a *manifest* form. The concepts *latent* and *manifest energy* are therefore important in our conceptualisation of human energy. Scholars such as Cleveland and Jacobs (1999) use the concept "potential energy" to describe what we choose to call latent energy.

Latent energy turns into manifest energy within organisations through interaction. As people interact, they experience the flow of energy within and between each other. The flow may be experienced as more or less intensive and over short or long periods of time. But the interaction also produces transformation within and between the interactants. In other words, there is a simultaneous process of transformation and manifestation of energy occurring through interaction processes among organisational members. It is this simultaneity of transformation and manifestation that produces differences in organisational asset management processes.

As noted earlier, organisational members may experience the transformation process of manifested energy as *invigorating* (i.e. positive and generative) or *weakening* (i.e. negative and draining). Consistent with this perspective, Dhawan *et al.* (2002) argue that psychic energy as reflected in different work activities in an organization is manifested in energy generating and energy draining activities.

The strength, intensity and pace of manifested energy can be illustrated with how participants behave during a meeting in an organisation. In situations where the energy in which the meeting is embedded is marked by strength and intensity, all the participants tend to be well prepared and focused. Everybody contributes to the discussions with openness and joy. Important decisions are made swiftly based on thorough and swift dialogue. But if the strength of the energy is low, most of the participants will appear to be less prepared and key persons may be absent from the meeting. Many participants may feel disorganised and frustrated, doing all other things than focusing on the central points of discussion – e.g. glancing through other papers, leaving to get some more coffee etc.

Energy Transmitters and Human Life Tendencies

We have argued earlier that individuals are transmitters of energy within organisations. The transmission takes place during interpersonal relations and/or group interactions. Here language and emotions combine to transmit the latent energy inherent within the individuals to one another. A typical situation in which energy transmission occurs within organisations is during interactions between personnel at different levels of organisational hierarchy (Bruch and Ghoshal, 2003). The transmission process is often self-reinforcing. That is, positive energy manifestation sets off a spiral of positive energies, while an initial negative energy manifestation produces the reverse effect (Dutton, 2003).

Whether or not an individual's behaviour manifests an invigorating (positive) or weakening (negative) energy in an organisation or a group will depend on four sets of factors: (1) the *basic life tendencies* of the individual; (2) the events in his/her *life history;* (3) the *manifested collective energy* within the ambient environment (e.g. organisation); and (4) the *socialisation process* or culture that has shaped his/her life. The diversity of individual life tendencies provides each organisation with unique potentials for transmission of energy. It is this feature that defines the degree of organisational agility, as well as the non-immutability and non-substitutability of organisational resources (Barney, 1991). That is, the ability of one organization to exhibit superior competitive capabilities over other organizations within a given industry and to manage linkages (local and international) may be understood through the psychic energy construct.

Individual life tendencies are shaped by events from history. Each individual's journey through life is laced with challenges from birth to death. During this span of life, the cumulative experiences (i.e. ways in which individuals tackle the complex set of events in their lives) provide the foundations of their basic life tendencies. Asian religious scholars suggest that some of these events may pre-date birth itself. They are also shaped by socialisation and upbringing, i.e. the culture of the societies within which a particular individual has been raised. This is combined (at work) with the patterns of socialisation and the rules of accepted behaviour that have guided the individual's life experience. Psychologists attempt to understand these basic tendencies as the individual's personality.

Borrowing again from Asian religious philosophies, we can analytically classify the fundamental life tendencies of human beings into ten hierarchically ordered categories: these are Hell, Hunger, Animality, Anger, Tranquillity, Rapture, Learning, Realization, Altruism and Wisdom/Compassion. The quality and value of the energy manifested through each life condition is different. Each life condition is thus considered to have its own type of catalytic potential. Technically speaking, the states of life condition are the fields through which the energies flow, not the psychic energies themselves. They are like doors which may be unlocked by certain conditions and circumstances. The ten life conditions can be divided in two broad groups, the lower level life conditions and the higher level life conditions, as explained below.

The Lower Level Life Conditions

The first six states are called the *six lower level life conditions*. These are hell, hunger, animality, anger, tranquillity and rapture. They have in common the fact that their emergence or disappearance is governed by external circumstances. Take the example of a firm with a strong desire to find someone to invest in a new risky idea. That desire reflects an organizational life condition akin to "hunger". If a manager finds an investor, especially after a long search, a feeling of ecstasy and fulfilment ensues (i.e. they find themselves in the state of rapture). By and by, potential rivals with similar ideas appear on the scene, and the managers become jealous (i.e. in the state of anger). The manifestation of the anger may drive the venture partner away. Crushed by despair (i.e. in the state of hell), the managers are filled with frustration. In this way, many of us – individually as well as collectively (in organisations) – spend time shuttling back and forth among the six lower level life conditions without ever realizing that we are being controlled by our reactions to the environment.

The Higher Level Life Conditions

The next two states – *learning* and *realization* – come about when top management of an organisation recognize that everything experienced in the six lower life conditions of the organizational life is impermanent, and they begin to seek some enduring or higher level vision that can drive its organisational life and development. These two states plus the next two – *altruism* and *compassion/wisdom* – may be called higher life tendencies. Unlike the six lower tendencies, which are passive reactions to the environment, these four higher tendencies are achieved through deliberate effort – i.e. proactive strategic orientation based on ethical probity. Organizations whose manifest collective energies are guided by the four higher life conditions are no longer prisoners to their own reactions. They are guided in their behaviour by transformational leaders.

The popularity of the concept of corporate social responsibility (CSR) as proactive strategic dispositions of organizations in recent decades is a general reflection of management desire to move their organizations to a higher level energy conditions. The CSR debate emphasizes the notion that organizations have a responsibility to maintain an equitable and working balance among the claims of the various directly interested groups – stockholders, employees, customers and the public at large. The ethical responsibilities of organizations define expectations that are not stipulated in laws, but are considered in a given society as being part of the morals, ethos or accepted rules of behaviour for employees and their organisations. These responsibilities are predicated on the view that businesses are moral and managers do what is right, just and fair. In specific terms, businesses are expected to engage in behaviours such as respecting people, avoiding social harm, and preventing social injury. Such responsibility is mainly rooted in religious convictions, humane principles, and human rights commitments (Lantos, 2001). The World Business Council for Sustainable Development (WBCSD, 1999) defines CSR as achieving commercial success in ways that honour ethical values and respect people, communities and the natural environment. Similarly, Steiner and Steiner (2000) argue that social responsibility is the duty a corporation has to create wealth by using means that avoid harm, protect, or enhance societal assets. This perspective is captured in what Epstein, (1987) refers to as the Social Contracts Theory.

Towards a Research Agenda

The discussions above suggest that the concept of human and organizational energy has a promise in opening up the hidden (and hitherto illusive) factor that explains the unique capabilities of some organizations to be agile, innovative and highly competitive. Although this line of research is gaining attention, it is still embryonic and requires more elaborate conceptualisation, theory building and empirical research direction. The outline above must be seen as an initial step in this direction. The rest of this section outlines some of the issues we consider to require immediate research attention that moves the field forward and positions it on the organizational research radar.

Human Energy in Specific Fields of Operation

It makes sense to expect organisational energy to impact different organisations differently, due to differences in the key functions that these organisations perform. For example, employees in a military organisation would experience energy flows in a manner different from business organisation. Similarly, personnel in the health service sector would experience different manifestations of organisational energy. Few people would disagree that compassion and comfort constitute important foci of care when illness is chronic or incurable. Approaching death can engender serious questions in life and these questions trigger anxiety, depression, hopelessness and despair. Difficult ethical dilemmas also emerge – e.g. decisions to withdraw treatment when death has not yet occurred. Unavoidably, such decisions challenge the personal values and beliefs of all involved – employees, patients and families. In such a context, abundant positive energy is required to manage relationships and reduce the incidence of burnout of key employees. These arguments justify a need for inter-sector/industry investigations into how organizational energy flows occur within and across sectors and strategies that can be adopted in the different sectors in order to ensure positive energy flows.

Impact of Human Energy on Leadership

Scharmer (2008) observes that we know a great deal about *what* leaders do and how they do it. But we know very little about the inner place, the source from which they operate. Business leaders are encouraged to find ways to energize themselves and their workers, to recoil to rooms of silence and to engage in meditation and self-reflection in order to sharpen their intuitive capabilities to make decisions that could change the fortune of their companies. Further research in this area would provide new perspectives to established modes of understanding the organisation of economic activities based on theories such as the agency theory, resource based theory and the myriad of other organisational theories of today.

The concept of transformational leadership is partly built on this understanding. Management literature describes transformational leaders as those who consistently transmit a sense of mission to their subordinates, eliciting extraordinary levels of motivation from them and encouraging them to excel beyond expectations. They do so partly by instilling pride, faith and respect for their efforts, providing them with mentorship where necessary and/or facilitate their knowledge acquisition and creative talent development (Politis, 2002).

Scholars of leadership have provided evidence to show that successful leadership depends on the quality of attention and intention that the leader brings to any situation. Two leaders in the same circumstances doing the same thing can bring about completely different outcomes, depending on the inner place from which each operates. Gumusluoghu and Ilsev (2009) argue that leaders must be very attentive and must create or "hold" a space that invites others in. The key to holding such a space is listening: to oneself (to what life calls the individual to do); to others (particularly others who may be related to that call); and to the voices that emerge from the organizations as entities. Doing so means leaders must keep their attention focused on the highest future possibility of their organizations. Similarly, Dahlberg (2004) argues that leaders with the right frame of mind and psychological dispositions can facilitate the flow of positive energy that improves organizational creativity. Such leaders can encourage divergent and convergent thinking, attitudes of curiosity, risk-taking, tolerance for ambiguity and openness among employees. This line of research also promises significant contributions to leadership theory.

Summary and Conclusions

The purpose of this paper is to introduce and highlight the concepts of human and organizational energy as overarching symbolisms in understanding contemporary organizations. With this concept, we hope to make explicit a notion that some have hitherto tacitly acknowledged and others have trivialised. The main thrust of the discussion here is that human and organizational energy is best seen in the relationships between people and organisations. It is not discernible within organisations. That is, we do not find it in systems and structures, but within and between persons that bring the system and structures to life. When systems are dismembered, energy disappears. Although the intangibility of energy makes it difficult for most organisational scholars to appreciate, to deny its existence is to fail to acknowledge the life-wire of organisations. Writers such as Wheatley and Kellner-Rogers (1996) have argued that human beings are identities in motion, searching for the relationships that will evoke more from them. Through these relationships they seek meanings, create systems and rearrange their lives. They invariably bring these characteristics into their work organisations, seeking from their co-workers, as individuals and collectives, the opportunities to explore their potentials in life. Organisational members are linked through energy flows and it is this energy that brings the organisation into life for its members.

The metaphysical conceptualization therefore extends existing discourses on learning in organizations. This perspective shifts the search for competitive advantages of organizations from such other resources as tangible assets and finance, to intangible and metaphysical process. The understanding is that, the ability of organizations to facilitate the flow of positive energy is critical to its long term survival and growth. This is especially important for business firms wishing to sustain a competitive advantage. Employees in organizations with positive energy flows would see their work as fulfilling a higher purpose and would be willing to do their very best in spite of challenging work conditions. They would focus on solutions rather than complain about problems.

But how does human energy play out in different types of organisations and in different societies and how best can management design strategies and nurture behavioural patterns that make optimal use of human energy? These are questions crying for answers from scholars.

Notes

1   Organisations learn independently of any single individual but not of all individuals (See Kim, 1993 for elaboration).

References

Arbaugh, J. B. (2001) "Reversing the Spirituality Lenses: Challenges and Opportunities for Developing a Spiritual Perspective on Strategy" Paper submitted for the 2001 Academy of Management Meetings Management, Spirituality, and Religion Interest Group Available at http://www. leaderu.com/offices/ben_arbaugh/ben_arbaugh-reversing.html downloaded on April 2, 2009

Barney, Jay B. (1991), "Organization Resources and Sustained Competitive Advantage" *Journal of Management* 17, pp: 99-120

Bruch, H. and Ghoshal, S. (2003) "Unleashing Organizational Energy" *MIT Sloan Management Review* Vol. 45No.1 pp: 45-51

Cameron, K. S., J. E. Dutton, and Quinn, R.E. (2003) *Positive Organizational Scholarship* San Francisco, Berrett-Koehler

Cavanaugh, Gerald. (1999). Spirituality for managers: Context and Critique. *Journal of Organizational Change Management*, Vol. 12 No.3 pp. 186-199

Cleveland, H. and G. Jacobs (1999) "Human Choice: The genetic code for social development." *Futures* Vol. 31 Nos.9-10 pp: 959-970.

Coase, Ronald H. 1937 "The nature of the organization" *Economica* 4 pp: 386-405

Dahlberg, Steven (2004) "Creativity by Choice, Not by Chance: Developing Imagination in the Intelligence Community" Available at www.applied imagination.org Assessed on 9 January, 2008

Dhawan, Sunil. K., Roy, Santanu and Kumar, Suresh (2002) "Organizational energy: an empirical study in Indian R&D laboratories" *R & D Management* vol. 32 No.5 pp. 397-408

Dutton, J. E. (2003 Energize Your Workplace: How to Create and Sustain High-Quality Connections at Work, Jossey-Bass.

Eisenhardt, Kathleen M. and Martin, J.A. (2000) "Dynamic Capabilities: What are they" *Strategic Management Journal* 21 pp: 1105-1121

Epstein, E.M. (1987) "The Corporate Social Policy Process: Beyond Business Ethics, Corporate Social Responsibility, and Corporate Social Responsiveness". *California Management Review.*

Grant, R. M. 1996. Prospering in Dynamically-competitive Environments: Organizational Capability as Knowledge Integration, *Organizational Science,* 7(4), 375-387

Gumusluoghu, Lale and Ilsev, Arzu (2009) "Transformational leadership, creativity and organizational innovation" *Journal of Business Research* 62 pp: 461-473

Kim, U., (1993) "Introduction to Individualism and Collectivism: Conceptual Clarification and Elaboration" (Paper presented at conference on Korean Culture, Copenhagen, May)

Lantos, G.P. (2002). The Ethicality of Altruistic Corporate Social Responsibility *Consumer Marketing* Vol.19, pp 205-232

Luthans, F., (2002) "Positive organizational behavior: Developing and managing psychological strengths". *Academy of Management Executive,* 16, 57-72.

Prahalad, C.K. and Hamel, Gary (1990) "The Core Competence of Corporations" *Harvard Business Review* May-June pp: 71-91

Penrose, Edith T. (1959) The Theory of the Growth of the Organization, (Oxford

Politis, John (2002) "Transformational and transactional leadership enabling (disabling) knowledge acquisition of self-managed teams: The consequences for performance" *Leadership and Organizational Development Journal* Vol. 23 Nos. 3&4 pp: 186-197

Scharmer, C. Otto (2008) "Uncovering the blind spot of leadership" Executive Forum Winter pp: 52-59

Spender, J.-C. (1994), "Organizational knowledge, collective practice and Penrosian rents", *International Business Review,* Vol. 3 No.4, pp.353-67

Steiner, G.A. and Steiner, J.F. (2000) Business, Government and Society: A Managerial Perspective, Irwin McGraw-Hill

Teece, D. J., (1980), "Economies of Scope and the Scope of the Enterprise" *Journal of Economic Behaviour and Organization,* 3 pp: 39-63

Wernerfelt, Birger (1984) "A Resource-based View of the Organization" *Strategic Management Journal* 5, pp: 171-180

Wheatley, Margaret J., and Kellner-Rogers Myron (1996) *A simpler way* (San Francisco, Berrett-Koehler Publishers Inc.,)

WBCSD (World Business Council for Sustainable Development) (2000) Corporate Social Responsibility: Making good business sense, available viahttp://www.wbcsd.ch (last accessed 10 June 2009).

Chapter 5

GLOBAL COMPENSATION SYSTEMS – A COMPARATIVE ANALYSIS ACROSS EU COUNTRIES

Magdalena Andrałojć

Introduction

In the contemporary world, especially in developed and developing countries in Europe and North America, we can observe common trends in compensating and rewarding: evolving pay-for-performance plans, increasing role of qualifications, more complex and sophisticated compensation package for high skilled workers, specialists and managers. Attention is being paid to the gap between women and men.

Companies are also looking for effective ways to motivate their employees. A survey of 400 of the Fortune 1000 companies indicates that more emphasis has been placed on at-risk pay and less on base compensation. This includes the adoption of so-called alternative pay strategies such as "broad banding" (the enlargement of pay ranges into broad bands, reducing the number of pay levels), "gainsharing" (Bowey, 2000) or "improshare" (Fein, 1991) (programmes designed to improve productivity or reduce costs and share the value of any productivity gains or cost savings with employees). Pay-for-performance programmes continue to be more and more popular.

Employees are paying more attention to professional career and improving their qualifications. High skilled workers and managers are offered better salary. The gap between high and low skilled workers, managers and non-managers, has become more significant in recent years. Discussions concerning management salaries stir up emotions. The heated debate over management compensation continues even now, four years after it peaked in the spring of 2002. It was triggered primarily by the ABB scandal (Reed and Sains, 2002; Woodruff, 2002). The sharpest criticism has been directed at the discrepancy between the salaries of managers and non-managers. In 1991, the average large company CEO received approximately 140 times the pay of an average worker. In 2003 the ratio was about 500:1 (Bebchuk and Fried, 2004).

Changing family characteristics and labour force trends suggest more flexible and more varied pay benefits packages. The big change is the rise in labour force activity among women. Since women entered the labour market the pay gap between genders has been one of the main subjects of discussion. Women, in general, earn less than men. Is this a matter of discrimination? There are a lot of international and national acts, decrees and legislative records forbidding gender discrimination on the labour market. It has resulted in gradual narrowing of pay gap (Shaw, Clark, 2000). Nevertheless, differences in pay between man and woman remain.

Despite the common trends concerning compensation, differences across countries remain. These differences may be observed in the following aspects:

- compensation package (e.g. fixed and variable components),
- pay structure (e.g. egalitarian vs. hierarchical),
- pay inequality (e.g. gender pay gap).

Successful techniques in compensating employees were not found to be uniformly effective across cultural borders. For instance, methods of individual performance appraisal that are widely used in the United States have not been successfully implemented in non-American companies outside the US (Erez and Erley, 1993). Failures in transferring compensating and rewarding methods across countries may suggest that culture plays important role in creating compensation system. There are, of course, other variables such as labour market characteristics: legislation, industry characteristics, ownership status, corporate culture, individual employees' behaviour, preferences and expectations (Aycan *et. al.*, 2000). Managing human resources in organization and setting effective compensation system requires understanding the influence of all these variables.

There are a lot of studies concerning culture as an important factor of human resource management (Smith, 1992; Hampden-Turner and Trompenaars, 1994; Brewster, 1996; Harris and Moran, 1996; Hofstede, 2001; Armstrong, 2002) and social behaviour (Triandis, 1994). But very little is known about the connection between culture and compensation system. The lack of research in this field may be due to limited access to cross-country comparable data. The existing databases are mostly at the national level. That is why a lot of researchers focus on describing compensation system in one country or try to analyze labour market factors influencing the pay level and structure in different sectors and occupational groups in the country of study.

The aim of this paper is to contribute to narrowing the gap in cross-country research concerning compensation system. The importance of culture factor in compensating employees is the focus of the study. Understanding and accepting cultural differences result in well-motivated and satisfied employees who contribute immensely to organizational performance (Tayeb, 1995; Budhwar and Debrah, 2001).

The first part of this paper provides an overall picture of compensation system. The concept, the role and the major factors that influence compensation are discussed. The second part focuses on culture as the determinant of pay model. It includes a step-by-step discussion that begins with presenting different approaches to the cross-culture study, then describing a cultural model and analyzing the potential cultural impact on compensation systems. The results of a cross-country study are then presented and discussed.

Compensation system

Compensation is a very complicated economic, social and psychological phenomenon (Borkowska, 2004). There are many synonyms of compensation in literature, with the most popular being: remuneration, pay, wage, salary and reward.

Are they equal? Remuneration refers to the total compensation received by an executive, which includes not only the base salary but options, bonuses, expense accounts and other forms of compensation. Compensation means all forms of financial returns and tangible services and benefits that employees receive as part of an employment relationship (Milkovich and Newman, 1990). This definition shows variety of compensation forms: direct compensation in the form of cash (e.g. base pay, incentives, and bonuses) and indirect compensations in the form of benefits and services (e.g. stock options, perquisites, health insurance, company car, mobile or computer for personal use).

Pay, wage and salary usually apply to cash compensation – the amount of money received by employee for performing his/her work. Salary is the pay calculated at an annual or monthly rate, whereas wage is the pay calculated at an hourly rate. In the United States, the distinction between periodic salaries (which could be paid regardless of hours worked) and hourly wages (meeting a minimum wage test and providing for overtime) was first codified by the Fair Labour Standards Act of 1938.

The reward system of an organization includes anything that an employee may value and desire and that the employer is able or willing to offer in exchange for the employee's contributions. Henderson follows Glinow (1985) to draw a distinction between compensation and non-compensation components of reward system (Henderson, 2003) – compensation being just one form of reward (Glinow, 1985). All rewards that can be classified as monetary payment or in-kind payment constitute the compensation system. Other forms of reward or returns that employees may receive – e.g. promotion, training, verbal recognition for outstanding work behaviours, social relationships with co-workers, supportive leadership and management as well as job satisfaction constitute non-compensation system. Any activity that has an impact on the intellectual, emotional, and physical well-being of the employee and is not specifically covered by the compensation system is part of the non-compensation reward system.

In sum, the different concepts that are used as synonyms for compensation may carry different meanings for different researchers. Each researcher should have it in mind while doing cross-country comparison. Reward has the broadest meaning; pay the narrowest. Pay (wage, salary) is the part of compensation (remuneration) system, and the compensation is part of total reward system. Compensation system may be described through:

- its elements (compensation package), and procedures used to set up these elements,
- the roles it plays in the organization and society, and
- determinants that influence the compensation structure and forms.

Compensation package

The shape of compensation package reflects the employer's belief about employees' needs and expectations concerning employee performance. It is very much connected with corporate culture (the culture of organization is reflected in compensation system and at the same time compensation system contributes to creating organization's culture). The adequate use of compensation elements plays important role in motivating employees and linking the individual employee goals with the company's strategy. The compensation package has been changing quickly – new elements appear the old ones evolve into new forms.

There is a variety of classifications concerning the compensation components. The most popular one divides compensation elements into two groups: direct and indirect elements (Robbins, 1996; Ivancevich, 1998; Milkovich and Newman, 1990; Henderson, 2003). For example, according to Henderson direct compensation includes base pay and cash incentives, and indirect – employee benefits paid for by an employer. Milkovich and Newman (1990) assume that base pay, merit pay, incentives and cost of living adjustment stand for direct compensation; protection programmes, reimbursed time away from work and employee services and perquisites stand for indirect compensation. According to Towers Perrin HR Services (one of the major international companies in HR consulting) total remuneration includes one of the following components: basic compensation, variable bonus, compulsory company contributions, voluntary company contributions, perquisites and long-term incentives. All in all, the compensation system is often built around the following elements:

- base pay,
- short-term incentives (Greenspan, 1991),
- long-term incentive plans (Hyman, 1991),
- perquisites,
- employee's services and social protection plans.

Base pay is the basic cash compensation that the employer pays for the work performed. This element tends to reflect the value of the work itself and generally ignores differences in individual contributions and effects. Some compensation systems set base pay as a function of the skills or education an employee possesses. Decisions concerning the pay structure in the organization (the array of pay rates for different work within single organization) should reflect similarities and differences in the work. Collecting and interpreting information about jobs is known as job analysis (Milkowich and Newman, 1990; Henderson, 2003). Job analysis provides the underlying information for preparing job description and evaluating jobs. It is a prerequisite for describing and valuing work and is highly related to the equity and efficiency of the pay system. It helps to achieve internal consistency – the pay relationship among jobs and skill levels within single organization. The last decade of the twentieth century saw a variation in pay grade development that was labelled broad-banding. Broad-banding groups a number of higher-paying grades into one broader pay grade band. This reduces the need to define and measure job differences more precisely and promotes paying the same rate of base pay for jobs that require different knowledge and skills. Using broad-banding an organization can reduce the number of pay grades included in the pay plan (Henderson, 2003). Both internal consistency and external competitiveness are necessary for the establishment of an appropriate pay structure (i.e. the pay relationships among organizations). What competitors are paying in the relevant labour market permits organizations to attract and keep key employees. Periodic adjustments to base pay may be made on the basis of changes in the overall cost of living or inflation, changes on the labour market or changes in employee's qualifications.

Short-term incentives tie pay directly to the performance and effects of work of an individual employee, a team of employees, a total business unit or all organization. Short-term incentives (e.g. cash bonuses and individual, team or company-based performance incentives, premiums such us pay for overtime work, shift work, weekend or holiday work, work that is offensive in any senses) are often given as lump-sum payment or as increments to the base pay (included in the payroll). They focus employee efforts on short-term goals and improve productivity. Productivity improvement programmes, such as gainsharing, allow both employers and employees to take advantage of increasing profits or reducing costs. The purpose of gainsharing programmes is to encourage employee involvement and commitment to improve the organization performance (Henderson, 2003).

Organizations sometimes call their short-term incentives variable pay. Such programmes are designed to benefit both employees and employers. If the variable pay plans are executed correctly, employees can be very goal-focused and motivated to meet and exceed their objectives and maximize their variable pay potential, and contribute to the success of the organization (Fay, 2003). A study presented by Fay reveals that 77% of the responding companies believe that the use of variable pay programmes helped to improve their business results. Meanwhile, 23% say that variable pay had no effect on their organization's results. For 33% of those organizations surveyed, variable pay was seen to have the greatest impact on rewarding top-performing employees.

Long-term incentives (e.g. stock options plans, stock appreciation rights, performance shares) are intended to focus employee efforts on longer range (a few years) results such as return on investment and market share. The size of reward is based on multi-year achievement of established performance-related goals. Long-term incentives are mainly offered to top managers or professionals (Balsam, 2002; Fried, 2004).

Perquisites include wide array of alternative compensation forms ranging from paid time away from work, the company car, a laptop or mobile for personal use to even club membership. Perks are usually offered to top-managers and executives; they reflect social status. Services (financial, legislative, taking care for children) and protection (medical care, life insurance, and pension schemes) are offered to all employees (Henderson, 2003). Since the end of the Second World War, employee services and protection plans have increased in importance as part of total compensation. Organizations purchase these goods and services for their members to take advantage of economies of scale through group purchasing and the benefits available through tax law and regulations. Many employers offer a "one size fits all" benefits plan, and, in doing so, fail to provide the benefits many of their employees really need or want. To meet an employees' need a cafeteria plan may need to be introduced. This plan empowers employees by allowing them to design their own benefit packages. Examples of benefits that may be offered under a cafeteria plan include coverage under a medical care, accident and health insurance, group-term life insurance, group automobile insurance, group homeowners insurance, vacation days, scholarships and fellowships, transportation benefits, educational assistance, employee discounts and retirement benefits. A big advantage for employees is that cafeteria plans allow them to choose the benefits they need. This may result in increased job satisfaction. Among the advantages for employers is saving on payroll taxes and better motivated employees. In addition, there may be a cost saving to the employer because the cost of benefits that employees do not want will be eliminated.

Compensation package may differ across countries. The reason is that the way the workers are compensated for their work may vary across types of economies. The social acceptance of different forms of pay may differ, as well. For example, in some countries workers get substantial payments "in kind", in others they do not, in some countries individual reward is more common, in others group rewards dominate, in some countries stock and options plans are popular, in others not. Systems of social insurance also differ between countries, which has an influence on compensation package. For example, in countries with high quality, governmental social insurance system such compensation elements as private pension plan or health care may not be so popular. One has to keep this in mind when comparing employee compensation for different countries.

Compensation role

Perceptions of compensation vary. Some may see it as income, some as a cost. For some people it is important motivator towards work; for others, it becomes a measure of equity and justice. All these perceptions reflect the different role of compensation. These include income generation, social welfare, cost creation, and motivation (see Table 1).

From the employee perspective the pay received for the work performed is usually the major source of personal and household income and hence a valid determinant of an individual's economic and social well-being (Nash and Carroll, 1975). According to The Canberra Group (an Expert Group on Household Income Statistics), household income, apart from compensation (income from employment), includes such components as: income from self employment, interest and dividends from invested funds, pension or other benefits from social insurance and other current transfers receivables. The economic well-being can be expressed in terms of access to goods and services. An employee is usually interested in increasing his/her income. The higher the income, the better will the economic situation be. The most important compensation component contributing to household income is base pay. As it has to be paid periodically it is very stable and a secure source of income.

Nowadays, a major problem facing developed countries is an increasing unacceptable difference between the incomes of the lower paid and the higher paid members of the workforce. The growing disparity of income between the lower-income and the higher income members of society relates directly to the increasing influence of higher levels of knowledge and skills in pay determinations. Those members of society who do not have an adequate or acceptable level of education find themselves in an unenviable position regarding current and future income opportunities (Henderson, 2003). Is there a minimum level of wage received by low skill employees? What is a fair salary? What is the acceptable level of pay inequality? Societies have been debating the question concerning fair salary and pay differences have been rising since the ages.[1] The focus of the discussion has been on the social role of pay. Some countries require an employee to receive a minimum base pay. The idea of minimum pay is to guarantee the financial security for working population. In 18 EU countries (Belgium, Spain, Estonia, Greece, France, Hungary, Ireland, Latvia, Lithuania, Luxembourg, Malta, the Netherlands, Poland, Portugal, Slovakia, Slovenia, Czech Republic and the United Kingdom) there is a statutory national minimum wage, based on collective bargaining. The other Member States do not have a statutory national minimum wage (Funk and Lesch, 2005; Regnard, 2006). Minimum wages apply to the majority of full-time employees. In some countries the minimum wage is applied to certain groups, taking into account the employee's age, length of service, skills or physical and mental capabilities, or the economic conditions affecting the enterprise.

Table 1: The different perceptions of compensation

Elements \ Role	Income-generating	Social	Cost-creation	Motivational
Point of view	employee	employee	employer	employer/employee
The essence	important component of household income, determinant of economic well-being	social security (at presence and in the future), measure of equity and justice (fair pay, discrimination), determinant of social status	important component of labour cost, determinant of economic success of organization and its competitiveness	important incentive to work; enable employer to create a desired employee attitude and behaviour
Main aim	maximize the income	support the idea of fair pay, counteract poverty and pay inequality	minimize the labour cost	combine employee's and employer's aims
Main compensation component	base pay	base pay, social protection plans	base pay	short- and long-term incentives, perquisites,

Source: author, on the basis of Henderson, 2003; Milkowich, 1990

In Greece, for instance, different rates of minimum wage apply to manual and non-manual workers. Many countries see the minimum wage agreed in terms of a monthly rate; while other countries (e.g. France, Ireland, United Kingdom) have the minimum wage fixed on an hourly rate. For purposes of comparison, the hourly rates for these countries are converted into monthly rates. In January 2006, statutory minimum wages across the EU countries varied between 129 euro (Latvia) and 1503 euro (Luxembourg) gross per month (Figure 1).

Figure1:   Statutory minimum wage (gross) in EU Members Countries, January 2006, in euro

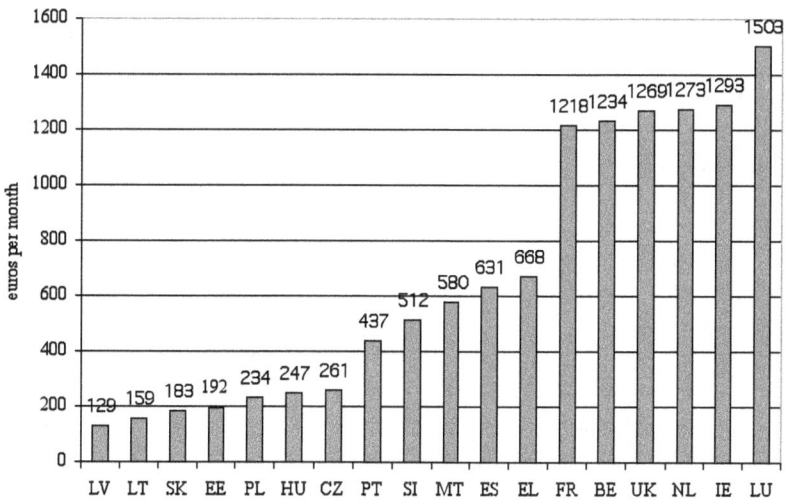

Source: Eurostat, database on minimum wages

National and international low indicate that all workers have the right to fair pay for the work that has been done. Pay discrimination based on sex, race, or national origin, and for other purposes is prohibited (equal pay for equal work).[2] Nevertheless, the differences in pay level and compensation components exist. In recent years pay inequality is the common subject of empirical research project (Galbraith, 2002).

Managers view compensation from two perspectives: firstly, as a major expense; and second, as a possible influence on employee work attitudes and behaviour. To survive in a complex global economy all organizations must be able to focus on the effective and efficient delivery of products they offer. Competitive pressures, both internationally and domestically, force managers to consider the affordability of their compensation decisions. Eurostat data show, that in 2000, in all sectors (except agriculture, fishing, public administration, private households and extra-territorial organizations) wages and salaries[3] accounted for 65-80 percent of labour cost (e.g. Hungary – 66.98, Spain – 75.04, Poland – 76.21, the Netherlands – 77.99, United Kingdom – 82.64, Cyprus – 85). Labour cost is an important component of overall organizational cost. Although organizations are searching constantly for ways to keep labour cost within acceptable limits, they must recognize that employee satisfaction relates directly to income obtained from work performed and the lifestyle opportunities made available to the workers and their families from this income (Henderson, 2003).

Well constructed motivating compensation system should attract talented people, retain key employees and motivate them to improve their work performance. In order to construct such compensation system managers have to understand how rewards affect motivation and modify employee behaviour. Over the years many researchers have made contribution to understanding why people behave the way they do. The dominant theories of motivation theories may be divided in two groups: *content theories* (e.g. Murray's Manifest Needs Theory, Maslow's Hierarchy of Needs, Herzberg's Two-Factors Theory, McClelland's Four Modes for Success, Alderfer's Three-Level Hierarchy); and *process theories* (Festinger's Cognitive Difference, Adam's Equity Theory, Hull's Drive Theory, Vroom's Expectancy Theory, Locke's Goal Setting Theory, Rend's Intellectual Theory, Skinner's Operant Conditioning).

Content theories of motivation focus on the needs individuals attempt to satisfy through various kinds of actions or behaviours. A primary contributor to the content motivation theories is Henry A. Murray, who identified an extensive set of needs. Abraham A. Maslow placed needs in a five-level hierarchy (physiological needs, safety and security, belonging, esteem, self-actualization). Different compensation components satisfy different needs. For example, basic pay satisfies mainly physiological, safety and security needs,[4] services and social plans satisfy safety and security needs, pay for-performance-plans – belonging needs, perks and pay increase, that reflect employee appreciation – esteem needs. For some, high level of pay may satisfy self-actualization needs. Frederic Herzberg repacked Maslow's hierarchy of needs and developed the concept of hygiene factors and motivators creating two-factor theory, where base pay is the hygienic factor. Process theories describe how the motivation process works and provide information on how to develop each part of the process. As far as compensation system is concerned, three theories are very important: Vroom's Expectancy Theory, Skinner's Operant Conditioning and Adam's Equity Theory. Expectancy represents ideas that are developed by individuals about the consequences of certain actions. Skinner's Operant Conditioning states that motivation is increased by accentuating desired behaviour through positive reinforcement (e.g. raises, performance bonuses, commissions, profit sharing, or any number of "extra benefits" like, automobiles, vacations, or other tangible items purchased and used as rewards). Pay-for-performance programmes will have more motivational influence when the employee recognizes a direct relationship between activities performed, results achieved and rewards gained. Adam's Equity Theory states that employees compare their compensation. When people perceive inequity in the workplace they will be motivated to reduce the tension created by the inequity.[5]

Compensation is the main source of employee income, and a very important component of labour cost. There is a conflict between employees and employers: employees want to increase their incomes, whereas employers are interested in reducing their labour costs. This conflict may be resolved if we look at the compensation as a motivator that combines the employees' and employers' goals. Employees' needs and employers' expectations may be covered by different compensation systems. The nature of compensation systems would depend on many variables, which are presented in the next section.

Determinants of compensation system

What should be taken into account while determining pay level and structure: employee contributions and value of the work performed or employee needs? There is no one simple answer. Having taken into account all variables that influence the compensation it could be good to find some balance, optimum solution. Compensation's determinants may be divided into three groups: individual, organizational and national (Figure 2).

The employees' compensation may be influenced by factors that characterize employees as individuals: their needs, expectations, age, gender, levels of education, skills, experience, position, performance and attitude to work. All kinds of pay discrimination (e.g. gender) are forbidden by law, nevertheless they exist and in some societies they are accepted to some extent. Using social connections (e.g. relatives on high position in the company) to get better compensation is not ethical, but it happens. It is commonly acceptable that highly qualified people, with more experience, holding a key position in a company will earn more (human capital theory). The allocation of compensation among pay forms to emphasize individual or group performance, qualifications, seniority, should be tailored to the needs of individual employees. Older, well paid employees may be interested in retirement plans, whereas younger ones, with high cash needs, may be interested in social package or educational support. The employees' needs are crucial while constructing compensation package (especially benefit plans). Pay system can be designed to permit employee choices. An example are the flexible benefit plans (cafeteria pay plans) that has been successfully adopted in many companies. In many organizations, employees' individual needs and preferences are ignored (Lawler and Hackman, 1969; Opsahl and Dunette, 1996).

Figure 2: Determinants of compensation system

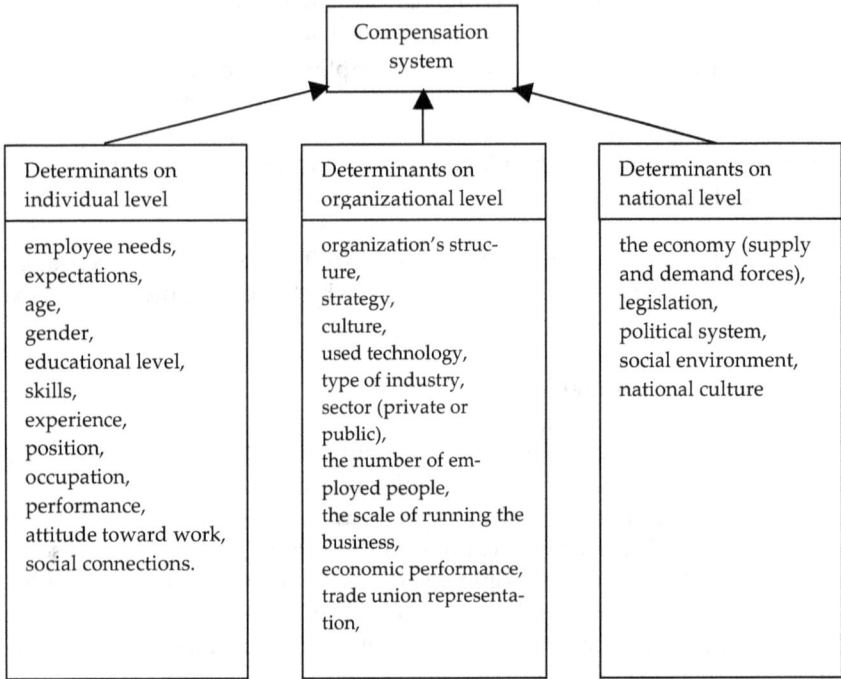

	Compensation system	
Determinants on individual level	**Determinants on organizational level**	**Determinants on national level**
employee needs, expectations, age, gender, educational level, skills, experience, position, occupation, performance, attitude toward work, social connections.	organization's structure, strategy, culture, used technology, type of industry, sector (private or public), the number of employed people, the scale of running the business, economic performance, trade union representation,	the economy (supply and demand forces), legislation, political system, social environment, national culture

Source: author, on the basis of Lupton and Gowler, 1969; Berg, 1976; Gerhart and Rynes, 2003; Borkowska 2004

To create effective compensation system managers have to answer the question: "For what do we want to pay in order to support the organization's strategy?". The greater the fit between the organization and compensation strategy, the more effective is the organization (Milkowich and Broderick, 1991). The organizational strategy may influence the level of base and variable pay, the compensation structure and forms of pay.

Compensation is just one of many systems that make up an organizational system. Its design is partially influenced by how it fits in with the other structures and systems in the organization and with corporate culture (Trice and Beyer, 1984). A highly centralized structure and hierarchical organization's culture is reflected in hierarchical compensation system – e.g. big differences in pay level between ordinary employees and managers, expanded managerial compensation package. A significant role in creating compensation systems is given to trade unions. They affect not only the level of pay, but the forms of benefits as well. The allocation between base pay and benefits has been greatly affected by unions (Freeman and Medoff, 1984; Mathieson, 2000). Unions have strong preferences for increasing base pay evolving social benefit plans, e.g. cost-of-living adjustment or heath care.

Organizations depend on the environment. Environment refers to economic factors (e.g. competitive pressure from product and labour market, and economic situation in the country), legislative factors (changes in legislation and policy) (Kavanagh and Elliott, 2000), and societal factors (changes in work force demographics, union-management relationship, national culture i.e. norms, customs and tradition). Pay differences were noticed in classical European economic literature – Adam Smith, David Ricardo, Karl Marx. Smith advocated that supply and demand are the main factors in setting wages. According to his theory, wages reflect a labour's worth (price) agreed between the buyer (employer) and the seller (employee). Smith did not address the issue of how supply and demand regulate wages. The issue of labour supply was addressed by Ricardo. He theorized that the wages of labour would always equal the amount necessary to buy goods that worker need in order to live at the subsistence level. Marx built his theory of surplus value on the basis of this understanding of labour. He said that under capitalism, wages will be based on exchange value (the agreement between employer and employee) and it will provide only subsistent wage. According to Marx, labour use value (the value or price ascribed to the use or consumption of labour in the production of goods or services) is higher than its exchange value. The surplus is pocketed by the employer, while it should be paid to the worker. Neoclassical economists explain away pay differences in terms of their worth to the organization and productivity (Bhagwati, 1984; Falvey and Gemmell, 1996). They evolved marginal productivity theory of wages. The introduction of supply-side approach to the wage problem was embodied in human capital theory. Earnings started to be seen as a reflection of human capital embodied in individuals, who invest in education and training. The assumption is that this investment raises productivity and hence the attractiveness of worker to employer who would pay higher wages to employ such a person.

The influence of individual, organizational, economic and legislative factors on compensation have been broadly discussed and analyzed in the literature. There is a lack of research taking into account culture as an important factor shaping the compensation system. National culture that manifests in common value system, customs and traditions, is important in analysing compensation from social and motivational perspective. Managers, mainly in multinational companies, need to take into account employees' cultural background in decision-making processes concerning earnings. In the next part of paper the culture concept is presented more precisely. Some assumptions concerning potential cultural impact on compensation system are also put forward.

Culture as a determinant of compensation system

Etic and *emic* approach towards cross-cultural study

Everybody can observe that people from different cultures act differently in many situations of life. People may have different problems and they may think differently about the same problems. Are these differences so deep that we cannot make any comparison, or is there something that may be compared? There is a tension between these two questions and two research traditions in cross-cultural study. Throughout the history of the study of culture there has been a dispute between those stressing the unique aspects of culture and those stressing the comparable aspects (Triandis, 1994).

The first approach is working intensively within a single culture in order to understand the indigenous phenomenon and how it is related in a cultural context. The second approach is working comparatively across the cultures in order to understand broad patterns of relationship between cultural variables and other phenomena. Some researchers perceive this methodological problem as *etic-emic* dilemma.[6] According to Pike, *emic* and *etic* views are not considered as opposites. He suggested that these two approaches describe the problem from two different standpoints, which lead to results, which shade into one another (Pike, 1971). In Table 2 *etic* and *emic* approaches have been compared.

Table 2:   *Etic* and *emic* approaches compared

Etic	*Emic*
Compare different aspect/dimensions across cultures.	Understand indigenous phenomenon in one culture.
Examine how culture influence individual behaviour.	Explain phenomenon of culture.
Culture seen as external factor influencing human behaviour.	Culture seen as integral part of human behaviour.
Researchers approach the question of cross-cultural study from a trans- or metacultural perspective.	Research attempts to view culture through the eyes of their subjects.
	Observations, interviews.
Surveys.	

Source: author, on the basis of: Pike, 1971

The example of *emic* approach is d'Iribarne's comparative study in three manufacturing plants of a French aluminium company in France, the

Netherlands and the United States (d'Iribarne, 1996/1997). Hofstede's research concerning culture's differences is example of *etic* approach. Both *etic* and *emic* approach have their specific advantage and shortcomings. The value of *etic* approach is fourfold. First, it provides a broad perspective about different events around the world, so that similarities and differences can be recognized. Secondly, techniques for recording differing phenomena can be acquired. Then third, an *etic* approach is the only point of entry, since there is "no other way to begin an analysis than by starting with a rough, tentative *etic* description of it" (Pike, 1971). And finally, an *etic* comparison of selected cultures may allow a researcher to meet practical demands, such as financial or time limitations. The most important *emic* advantages are the following: it permits an understanding of the way in which culture is constructed; it helps one to understand individuals in their daily lives, including their attitudes, motives and interest; and this approach "provides the only basis upon which a predictive science of behaviour can be expected to make some of its greatest progress, since even statistical predictive studies will in many instances prove invalid" (Pike, 1971). These advantages aside, each approach has its shortcomings. Through an *etic* approach it is easy to overlook the differential effects of cultural impact (Harris, 1999). The *emic* treatment tries to compensate for culture-boundness by giving their own say the individuals under study. The difficulty in *emic* approach is that biases, which limit self-determination and self-reflection, are ignored.

As the aim of the chapter is to address the question as to whether cultural differences across countries correspond to differences in compensation systems, the etic approach towards cross-culture study will be used. Hofstede's culture dimensions have been chosen to describe the culture of the countries analysed.

The concept of culture

Culture is a complex concept. It has been defined in many ways. From anthropological point of view culture describes patterned ways of thinking, feeling and reacting, acquired and transmitted mainly by symbols, constituting the distinctive achievements of human groups, including their embodiments in artefacts. The essential core of culture consists of traditional (i.e. historically derived and selected) ideas and, especially, their attached values (Kluckhohn, 1951). Culture has tangible (artefacts) and intangible (the philosophy of life, values) aspects. Through human behaviour, the language people speak and their relationships with their environments, researchers may guess the life philosophy and values underlying artefacts in human societies. The artefact and social constructs (such as compensation system) may reflect national culture. Culture distinguishes one group or category of people from another. The distinction can be made on three different levels: national, regional organizational.

Some researchers state that culture changes continuously (Gullestrup, 2001), while other argue that a stable unit is difficult to change (Hofstede, 2001). Artefacts and human behaviour may be changeable, but values, attitudes, beliefs shared within society are more entrenched (Hofstede, 2001). The fact that culture is difficult to change, or change is very slow at least, is the basis for further analysis; this will use Hofstede's culture indexes in five culture dimensions.

Hofstede's model of culture

The base data for Hofstede's study was collected in 1980 at IBM, a large multinational corporation residing in over 40 countries (Hofstede, 2001). An extensive analysis of questionnaire responses from IBM employees and historical analysis of culture differences suggested that differences in national cultures can be thought of as varying along five dimensions:

- Individualism – Collectivism (IDV),
- Power Distance (PDI),
- Uncertainty Avoidance (UAI),
- Masculinity – Femininity (MAS),
- Long-Term/Short-Term Orientation (LTO).

Individualism – Collectivism refers to the role of the individual and group, and which interest prevails over the other. Hofstede's research shows that in individualistic cultures employees perform best as individuals; direct appraisal of performance tended to improve productivity, qualifications for jobs were reflected by performance in previous tasks. Also, employees saw earnings as a more important aspect than interesting work. Collectivistic cultures assign a great deal of importance to training and use of skills in jobs, employees perform best in groups, and direct appraisal of performance is perceived as a threat to harmony (Hofstede, 2001). On the basis of Hofstede's individualistic-collectivistic analysis some assumptions concerning compensation's preferences can be made. In individualistic cultures, employees probably would like to be paid on individual basis, rather that collective one. Pay-for-performance plans and variable pay is going to be common (more common than in collectivistic cultures) and the wage differentials may be high (higher than in collectivistic cultures).

Power Distance reflects the degree to which people believe how institutional and organizational power should be distributed (equally or unequally) and how the decisions of the power holders should be viewed (challenged or accepted). Hofstede's research shows that in cultures where the power distance is high, subordinates do not express disagreement to their managers and expect to be told what to do; privileges and status symbols are expected, hierarchy in organizations reflects natural differences and inequalities between people are expected and desired. Cultures with low power distance saw subordinates express their disagreement to their managers. Subordinates expect to be consulted, privileges and status symbols are not expected, managers expect initiatives from subordinates, hierarchy in organizations is seen as exploitative, inequalities between people should be minimized (Hofstede, 2001). There may be some reference to the compensation system, based on Power Distance dimension. In cultures where power distance is high, managers may have more additional bonuses and rewards than subordinates. It may have reflection in high wage differentials between managers and non-managers (the differentials are going to be higher in the high Power Distance cultures).

Uncertainty Avoidance refers to the extent to which people feel threatened by ambiguous, uncertain situations and try to avoid them by establishing more structure. Hofstede's research shows that in cultures where the uncertainty avoidance is high, many rules are established. There tends to be a low tolerance of deviant ideas and resistance to change. Cultures with low uncertainty avoidance display few rules, high tolerance of deviant, innovative ideas coming from employees and much risk taking (Hofstede, 2001). In cultures with high uncertainty avoidance, employees may prefer to receive a high (fixed) wage and maybe reluctant to take variable pay. Employees with low uncertainty avoidance cultural background may prefer variable pay that one month may be very high, but the next month it may be very low.

Masculinity – Femininity refers to expected gender roles in a culture. In masculinity cultures there is strong gender differentiation in the socialization of children, different role models for men and women and people live in order to work. The level of pay is also important. Feminine cultures saw weak gender differentiation in the socialization of children, similar role models for men and women, people work in order to live and the quality of work matters (Hofstede, 2001). In masculine cultures, there could be a larger gender wage gap and higher social acceptance of such differences than in feminine cultures.

In long-term oriented cultures most people believe that the most important events in life will occur in the future and people are more willing to save. Short-term cultures tend to believe that the most important events in life occurred in the past or occur in present; people are a lot less willing to save (Hofstede, 2001). In long-term oriented cultures, long term compensation (such as shares, options, pension or saving plans) may be more common than in short term oriented cultures

Although Hofstede made a major contribution to the study of organizations and cultures, there are some shortcomings in this approach. Researchers, who criticize Hofstede's model of culture, raise some questions. Are surveys a suitable way to measuring cultural differences? Is the nation the best unit to study culture? Can an IBM sample be representative for particular cultures? What results could be obtained if he had chosen other sample?[7] Are Hofstede's dimensions the main ones or the only ones upon which we should be focusing on? Has increasing modernity reduced or changed the types of cultural differences which were apparent at the time when Hofstede conducted his research? Some of these questions concern *etic* approach toward cross-culture study, some have been answered by the Hofstede himself (Hofstede, 2002).

Variable versus base pay; Individualism-Collectivism, and Uncertainty Avoidance cultural dimensions

Managers frequently face this dilemma: how to compensate in order to meet organizational and employees' goals at the same time. Pay-for-performance programmes seem to be fair (employee is paid for effective work and results) and efficient if the condition of clear and commonly accepted rules are in place. Employers are willing to use these programmes, but employees are not so enthusiastic about them. Why? Variable pay differs from month to month – one time it may be very high, another very low. It is uncertain. Some employees prefer lower, but more stable pay. The share of variable pay in total compensation differs between countries. Is this due to cultural differences?

An empirical analysis in this section uses data from Worldwide Total Remuneration 2005-2006 report, prepared by Towers Perrin – the leading company in HR consultancy services.[8] The report highlights the various compensation and benefits practices in 26 representative locations around the world. For the purposes of this paper, nine European countries, the US and Japan were chosen. The data in this report estimates the typical pay for local national employees in April 1, 2005, in locally headquartered companies with approximately $500 million in worldwide annual sales.

Variable pay is important component of managers' compensation. Its share in total managerial cash compensation is significant in all analysed countries, but it varies significantly (from 28% in Japan and 40% in Poland till 70% in US) (Figure 1).

According to Hofstede, the Japanese and Polish cultures are character-ised by high UAI index (respectively 92 and 93), whereas US has a lower UAI index (46). Moreover Japan and Poland are collectivistic countries (IDV for these countries is 46 and 60), whereas US – individualistic (IDV=91). Uncertainty Avoidance and Individualism-Collectivism are negatively correlated (the Pearson correlation coefficient equals -0,14), which means that the less uncertainty avoidance the more individualistic the culture is.

Countries presented in the Graph 1 are sorted in terms of IDV from the most individualistic country to the less individualistic. Looking down the graph, the share of variable pay in general decreases. It implies that there is a connection between IDV and variable pay (see graph 2). The higher the degree of individualism the higher percentage of variable pay in total cash payment will be. There is a positive correlation, the Pearson correlation coefficient equals 0,56 between IDV and share of variable pay.

Graph 1: CEOs' variable and base pay as a percentage of total cash pay, IDV and UAI indexes in nine European countries, US, and Japan in 2005

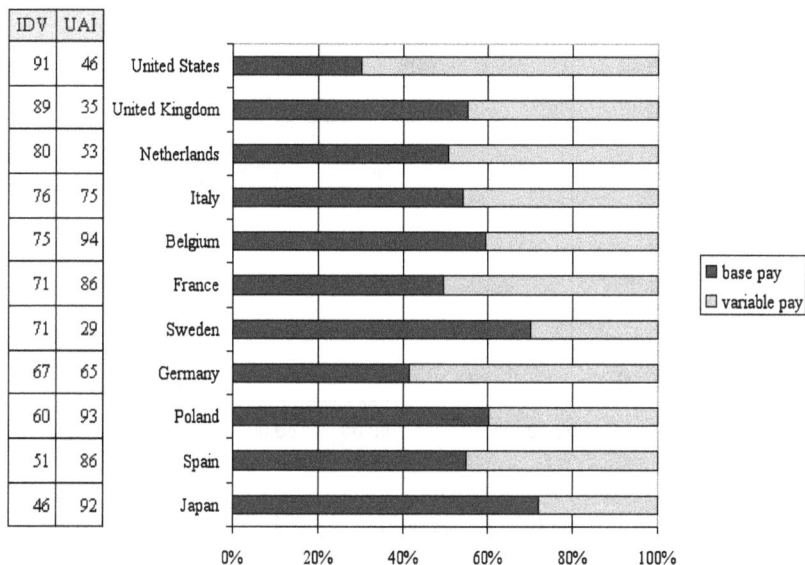

IDV	UAI		
91	46	United States	
89	35	United Kingdom	
80	53	Netherlands	
76	75	Italy	
75	94	Belgium	
71	86	France	
71	29	Sweden	
67	65	Germany	
60	93	Poland	
51	86	Spain	
46	92	Japan	

Legend: ■ base pay □ variable pay

(Horizontal axis: 0% 20% 40% 60% 80% 100%)

Source: Worldwide Total Remuneration 2005-2006, Towers Perrin, Hofstede 2001

Graph 2: Relation between CEO's variable pay and IDV

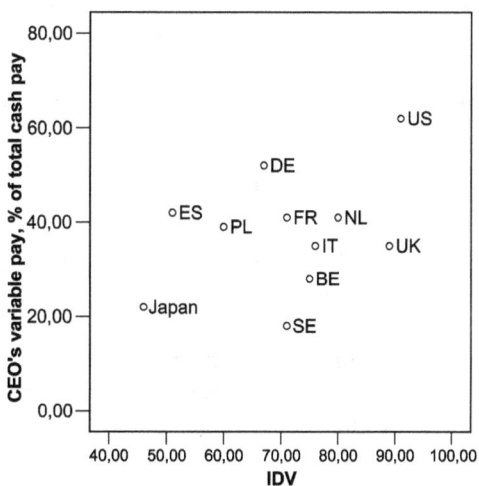

(Scatter plot: vertical axis "CEO's variable pay, % of total cash pay" from 0,00 to 80,00; horizontal axis "IDV" from 40,00 to 100,00)

Data points:
- US (~92, ~60)
- DE (~70, ~51)
- ES (~51, ~40)
- PL (~58, ~38)
- FR (~71, ~40)
- NL (~80, ~40)
- IT (~75, ~35)
- UK (~89, ~35)
- BE (~75, ~32)
- Japan (~46, ~22)
- SE (~71, ~20)

Graph 3:   Relation between CEO's variable pay and UAI

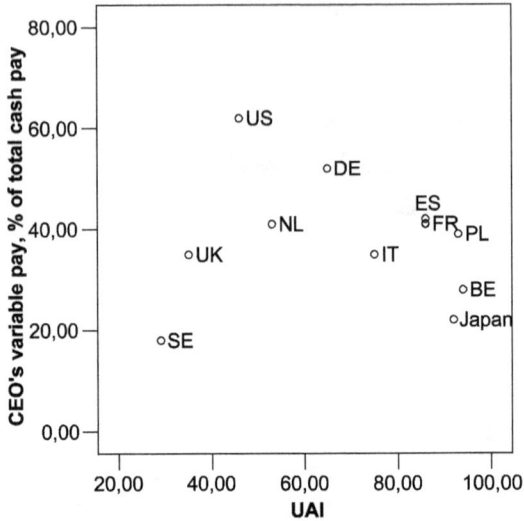

Source: Worldwide Total Remuneration 2005-2006, Towers Perrin, Hofstede 2001

Graph 3 shows the relation between uncertainty avoidance and share of variable pay. Negative correlation (r = -0.14) suggests that high uncertainty avoidance is associated with lower share of variable pay. This does not, however, apply to all countries. Sweden, for instance, has relatively low UAI index and relatively high IDV, but variable pay accounts for only 30 percent of total cash compensation. This may be explained by very low masculinity index (MAS index for Sweden is 5, while the average MAS index for the analysed countries is 53). According to Hofstede, people in feminine societies (low MAS index) are not very much interested in getting high salary. The work and earning money is not a priority. The very important issue is harmony. When employees are compelled to make a choice: either compete with his/her colleague to get a higher salary, or obtain a smaller salary with a nicer atmosphere at work, he/she probably would choose the second solution (under the condition that the base salary is high enough).

Egalitarian versus hierarchical compensation structure and Power Distance culture's dimension

Ford CEO Jacques Nasser's retirement package, as reported in the Wall Street Journal in 2002 was the following: one car a year from Ford with the option of buying several more at discount, financial planning assistance, executive office at headquarters with administrative assistant, a scholarship at an educational institution of his choice founded by the company and an annual pension of $1.27 million.

Everybody, at first glance, dreams about such compensation package and pay level. At second glance, having taken into account: the scale of responsibility, working hours, availability to the company (almost 24 hours per day and 7 days per week), the scale of consequences of decisions that have to be made every day – some people stop dreaming about being Ford CEO. In general, people accept the differences between managers and non-managers (especially if the person is a manager). But to what extent? The range of acceptability may differ across countries.

Egalitarian philosophy implies a belief that all workers should be treated equally (equal pay for jobs of equal worth). Some believe that more equal treatment will improve employee satisfaction and subsequently affect workers' performance. More egalitarian pay structures would have fewer levels and smaller differentials between levels and between managers and none-managers. By contrast, hierarchical structures have more levels and greater differentials among them. All pay structures by definition have some degree of hierarchy. The case is that some have more than others. Table 3 and figure 4 show the pay gap between managers and non-managers in 12 European countries in terms of Power Distance index. The smaller the gap the more egalitarian the compensation system is.

The empirical analysis in this and next section is based on European Community Household Panel database (ECHP UDB) and WageIndicator data. The ECHP is a standardized survey conducted in EU member states under the auspices of the Statistical Office of European Commission. Each year from 1994 to 2001 interviews were conducted with the representative panel of household and individuals. The database is a main source of comparable information across member states on income, work and employment, poverty, health and many other social indicators.

The gap within one country through the five year period remained stable. Denmark is the country with lowest pay gap between managers and non-managers (about 34%). The highest pay gap index was observed in Portugal (about 60%). There are no significant changes in the countries' ranking from one year to another. The first position was permanently held by Denmark and the last one by Portugal. Netherlands is an exception – there was some slight increase in the pay gap in 2001, which caused the drop in the ranking (from 5th position in previous years to 11th in 2001). Graph 4 shows pay gap between managers and non-managers. Countries are sorted by Power Distance Index (PDI). Some countries' culture correspond with the differences in managers' and non-managers' compensation (e.g. Denmark, Finland are countries with low PDI and relatively low pay gap on the one hand; and Spain and Portugal – countries with high PDI and relatively high pay gap on the other). Graph 5 shows the relation between managers pay gap and PDI. Differences in managers' and non-managers' pay are bigger in countries with higher PDI (Pearson correlation coefficient equals 0.52).

Table 3: The pay gap between managers and none-managers in 1997, 1998, 1999, 2000 and 2001

Country	1997		1998		1999		2000		2001		PDI
	index	rank	index	rank	index	rank	index	rank	index	rank	
Denmark	34%	1	34%	1	34%	1	34%	1	35%	1	18
Italy	41%	2	42%	2	43%	2	42%	3	42%	2	50
Finland	42%	3	42%	3	43%	3	41%	2	42%	3	33
Belgium	43%	4	44%	4	43%	4	43%	4	44%	4	65
Netherlands	46%	5	46%	6	44%	5	46%	5	55%	11	38
Austria	46%	6	45%	5	47%	6	46%	6	45%	6	11
Ireland	50%	7	47%	7	48%	7	49%	7	48%	7	28
UK	50%	8	51%	8	50%	8	49%	8	49%	8	35
Greece	51%	9	52%	9	51%	9	51%	10	45%	5	60
France	52%	10	52%	10	51%	10	49%	9	50%	9	68
Spain	59%	11	57%	11	56%	11	55%	11	53%	10	57
Portugal	63%	12	60%	12	60%	12	57%	12	60%	12	63

Note: the pay gap index is calculated as follows: managers' gross hourly wages in national currency minus non-managers' gross hourly wages in national currency divided by managers' gross wage
Source: ECHP database, Hofstede 2001

Graph 4: **The pay gap between managers and none-managers in 1997**

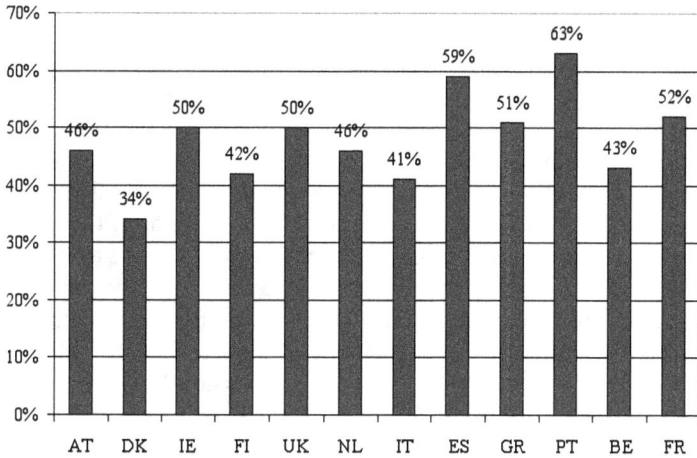

| PDI | 11 | 18 | 28 | 33 | 35 | 38 | 50 | 57 | 60 | 63 | 65 | 68 |

Source: ECHP database 1997, Hofstede 2001

Graph 5: **Relation between managers pay gap and PDI – ECHP database**

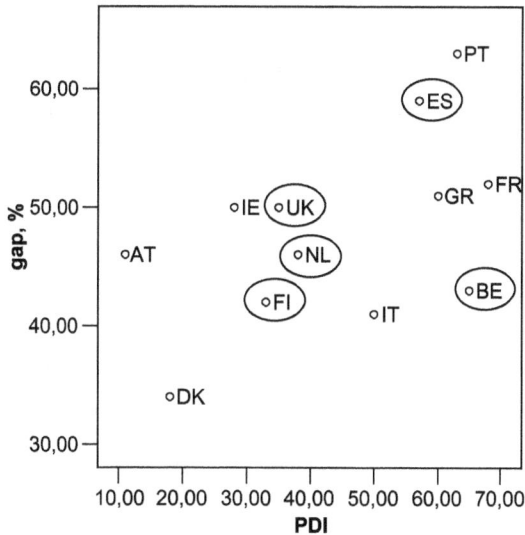

Source: ECHP database 1997, Hofstede 2001

ECHP has some restrictions, especially as far as wage analysis is concerned. Although the questionnaire is standardized, it may not give the identical information among countries. This is due to the different legal and institutional definitions of the same notions, e.g. gross and net employment income may be defined differently in different countries (net income in Germany means income after taxes and social security contributions, and in France – after social security contributions, but prior to taxation). Because of these shortcomings it is good to take other data into the consideration.

Graph 6 shows pay gap between managers and non-managers in 2005. The analysis was done on the basis of WageIndicator database. The data come from online questionnaires, which can be found on the websites of countries taking part in the WOLIWEB project.[9] Woliweb is an acronym for WOrk LIfe WEB. It aims at contributing to the understanding of citizens' work life attitudes, preferences and perceptions through a cross-country comparative research by means of European-wide data collection with regard to work life. In 2005, almost 70 thousands employees in seven European countries answered the questionnaire. The pay gap between managers and non-managers, according to WageIndicator data, is lower than the pay gap calculated on the basis of ECHP data. However, the country relative positions in the ranking are more or less the same (Finland and Belgium have got low pay gap index, whereas those of UK and Spain were higher). The differences in pay gap level between WageIndicator data and ECHP data may be explained by different definition of manager and non-managers. In ECHP questionnaire respondent indicated whether he/she has a supervisory position, intermediate or non-supervisory position. There were three levels of positions that were held by the respondents. Only those with supervisory positions and non-supervisory position were included in the analysis. In WageIndicator questionnaire respondents were asked the question: "how many people do you supervise?" Of those who answered – 0 (nobody) were considered as non-managers; those, who answered – 1 and more were considered managers.

Graph 6 shows the pay gap between managers and non-managers in different countries, and graph 7 – relation between the gap and PDI. As the second graph shows, the analyzed countries may be divided into two groups: with low and high PDI. Finland, Germany, UK, and the Netherlands belong to the first group, Spain Belgium and Poland – to the second one. The pay gap between managers and non-managers in general is lower in the first group and higher in the second group (Belgium is an exemption). The Pearson correlation coefficient equals 0,48.

Graph 6: **The pay gap between managers and non-managers in 2005 and PDI**

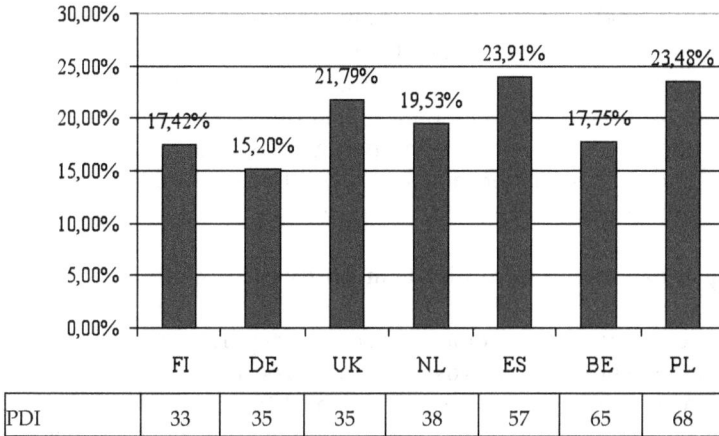

	FI	DE	UK	NL	ES	BE	PL
PDI	33	35	35	38	57	65	68

Source: WageIndicator-2005, Hofstede 2001

Graph 7: **Relation between managers pay gap and PDI – WageIndicator-2005 database**

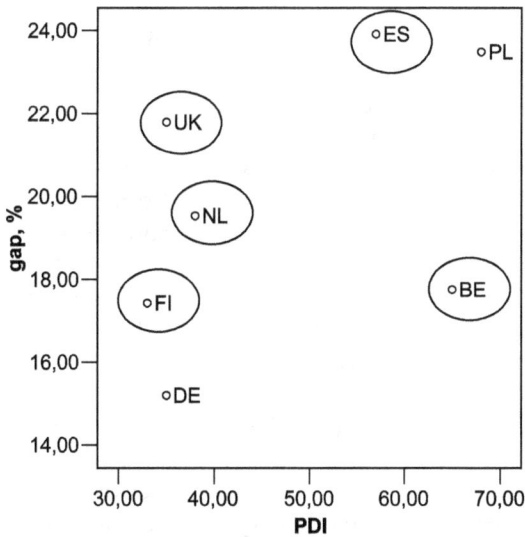

Source: WageIndicator-2005, Hofstede 2001

It is interesting to compare the results of analysis from the two sources of data – ECHP database, and WageIndicator database (graph 5 and 7). It would be less useful, of course, to compare the pay gap between these two databases (the gap was calculated differently). But as far as culture differences is concerned, it is worthy to analyze the relative positions of each country with reference to each other. Countries which were included in both databases are shown in the graphs in the circle. There were five such countries: Belgium, Finland, The Netherlands, Spain and UK. The relative position of these countries is the same in the two graphs. It is one, out of others, evidence, that culture matters as far as pay differences between managers and non-managers are concerned.

Gender pay gap and Masculinity-Femininity culture dimension

In the European Union women earn on average 16% less than men (raw or unadjusted gender gap in gross earnings). The study conducted by German researchers show that at most 50% of the difference in pay between the sexes can be attributed to differences in women and men characteristics (Beblo *et. al.*, 2003). Although there are a lot of studies on gender pay gap, and many attempts to explain it, some unexplained part remain. Apart from taking into account gender characteristics (e.g. education, professional experience, position, occupation, the type of contract, working hours) it might be interesting to consider others: mainly values, needs and attitudes. The women's situation on the labour market may, to some extent, reflect a common value system, behaviour patters and believes. For example, in some cultures women are expected to take care of children, so they stay at home and decide to suspend their professional career for some time. Such situations, even if commonly acceptable by the society, contribute to differences in women and men earnings.

Table 4 shows gender pay gap in 13 EU countries at the turn of the millennium (in 1999, 2000, 2001). The situation did not change very much in most these countries during the three years period. Spain, Greece, Denmark, and the Netherlands saw the gender pay gap increased slightly. The ranks of the countries (where first means the lowest gender pay gap, and 13 – the highest) remained almost the same. Diversity in the value of the gender pay gap index among countries was huge. The country with the lowest differences between men's and women's earnings was Portugal; the highest was the UK. The masculinity index (MAS) in Portugal is relatively low, in the UK it's high. But in general, correlation between gender pay gap and MAS was not observed (e.g. in Italy, where MAS is relatively high gender pay gap was low, in the Netherlands – the other way round – low MAS and high pay differences between men and women). The Pearson correlation coefficient was 0.06.

Table 4:   **The gender pay gap in 1999, 2000 and 2001**

	1999		2000		2001		MAS
	GPG	rank	GPG	rank	GPG	rank	
Portugal	1,69%	1	1,18%	1	1,55%	1	31
Italy	6,51%	2	4,94%	2	5,74%	2	70
Spain	8,91%	3	11,71%	4	14,33%	5	42
Greece	9,28%	4	10,46%	3	14,91%	8	57
Belgium	12,06%	5	12,32%	5	12,92%	3	54
France	12,65%	6	12,51%	6	13,12%	4	43
Denmark	13,72%	7	15,25%	7	14,45%	6	16
Ireland	15,97%	8	16,71%	8	14,67%	7	68
Finland	18,46%	9	17,23%	9	18,46%	9	26
Netherlands	18,79%	10	17,52%	10	20,03%	13	14
Germany	19,17%	11	19,09%	11	19,07%	10	66
Austria	20,09%	12	19,20%	12	19,69%	12	79
UK	21,57%	13	20,33%	13	19,51%	11	66

Note: gender pay gap index is calculated as followed: male minus female gross hourly wage in national currency divides by male gross wage. MAS – Masculinity Index – the higher index, the more masculine culture

Source: ECHP data

WageIndicator data that comes from a more homogenous group (young, well educated people) shows some correlation between gender pay gap and MAS (the Pearson correlation coefficient equals 0, 66). In Finland, the less masculine country (MAS=14), the lowest gender pay gap index (16, 64%) was observed, whereas in Poland, where MAS is relatively high (64) gender differences in earnings was the highest (25,49%) (see Graph 8).

Graph 8: Relation between gender pay gap and MAS

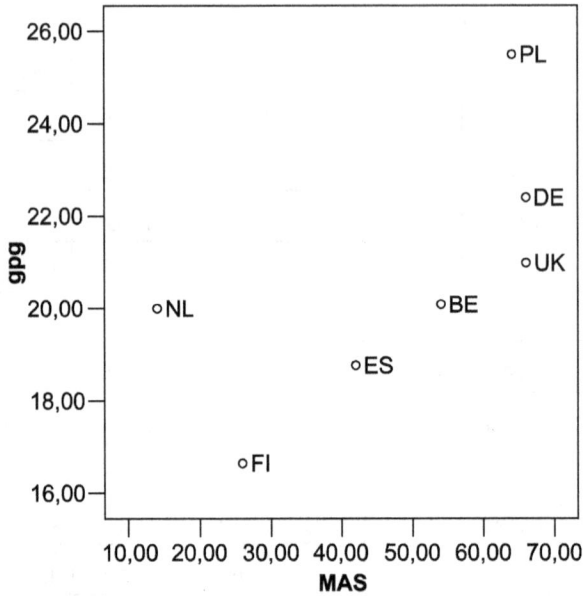

Source: WageIndicator-2005, Hofstede 2001

Conclusions and further research

One of the most important shortcomings in compensation's comparative analysis across countries is lack of comparable data with all important compensation system characteristics derived from one database and the same time period. Because of that, we had to use three data bases in order to analyse three main compensation system characteristics. For measuring the shares of base and variable pay – data from Towers Perrin's Managing Global Pay and Benefits Report (11 European countries, Japan and US were used). For analysing the difference between managers' and non-managers' compensation, two databases were used: ECHP (12 European countries) and WageIndicator (seven European countries). For analysing raw gender pay gap the same as for managers' pay differences database were used: ECHP (13 European countries) and WageIndicator (seven European countries). The data were available for different time period: Tower's Perrin Report – 2005, ECHP database – 1994-2001 (as the country taking part in the survey were changing, the years 1997-2001 for analysing pay difference between managers and non-managers, and 1999-2001 for analysing gender pay gap have been chosen), and WageIndicator database – 2005.

The main aim of this paper was to answer the question: whether differences in compensation systems' characteristics reflect differences in the cultural dimensions identified in Hofstede's? There is no one simple answer, but there is some temptation to say "yes". This is due to evidence. Analysis shows that there is a positive correlation between IDV and the share of variable pay, implying that variable pay makes up greater percentage of total pay in more individualistic countries. The correlation between UAI and the share of variable pay is found to be negative, implying that the greater uncertainty avoidance in a country the lower the share of variable pay in total compensation in that country. The correlation between PDI and the pay gap between managers and non-managers was positive, meaning that the strongest power distance the higher the pay gap between managers and non-managers. The correlation between MAS and gender pay gap is positive, indicating that there is some association between masculinity and greater pay gap between men and women). The correlations were, however, not significant seen from a statistical point of view.

Countries may be divided into the groups as far as culture and compensation system is concerned. Hierarchical cluster analysis shows that six countries that were taken into account create the following groups: 1) Belgium and Poland; 2) Germany and United Kingdom; 4) the Netherlands; 5) Spain. As culture dimensions are concerned, we have following groups: 1) Belgium and Poland; 2) Germany; 3) United Kingdom; 4) the Netherlands and Spain. As compensation system is concerned, the groups are similar, so it is difficult to draw any significant conclusions.

It is evident from the results that some degree of association exists between some types of compensation systems and the various cultural dimensions used in the study. But more in-depth analysis in this field is necessary. It would be interesting to conduct more broad descriptive analysis, using other cultural model, and cultural dimensions.

The culture manifest itself in different aspects of human's social and economic life. A lot of researchers and managers notice its importance in contemporary cross-national management practices. There is no doubt that, to some extent, culture influences these practices. The question is: how to prove it?

Notes

[1]   This question has been already discussed in New Testament: Matthew, chapter 20, verses 1-16, for a history of the different standards for pay see: Tolles, 1964,

[2]   Examples are UN Universal Declaration of Human Rights (1948), UN International Covenant on Economic, Social and Cultural Rights, The European Convention on Human Rights, ILO Convention 100: Equal remuneration, ILO Convention 111: Discrimination (employment and occupation), Directive 2002/73/EC of the European Parliament and of the Council of 23 September 2002 amending Council Directive

76/207/EEC on the implementation of the principle of equal treatment for men and women as regards access to employment, vocational training and promotion, and working conditions, National Constitutions

[3] According to Eurostat wages and salary include: direct remuneration, bonuses, payments to employee saving schemes, payments for days not worked, wages and salaries in kind, company products, staff housing, company cars, others.

[4] Psychological research studies shows that pay is associated with the satisfaction of some psychological needs such as security, esteem, status, recognition (Lawler, 1971),

[5] More about motivation theories: Bowey, Thorpe, 2000, pp. 81-101

[6] These terms were introduced into anthropology in the 1960s by the linguist Kenneth Pike. They were extrapolated from distinction in linguistic between *phonetic* and *phonemic*.

[7] Some researchers have tried to use Hofstede's questionnaire with different samples of respondents, and the results were similar (e.g. Hoppe, in 1990, surveyed 1544 very senior administrators from business, government, academia and non-profit organizations, who had attended a series of seminars in Salzburg, Austria), see: Smith, 1996,

[8] The report can be found on the web site www.towersperrin.com

[9] www.wageindicator.pl

References

Aycan, Zeyneb, Rabindra N. Kanungo, Manuel Mandoca, Kaicheng Yu, Jurgen Deller, Gunter Stahl, Anvar Kurshid (2000), "Impact of Culture on Human Resource Management Practices: A 10-Country Comparison" *Applied Psychology: An International Review*, vol. 49. no 1, 192-221.

Balsam, Steven (2002), An introduction to executive compensation, Academic Press.

Bebchuk, Lucian and Jesse Fried (2004), *Pay without performance. The unfulfilled promise of executive compensation*, Harward University Press, Cambrige, Massachusetts, London, England.

Beblo, Miriam, Denis Benninger, Anja Heinze, Francois Laisney (2003), *Methodological issues related to the analysis of gender gaps in employment, earnings and career progression*, Project carried out for the European Commission, Employment and Social Affairs DG, Final Report.

Berg, Gary (1976), *Managing Compensation*, Amacon, New York.

Bhagwati, Jagdish N. (1984), "Why are services cheaper in the poor countries?" *Economic Journal*, No. 94, pp. 279-286.

Borkowska, Stanislawa (2004), *Compensation strategy* (in Polish), IPiSS, Warszawa

Bowey, Angela (2000), *Gainsharing, in: Strategic reward systems*, ed. Richard Thorpe, Gill Homan, Prentice Hall, Pearson Education Limited, pp. 330-340.

Bowey, Angela, Richard Thorpe (2000), *Motivation and reward, in: Strategic reward systems*, ed. R. Thorpe, G. Homan, Prentice Hall, Pearson Education Limited.

Brewster, Chrees (1996), "Comparative research in human resource management: a review and an example", *The International Journal of Human Resource Management*, September Vol.7, No. 3.

Budhwar, Pawan S. and Yaw Debrah (2001), "Rethinking comparative and cross-national human resource management research" *International Journal of Human Resource Management*, May, vol. 12, no 3, pp. 497 – 515.

Erez, Miriam and P. C. Earley (1993), *Culture, Self-identity, and work*, New York, Oxford University Press.

Falvey, Rodney E. and Norman Gemmell, A formalization and test of the factor productivity explanation of international differences in service prices, International Economic Review, February, vol. 37, no 1, pp. 85-102.

Fay, H. (2003). "Currents in compensation and benefits" *Compensation and Benefits Review* Vol. 36, no 6, pp. 7-27.

Fein, Mitchell (1991), *IMPROSHARE: a technique for sharing productivity gains with employees, in: The compensation handbook*, ed. Milton L. Rock, Lance A. Berger, third edition, McGraw-Hill, pp. 159-175.

Final Report and Recommendations (2001), *Expert Group on Household and Income Statistics*, The Canberra group, Ottawa.

Freeman, Richard B., James L. Medoff (1984), *What do unions do?*, New York: Basic Books.

Funk, Lothar and Hagen Lesch (2005), "Minimum wages in Europe, European industrial relations observatory" on-line http://www.eiro.euro found.eu.int/2005/07/study/tn0507101s.html

Galbraith, James K. (2002), Inequality and globalization: judging the data, A presentation prepared for a conference etc., The University of Munich, Germany, November.

Gerhart, Barry and Sara L. Rynes (2003) *Compensation, Theory, Evidence, and Strategic Implications*, Sage Publications, Thousand Oaks, London, New Delhi.

Glinow, von Mary Ann (1985), "Reward strategies for attracting, evaluating and retaining professionals" *Human Resource Management*, Summer, pp. 191-206.

Greenspan, Ike (1991), *Short-Term Incentives, in: The compensation handbook*, ed. Milton L. Rock, Lance A. Berger, third edition, McGraw-Hill, pp. 266-289.

Gullestrup, Hans (2001), The complexity of intercultural communication in cross-cultural management, International Business Economics, (Reprint Series, Aalborg Universitet)

Hampden-Turner, Charles and Fons Trompenaars (1994), *The seven cultures of capitalism*, Piatkus, London.

Harris, Philip R. (1999), *Theories of Culture in Postmodern Times, Altamira Press, A Division of* Sage Publications, Inc., Walnut Creek – London – New Delhi.

Harris, Philip R. and Robert T. Moran (1996), *Managing Cultural Differences*, Gulf Publishing Company, Houston-London-Paris-Zurich-Tokyo.

Henderson, Richard I. (2003), *Compensation Management in a Knowledge Based Society*, Prentice Hall, Upper Saddle River, New Jersey.

Hofstede, Geert (2001), *Culture's Consequences*, Second edition, Sage Publication, Thousand Oaks, London, New Delhi.

Hofstede, Geert (2002), "Dimensions do not exist: A reply to Brendan McSweeney", *Human Relations*, vol. 55, no 11.

Hyman, Jeffrey S. (1991), *Long-Term Incentives, in: The compensation handbook*, ed. Milton L. Rock, Lance A. Berger, third edition, McGraw-Hill, pp. 338-354.

d'Iribarne, Philippe (1996/1997), "The usefulness of an ethnographic approach to the international comparison of organizations", *International Studies of Management and Organization*, White Plains, Winter.

Ivancevich, J. M. (1998) *Human resource management*, Irwin/McGraw-Hill.

Kavanagh, Catherine and Robert Elliott (2000), *Economic policy, the labour market and reward, in: Strategic reward systems*, ed. Richard Thorpe, Gill Homan, Prentice Hall, Pearson Education Limited, pp. 63-80.

Kluckhohn C., (1951), *The study of culture, in: The policy sciences*, ed. D. Lerner, H. D. Lasswell, Stanford University Press.

Lawler, Edward E. III (1971), *Pay and organizational effectiveness:* a psychological view, McGraw-Hill, New York.

Lawler III, Edward E. and Richard Hackman (1969), "The impact of employee participation in the development of pay incentive plans: a field experiment", *Journal of Applied Psychology*, no 53, pp. 467-471.

Lupton, Tom and Dan Gowler (1969), *Selecting a wage payment system*, Kogan Page (Associates) Ltd.

Mathieson, Hamish (2000), *Trade unions and reward, in: Strategic reward systems*, ed. Richard Thorpe, Gill Homan, Prentice Hall, Pearson Education Limited, pp. 179-198.

Milkowich, George T. and Renae F. Broderick (1991), "Developing a compensation strategy", in: The compensation handbook, ed. Milton L. Rock, Lance A. Berger, third edition, McGraw-Hill, pp.24-39

Milkovich, George T. Jerry M. Newman (1990), *Compensation*, 3rd edition, Richard D. Irwin Inc.

Nash, Allan N. and Stephen J. Carroll (1975), *The Management of Compensation*, Boos/Cole Publishing Company Monterey, California.

Opsahl, Robert L. and Marvin D. Dunnette (1996), "The role of financial compensation in industrial motivation", *Psychological Bulletin*.

Pike, Kenneth Lee (1971), Language in relation to a unified theory of the structure of human behavior, The Hague – Paris: Mouton.

Robbins, Stephen P. (1996) *Organizational behavior*, Englewood Cliffs New Jersey, Prentice Hall.

Reed, Stanley A. Sains (2002), "Outraged in Europe over ABB", Business Week online, March 4, http://www.businessweek.com/magazine/con tent/02_09/b3772140.htm.

Regnard, Pierre (2006), Minimum Wages 2006, *Statiscits in Focus, Population and Social Condition*, Eurostat, no 9.

Schneider S. C., (1992), National vs Corporate Culture: Implications for Human Resources Management, in: Globalizing Management, ed. V. Pucik, N. Tichy, C. Barnett, John Wieley&Sons, New York.

Shaw, Sue and Mary Clark (2000), "Women, pay and equal opportunities", in: *Strategic reward systems*, ed. Richard Thorpe, Gill Homan, Prentice Hall, Pearson Education Limited, pp. 199-216.

Smith, Peter B. (1996), National cultures and the values of organizational employees: time for another look, in: Managing Across Cultures: Issues and Perspectives, edited by P. Joynt, M Warner, International Thomson Business Press.

Smith, Peter B. (1992), "Organizational Behavior and National Cultures", *British Journal of Management*, vol. 3, pp. 39-51.

Triandis, Harry C. (1994) *Culture and Social Behavior*, McGraw-Hill, Inc.

Tayeb, Monir (1995), "The competitive advantage of nations: the role of HRM and its socio-cultural context", *The International Journal of Human Resource Management*, September, vol. 6, no. 3, pp. 588 – 605.

Tolles, Arnold (1964), *Origins of modern wage theories*, Englewood Cliffs, NJ: Prentice-Hall.

Trice, Harrison M. and Janice M. Beyer (1984), "Studying organizational cultures through rights and ceremonials", *Academy of Management Review*, October, pp. 653-669.

Woodruff, David (2002), "Esteem of business leaders sinks via corporate scandals", http://www.careerjournaleurope.com/myc/survive/20020627-woodruff.html,

Worldwide Total Remuneration (2005-2006), *Managing global pay and benefits.* Towers Perrin HR Services.

Chapter 6

WEBSITES IN A CROSS-CULTURAL PERSPECTIVE[1]

Malene Gram

Introduction

Communicating with customers and potential customers on the Internet is a relatively new phenomenon and the Internet is still – even in recent marketing books – considered a "new media". The broad commercial use of the Internet is just around 10 years old, yet today every serious company has its own website. The media transcends borders and has become a symbol of globalization, and the fact that users across the globe can access a company's website is a great advantage but this also poses a number of challenges.

In this article it is examined how a number of Danish companies deal with language and culture on their websites aiming at a cross-cultural audience – the Danish food company Tulip is used as a case study. A study is made as to how culture and websites are linked in the research literature and the article invites to reflect on companies' need to localize their websites and on how ideas about culture can be operationalized within two different ways of seeing culture (emic and etic approaches).

The article is based on a literature study on culture and websites. The empirical data consist of an explorative study of Danish corporate websites, interviews with heads of communication of the Danish companies Arla, Vestas and Tulip, mail contacts with the Danish companies Aalborg Industries and Aalborg Portland and a study of Tulip's homepage.

Case: Tulip Food Company

The Tulip Food Company is a Danish company which produces and markets chilled, frozen and canned meat products with its own label, as well as private labels, to more than 130 markets. The company has sales subsidiaries in nine countries and a representative office in Russia. The Nordic region, particularly Denmark, is regarded as the company's home market. Other European markets, including Germany, France, Italy and the U,K are also important. Moreover, Tulip Food Company is a supplier to overseas markets, including the US and Asia (www.tulip.dk, January, 2006).

Tulip's website

Until around 2003, Tulip Food Company's home page was merely a business card, static and non-interactive. At this stage, the home page was made in an HTML-based system, common at the time. This system was not user-friendly; whenever changes had to be made, Tulip had to contact the advertising agency who created the site and had to pay to have changes made. In 2003, Tulip changed to the Windows-based system it has today. This system is simple to work with. It consists of several templates, and these templates can be filled in, updated and changed by Tulip employees.

On Tulip's home page (www.tulip.dk January 2006) there is a strong focus on Tulip's meat products. This home page shows a happy mother and three children, a selection of recipes, a competition and a link to Tulip's television commercial. According to Pernille Kroer, head of communication at Tulip, the main aim of the Danish website is to create a preference for Tulip's brand. To cater for B2B buyers and sellers, a special link ("Samhandelspartnere") is offered, where more specific information can be found regarding Tulip's products and services. There is also a photo archive which can be used – e.g. by retailers and wholesalers, and a direct link to Tulip's "Slice calculator" (helping buyers from industrial kitchens to find out how to buy Tulip's products the cheapest way).

Tulip has to handle the fact that the users of its website are not all Danish. Pernille Kroer states:

> Our homepage exists in a Danish, German and English version. Furthermore we have 'local' homepages in the countries where we have subsidiaries. The Danish site is a group homepage with a number of target groups. We get quite a lot of requests from the whole world through this group homepage. That's why we have found it relevant to have this site in several languages. However, the German and English version is not completely identical with the Danish version, which is bigger. The local sites are primarily directed at customers and consumers in each country.

In the English version of the Danish home page Tulip has chosen to show its main products. Danish television commercials are not part of this site. Apart from this difference the English site on the Danish main site is a more limited version of the Danish site, with the same design.

Tulip's subsidiaries' local websites

The local websites in Germany and the United Kingdom are similar to the Danish main-site, even though the subsidiaries have autonomy when it comes to filling in the ready-made templates. The French and Italian websites are still based on the system from 2003, but changes are planned.

The British subsidiary's site is managed by the British subsidiary and adapted to the British market even though a fair share of the information on the site is translated from the Danish site (e.g. the section on food safety). This site is aimed primarily at the British B2B market. In Britain Tulip Food service is only selling to the B2B market, a sister company is dealing with the British consumer market.

In Sweden, however, the local management felt that the Danish site-template did not live up to Swedish expectations of interactivity and the Swedes were allowed to make a more challenging site for the Swedish users. The local management in Tulip's subsidiaries (Germany, Britain and Sweden) are responsible for the main export markets assuring that these sites are acceptable to their national audiences. The localizations are primarily made in the B2C part of the websites, not in the B2B part.

The Swedish subsidiary has had relatively free hands to make websites promoting Tulip's products. The local sites are all managed by the local subsidiaries but follow the broad lines of the parent company in Denmark.

In Tulip's markets outside of Europe, no websites exist. In several of these markets contacts with agents and supply agreements with big wholesalers mean that hardly any market communication exists. Furthermore, in some of these markets, e.g. Mexico, the online population is still very small. Tulip has no dot-com address since tulip.com is occupied by a Dutch computer company. Tulip has, however, reserved the new European counterpart to dot-com: dot-eu.

Apart from what the local managements do to adapt the websites, Tulip has not given priority to adapting the sites much to local tastes. Pernille Kroer explains:

> We are so small in the German and French markets. Even though we have a good turnover in these markets we will never become a big player as we are in the Danish market.

Strategic choices

Creating a website is a difficult discipline because it is expensive and there are limits as to how many times users of the sites can be expected to click themselves further into the site. Pernille Kroer explains that Tulip has – as any other company creating a website – had to make a number of strategic choices. Tulip has chosen to focus on home and neighbouring markets. At the moment, the marketing department at Tulip has chosen to target end-users at its home page to aim at creating preferences for its brands.

Big companies like Tulip have resources to manage both a main corporate website with versions in German and English, and local subsidiary home pages managed locally. Even though Tulip has, till now, according to Pernille Kroer, not given high priority to cultural adaptation, and particularly not to the B2B segments, the mere fact that local subsidiaries are responsible for the local sites assures that the content is acceptable in a given cultural context. But for small and medium sized companies (SMEs), resources are seldom available for such an elaborate system of websites.

Culture matters – also on websites

For some reason there has been a tendency to perceive the Internet as "culturally neutral" (Zhao *et al.* 1998). This is probably due to the fact that it is considered that the users of the Internet have access and skills to handle the same technology and that they are possibly often relatively well educated. Still a number of studies show that various cultural groups have different expectations of a website (Hart, 1998), and that non-English speaking groups stay twice as long on localized websites (Singh and Pereira, 2005). A number of researchers argue that it is necessary to use local values and symbols to have impact (Luna *et al*, 2002).

Cultural preferences seem to matter on websites. Even though a number of studies show that websites of various global companies and brands are not adapted to specific cultural communication styles (e.g. Hermeking, 2005), other studies find that local country websites depict the cultural values of that country. Singh and Pereira (2005) write, after having compared the US, India, China and Japan, that even within the Asian region: "there is considerable variation in the depiction of cultural values on the web" (p. 141). This indicates that different cultural tastes exist when it comes to websites.

Challenges for Tulip's websites

Within neighbouring markets, Tulip plans changes in the near future to profit better from the possibilities of interactivity for visitors on its website – and also offering more attention to its B2B visitors. Tulip faces a number of challenges when creating and maintaining its websites. Tulip has to deal with:

- Developing a site or sites, choosing between numerous options: moving from an online business card in less than three years to an advanced interactive site is a big step.
- B2C and B2B target groups. Are these user groups' needs and ways of using websites very different? And are both groups sensitive to culture?
- Considering home market, neighbouring markets, foreign markets with varying cultural backgrounds and language skills. Should web content and layout be adapted? How can a cultural sensitive approach be integrated in corporate websites?

This article digs into these challenges by giving a brief overview of the website as a communication channel in an intercultural perspective, by showing how a number of other Danish companies have dealt with the challenge of multicultural readers and by presenting what has been written about websites and intercultural communication.

New media, old challenges

The obvious advantage of Internet communication is that anyone can access a website from anywhere in the world. This does, however, pose a number of challenges for the website owner, not least regarding the intercultural communication, which might follow from this. A number of these challenges are similar to considerations which have existed for decades with regard to other media (catalogues, ads, direct mail, TV commercials, etc.).

The opportunity of direct contact with customers is obviously a strength; but this can also cause problems. Replying to e-mails from users asking questions or demanding catalogues can be difficult to handle because it demands manpower of varying intensity and e-mail users expect a fast response (Hanna and Millar, 1997). The global nature of the audience who can access a website plays a role for the page content (e.g. language, cultural considerations, and simple linguistic considerations as the use of abbreviations, contact details).

B2B and B2C web visitors

How about the differences between B2B and B2C visitors to websites with regard to influence of culture? By some, B2B-buyers are considered as being very different, more "rational" buyers than B2C-buyers, by others they are considered as being just as anchored in a cultural context as B2C buyers: influenced by ideas about which sales arguments are valid in the context of a given product or service; which communication style is acceptable; which pre-understandings he or she has for example of a Danish company. In this article, the assumption is that a B2B buyer is also sensitive to cultural differences and that it is therefore relevant also to consider culture when creating a website in a B2B context.

Language strategies

How do Danish companies address potential or current website visitors? Danish companies interested in attracting foreign customers need to do so in a different language, because so few people speak and read Danish. An infinite amount of money can be used to develop websites, and obviously few companies, particularly small and medium sized companies, have large amounts of money to spend on their websites. Therefore it is necessary to prioritize their needs according to their actual contacts and future aims and ambitions as we saw in the Tulip case. In the following, a number of examples of different language strategies of how to deal with non-Danish visitors to websites are explored from locally centred to the most globally oriented companies.

In the first example of a language strategy the website is a primarily Danish site with less elaborate sites for main foreign markets for example in English and German.

Figure 1: **Main focus on home market, and smaller versions for main markets, possibly link to local sites for main export markets (inspired by Hillier, 2003). DK means Danish, E means English.**

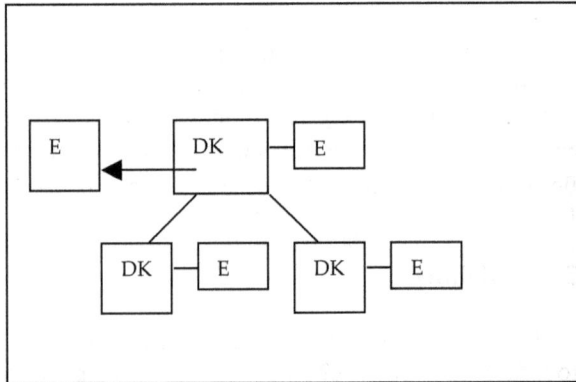

This language strategy can be relevant when the home market is most important, and further resources are then prioritized to main export markets. For some companies, agents and other partners deal with the export markets locally, and the main home page serves to inform or perhaps redirect people to a market served by an agent or a subsidiary. This strategy is for example applied by Tulip as presented in the case above.

A second way of handling non-Danish visitors on the company's website is to have a dot-dk or dot-com address with an English and Danish language option. Danish text would make it possible for Danish readers to quickly navigate towards the Danish language site, and English text for non-Danish speakers. Here the approach is global, but the company still demonstrates that Danish readers have a priority. An example of this is the Danish cement manufacturer Aalborg Portland (aalborg-portland.com, January 2006).

Figure 2: **Equal focus on non-Danish and home market visitors (Inspired by Hillier, 2003).**

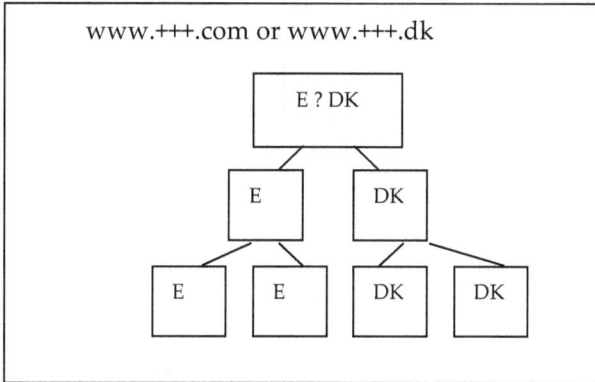

```
www.+++.com or www.+++.dk

          E ? DK

      E          DK

  E     E     DK     DK
```

A third language strategy is a dot-com address with a world map or a row of different national flags, making it possible to click into the relevant area of the world. This click might link to elaborate sites for various national markets e.g. www.arla.com (January 2006) (or elaborate sites for main markets and less elaborate sites, just addresses of agents for "other markets", or it can link on to just addresses of agents). This world map entry site can be supplemented by a Danish site, giving special priority to the home market as www.arla.dk (January 2006) does.

Figure 3: **"World map" dot-com leading to local sites or contacts supplemented with Danish site for home market.**

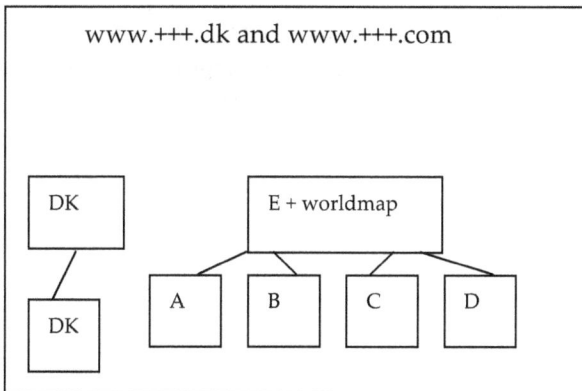

```
www.+++.dk and www.+++.com

  DK                E + worldmap

  DK          A     B     C     D
```

A fourth language strategy is a choice of an all English website with no Danish or other language options.

Figure 4:   **The all global no local approach.**

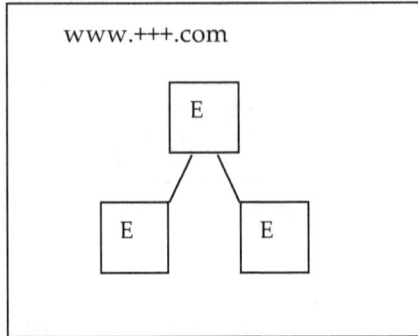

An example of this language strategy is Aalborg-Industries (aalborg-industries.com, January 2006) The aalborg-industries.dk address links on to the dot.com address, and this language strategy does not focus on its home market but has a global approach.

These different language strategies in corporate websites reflect the companies' strategic priorities. The various strategies can be found both in very modest and very sophisticated versions.

Summing up typical language strategies on Danish websites are one of the following. The website has:

1. Main focus on home markets with home page in Danish, offering smaller versions for main export markets (possibly supplemented with links to local websites).
2. Equal focus on non-Danish speaking and Danish speaking visitors with a main home page where the visitor has to choose between an English language or a Danish language site.
3. "World map" dot-com address, making it possible to click into the relevant area of the world, possibly supplemented with a dot-dk address with a Danish site for the home market.
4. All English, no Danish or other languages options.

Culture in websites

However, handling non-Danish visitors is not just about language. The content of the website can be read in a number of different ways depending on the reader's horizon of understanding and world-view. A number of authors claim that cultural differences and expectations must be taken into account. Hillier writes:

> "a mismatch between the cultural context of the site design and a set of translated text would cause 'inconsistencies' and 'uncomfortableness' to arise in the mind of the user" (2003: 11).

Figure 5 illustrates that communicating on websites demands more than adaptation of language. But how can we deal with culture on websites?

Figure 5: **Mismatch of language and cultural context in translated website (Hillier, 2003: 11).**

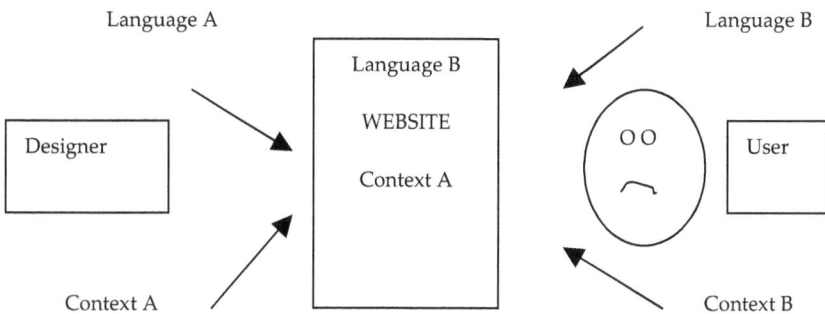

Hofstede and Hall: mainstream, but adequate?

Most studies on websites and culture have been made within the functionalist paradigm using primarily Hofstede and Hall's cultural models as frameworks. The functionalist studies identify general differences within values and within communication styles. This general approach has several limitations (a static view of culture, focus on national cultures, search for universal traits rather than looking out for what is special in a given context), but still a number of findings from these studies will be outlined below because they are used widely and with the limits in mind they might be inspiring when considering culture on websites.

Singh and Baack (2004) compared Mexican and American websites and found that the use of family and tradition as a theme (Collectivism vs. Individualism), titles and rank or prestige of the company (Power distance) differed between American and Mexican sites. In the Mexican sites, it was found that company titles, and in addition to plain titles the professional degree of individuals such as "Liecenciado", "Ingerniero" and "Doctor" was used far more frequently than on the US sites. The tradition theme was applied more in the Mexican context by using legacy statements of the founding fathers of the company and pictures of the founding Chairman (Uncertainty avoidance). Finally, gender roles were used in a different way (Masculinity vs. Femininity). According to Singh and Baack, men play a predominant role in the pictures on the websites, often shown conducting most of the company operations. Women, on the contrary, were seldom depicted, and if they were, they were shown in traditional roles on the Mexican sites.

Hermeking (2005) finds that many websites are characterized by a low-context style (i.e. very text heavy, deeply structured content). Hermeking sees these websites as strongly standardized and not taking into account the so-called high-context cultures who, according to Hermeking, prefer visual and less structured content elements on sites with a stronger emphasis on entertainment and emotional aspects. Hermeking calls this a "less print, more TV style", which he claims is better catered for in B2C contexts (especially regarding non-durable products) than in B2B contexts (particularly not industrial products).

Furthermore, differences in communication styles and values play a role when communicating on websites. Singh and Baack (2004) enumerate a number of differences found on websites in various cultural contexts. Readers across cultures might have different expectations and habits when it comes to web page layout for example when translating Roman-based alphabets (English, French, German, etc.) to non-Roman based alphabets (Chinese, Japanese, Korean, etc.). These readers have diverging rules of bolding, underlining and capitalizing and font selection vary between these two sets of alphabets (Rockwell, 1998 quoted in Singh and Baack, 2004). Singh and Baack also quote studies, which show that people who are used to reading from right to left prefer navigation bars in a similar sequence. As with other kinds of market communication, culturally bound traditions for making market communication must be taken into consideration along with translation equivalence, country-specific symbols, varying connotations associated with colours and icons with a special meaning in a given cultural context.

Alternative paradigms

While useful to consider, functionalist approaches to handling culture on the Internet seem like a limited approach to the complexities of cultural differences. The approach is most often an etic approach, looking for the same elements in various cultural contexts (e.g. that high power distance and high context communication are valid in all Mexican websites regarding all products) and it is static not taking into account that culture is dynamic.

According to modern anthropologists and sociologists culture is perceived as being dynamic and heterogeneous. In this view culture is perceived as meaning and collective subjectivity and culture is considered a social construction. Communication is considered a merging of horizons rather than sending a message to a receiver.

In this view it is clear that we cannot just consider cultural preferences as something fixed and static. The readings and reactions to websites are dependent on the readers' dynamic pre-understandings and expectations, experiences and values related to a given consumption context along with the words and images offered on the website.

The interpretive or symbolic approach – in contrast to the functionalist approach takes into account that cultures – and therefore readers of websites – are dynamic. Website creators take their point of departure in what they themselves think is good and appropriate communication when they create websites. Readers take their point of departure in what they think is good and appropriate when they evaluate websites. Furthermore Internet-users zap easily from context to context on the Internet and are used to reading contents and communication styles with various origins. This makes them competent readers, but they are still anchored in a cultural context.

When websites are created web designers and creators of web content automatically communicate from their own cultural horizons. The image they themselves hold of the company and the image they think others, e.g. people within different national settings, have of them as Danes and as part of a given business segment will play a role for how they orchestrate themselves on the website.

The meaning of horizons in the creation of websites

When creating websites the users and their various cultural backgrounds must therefore be considered. Who are the target groups? What are their horizons? Which experiences and expectations do they have towards the given products, situation of use, the nationality of the users and producers, etc.

111

Figure 6: **Website creators' and visitors' expectations and understandings of websites.**

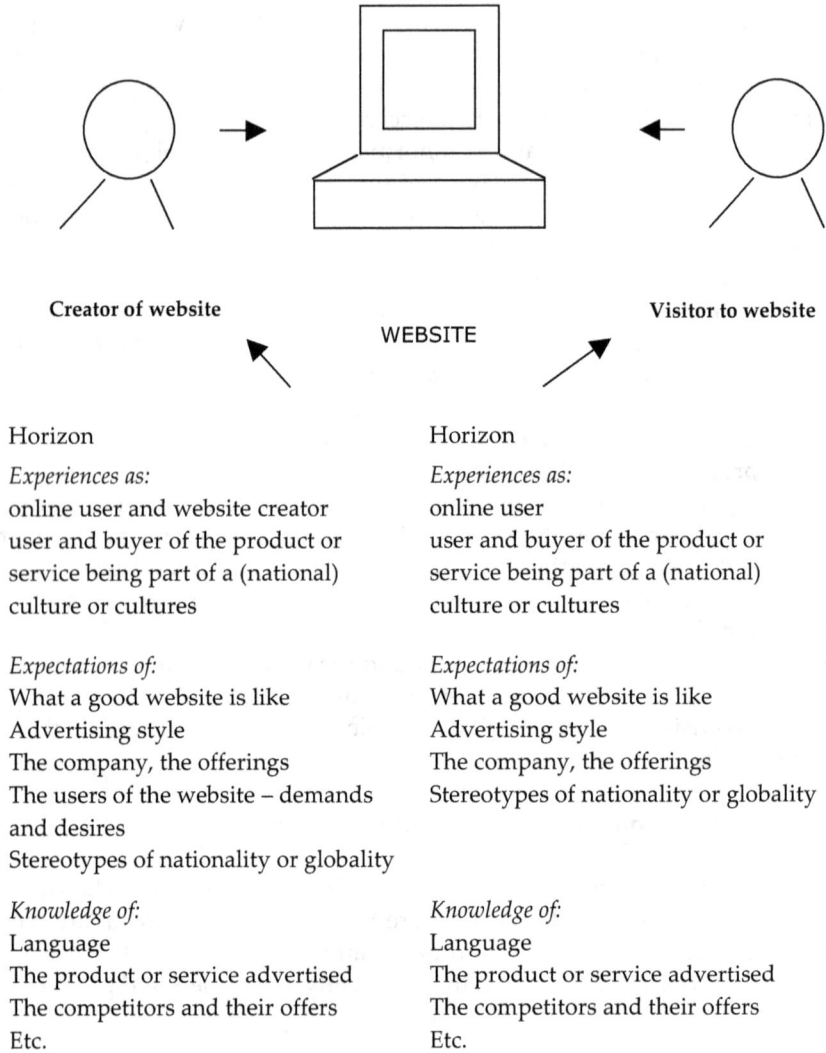

Creator of website	Visitor to website

WEBSITE

Horizon

Experiences as:
online user and website creator
user and buyer of the product or
service being part of a (national)
culture or cultures

Expectations of:
What a good website is like
Advertising style
The company, the offerings
The users of the website – demands
and desires
Stereotypes of nationality or globality

Knowledge of:
Language
The product or service advertised
The competitors and their offers
Etc.

Horizon

Experiences as:
online user
user and buyer of the product or
service being part of a (national)
culture or cultures

Expectations of:
What a good website is like
Advertising style
The company, the offerings
Stereotypes of nationality or globality

Knowledge of:
Language
The product or service advertised
The competitors and their offers
Etc.

By considering background knowledge of the consumption context (e.g. local food culture, if the product is foodstuffs, local working place relations, if the product is related to office equipment), other websites for similar products, other kinds of advertising for similar products if this exists in the target culture, a valuable insight can be obtained, which is more nuanced than the functionalist dimensions of culture or rough how-to-do advice.

Most often the functionalist approaches ignore the contexts of reading the websites, contexts of consumption, cultural-bound expectations of a product, a service or a website. Still some of the findings from functionalist studies might be inspiring and helpful, for example differences found in preferences regarding text versus pictures and graphics, emphasis on some values rather than others, etc. The best result is no doubt gained by including as much knowledge as possible from studies already made and combining these findings with an emic and open approach (what is special in a given cultural context?) and a feel for the ever-changing horizons of understanding among the target audience of the websites.

Tulip revisited

If Tulip decides to make a more developed and localized site e.g. to the French market, it could be relevant to dig into the issue of French food culture. Today this culture is torn between old and proud traditions of good ingredients and refined cooking and the busy lifestyles of not least French women (most often fulltime employees and housewives). The lack of time makes it difficult – if not impossible – to live up to the traditions of proper and well-prepared meals of earlier days. With its offer within precooked and convenience products, Tulip might very well fit nicely into this dilemma.

French consumers have a particular view on the importance of a meal being balanced ("un repas équilibré") i.e. combined by the right elements. To encounter these French expectations of what good and proper meals are, and what looks delicious, Tulip might want to integrate this more explicitly in its French website (e.g. by showing more vegetables along with the meat products presented, and possibly smaller helpings (there has to be appetite for the hors-d'oeuvre, cheese and dessert)). Also, the social aspect of eating is very strong in France, an aspect, which could also easily be integrated visually. That the website reflects an adequate presentation of food to a visitor from a French context might very well play a role for how images and sales arguments are assessed – also in the French B2B context.

The communication style of the French is known to be more poetic and emotional in advertising, but at the same time more formal and polite than the Danish context. If it holds true that markets known to be high context in Hall's terminology is more visually oriented this could be a clue for Tulip in the creation of the French website. Of course, this communication style is developing and changing, and a close look on similar French websites will provide Tulip with ideas to find a suitable approach and tone in the French version of its website, assuring a cultural sensitive approach to the French market.

Conclusion

Making corporate websites is still a new discipline, a discipline which is developing rapidly. Websites are cultural zones, like any other zones, and even though Internet users – both in B2B and B2C contexts – are more used to seeing web communication from various contexts, studies indicate that different cultural values, traditions and communication styles play a role.

A number of different language strategies from Danish companies' websites were presented in this chapter demonstrating different ways of dealing with non-Danish site visitors. Some corporate sites give highest priority to the home market with a little room for neighbouring markets, whereas other sites give no attention to the home market but have a focus in the website of being a global corporation with all communication in English. Danish companies have chosen a number of different ways of dealing with non-Danish visitors because they represent different missions and visions, different strategies, resources and priorities.

From an explorative view on Danish websites it seems that several companies have translated sites, but less so culturally adapted sites and in a number of cases the company seem to communicate with one "global" English-speaking person.

In the studies made regarding culture on corporate websites, it is found that cultural differences matter and different traditions already exist in different markets, as has been known for long in advertising research. The main part of studies made regarding culture on the websites are anchored in a functionalist tradition referring to Hofstede and Hall's notions of power distance, individualism vs. collectivism, high and low context communication, etc. These etic studies point out that different preferences exist when it comes to the use of visuals vs. text, weight on tradition vs. innovation, hard vs. soft sell, etc.

It seems obvious, however, that an eye for unique values, traditions and knowledge in a given segment, context of use of the product or service being promoted, unique traditions of market communication (traditions for use of humour, the use of authorities and experts to recommend products and guarantee quality, etc.) a so-called emic approach, is a valuable method when assuring the necessary knowledge about web target groups across borders. Relevant questions to ask are what is special for the targeted readers of a company's website, what are their associations linked to the product or service in question and what is changing in the experiences and expectations of the readers. Without any doubt, more emic studies could enhance approaches the Internet in an intercultural perspective to make the websites more culturally sensitive and possibly more powerful.

Whether or not a website should be localized to a local market is a much debated question. Clearly some benefits can be gained from using a country-of-origin approach (Danish Design, Danish Bacon), at least for some countries. However, in order to avoid offending or provoking or making the site illegible, it is relevant to understand the local culture and the local communication style (Is it e.g. acceptable to be emotional? Authoritarian? Direct? Are our sales arguments valid?). Websites with special domains for different languages or cultural areas have the option of localizing. This is more difficult with one global and standardized approach.

Another snag of creating various localized versions of the corporate website is that it is easy for readers of sites to click from one national version to another and may be puzzled if there are too great differences from one site to another. The question of how to handle the corporate image is therefore much more pressing regarding the creation of websites than when catalogues are sent out to different corners of the world. At the same time it is easy to check out one's competitors to see how they handle their web communication. This all adds to the excitement of intercultural communication in cyberspace.

Notes

[1] This article is a more elaborated version of a chapter in the book Meanings and Messages edited by Inger Askehave and Birgitte Norlyk (2006). The publisher Academica has kindly permitted the use of it here. The article was presented in Rebild, Denmark at the conference Internationalisation of Companies and Intercultural Management the 27th of October 2006.

References

Hanna, J.P.R. and R. J. Millar (1997): "Promoting tourism on the Internet", *Tourism Management*, Vol. 18, pp. 469-470.

Hermeking, M. (2005): "Culture and Internet Consumption: Contributions from Cross-Cultural Marketing and Advertising Research", in *Journal of Computer-Mediated Communication*, 11, 1, pp. 1-31.

Hillier, M. (2003): "The role of cultural context in multilingual website usability", in *Electronic Commerce Research and Applications*, 2, pp. 2-14.

Singh, N., Hongxin, Z. and Xiaorui H. (2005): "Analyzing the cultural content of websites. A cross-national comparison of China, India, Japan and US", in *International Marketing Review*, 22, 2, pp. 129-146.

Singh, N. and Baack, D. W. (2004): "Website Adaptation: A Cross-Cultural Comparison of US and Mexican Websites", in *Journal of Computer-Mediated Communication*, 9, 4.

Chapter 7

THEORETICAL REFLECTIONS ON COMMON FEATURES IN EUROPEAN CULTURES AND THEIR IMPLICATIONS FOR DEVELOPMENT IN SOCIETY

Hans Gullestrup

Introduction

Recent debate about Denmark's position in Europe has presented the discussion in terms of Denmark and Europe. I actually do not know why the debate has focused on this dichotomy – for we should rather discuss Denmark *in* Europe, or Europe *in* Denmark. The current debate presents Denmark *and* Europe as if Denmark were an entity that in actual fact could be separated from Europe. But in actual fact, we cannot use this approach! First and foremost, Denmark is already *part of* Europe, whether we want it or not. Denmark is in Europe or rather Denmark is part of Europe, both geographically and historically.

No one can challenge the geographical affiliation that Denmark is part of continental Europe, and no one with historical insight can reasonably challenge the fact that Demark has been an actor in European history for centuries. Just think of the many Danish victories and defeats there have been in wars and conflicts with Germany, England and Ireland, and what we today call the Baltic countries – not to mention all the many conflicts with Sweden. And just think of the Viking settlements in Normandy in France, in the areas south of the Naples in present-day Italy, and in England, and Ireland. Indeed, all the way down to 'Miklagaard' – the name the Northmen used for Constantinople or present-day Istanbul on the border between Europe and Asia. Or think of the proliferation of Hans Christian Andersen and Kierkegaard's thoughts and works around Europe, and let us not forget the age-long export of Danish agricultural produce, know how, and industrial products to countries in Europe.

So, Denmark is both geographically and historically already part of Europe!

But is Europe part of Denmark, then? Yes, and the answer must be a definite 'Yes'. Since most of what we refer to as Danish today, actually have come to Denmark from the outside in the form of goods, technology, science, art, and not least in terms of people with ideas and commitment. Ideas and commitment which have shaped the historical development in Denmark to such an extent that without these Denmark would not have been the Denmark that we know today. Europe, then, has continuously brought things, ideas, and commitment to Denmark. These have, admittedly, been assessed, modified and adapted to various degrees, but have then moved on to be considered as something typically Danish. European people, their ideas, and new knowledge have become Danish to such an extent that in many cases we have totally forgotten the origin of 'Danish' ideas, and the biological and spiritual kinship that many Danes have with the rest of Europe. Indeed, many Danes are in kinship with people from many other countries across the globe. We need only to remind ourselves that the Danish nobility that was behind the big and important agricultural reforms about 200 years ago originally came from Germany, and the cultivation of the moors of Jutland, and the development of Lolland/Falster in large parts were initiated by (potato) Germans and sugar-beet workers from Poland. Similarly, Sweden, Norway and the Netherlands have made contributions to Danish ancestral cradle. It is also worth remembering that Danish music, the music for the folk play of Elverhøj [Elves on a hill] was actually composed by an illegal immigrant from Germany: Kuhlau. Even the highest ranks of the Danish establishment – the royal family – have a good deal of their roots planted deep in the European soil outside Denmark; most recently in the French soil, and even much farther away, namely in the 'European cultural pockets' of Hong Kong and Australia.

So, indeed Europe is definitely also part of Denmark!

But besides the historical and geographical aspect, how much is Europe then part of Denmark? And how much is Denmark part of Europe? Or put in another way, how much do we Danes in Denmark have in common with other Europeans of today?

One of the ways we can approach an answer to this question is by means of the concept of culture. Is it, for instance, reasonable to speak of a common European culture – of common European values, or even of a common European identity?

Much has been written about this issue over time and in recent years in particular[1]. The present chapter explores some aspects of the debate. I will initiate the discussion with a presentation of my perspective on the concept of culture. This is followed by my reflections on some common features of the European culture and their implications for development in Europe and the rest of the world. The main thrust of my argument is that our cultures encourage us to perceive, acknowledge and define relevant issues in our societies. By doing so we select the kind of knowledge and insights that we think we need through research and developmental initiatives. In so doing we tend to ignore insights that we do not recognise we lack. This selective process of knowledge acquisition shapes the manner in which we formulate (or ignore) policies that guide developments in our societies. I will primarily reflect on which impact the common cultural features in Europe exert on how we in Europe – by using Denmark as an example – shape our development process. Finally, I will present three proposals on how, in Denmark, to a larger extent, we can rid ourselves of the restrictions of these cultural common features whereby we identify essential issues in society, and thus get rid of the culturally embedded solutions that we normally perceive to be the only relevant and realistic ones in the social debate in Denmark.[2]

A Model for cultural understanding

The concept of culture is difficult to define by researchers in the fields of humanities and the social sciences. Nevertheless, or perhaps for this very reason, it is a concept that many researchers from many different schools have worked with, and in which many researchers are still deeply involved. If one is to attempt to explain why it is so, it must be that culture is something that is relevant to all of us. It is something that we all have, and something which we want to preserve, and at the same time try to change, consciously or unconsciously. Culture provides security and gives us a feeling of belongingness in the company of some people and a feeling of distance to others. But, for better or worse, culture is also a strong guide for our way of being and our way of perceiving 'reality'.

If we are to understand much of what is happening in the world today we have to take into account the concept of culture. If we are to understand the situation in the Middle East, and what is happening and has happened in ex-Yugoslavia, in Palestine and Israel, or if we are to try to understand the debate about the Muhammad cartoons in the Danish Daily *Jyllands-Posten*, and the whole debate about refugees and immigrants in Denmark, we have to deal with the concept of culture. In recent years, the concept of culture has also become part of a tool in understanding organisational development and international cooperation in different types of organisations.

But what does the concept of *culture* mean? Well, to me culture is:

> The world conception and the values, moral norms and actual behaviour – as well as material and immaterial results thereof – which people (in a given context and over a given period of time) take over from a past generation, which they – possibly in a modified form – seek to pass on to the next generation; and which in various ways make them different from people belonging to other cultures.

Culture is by this definition man made and acquired, and thus in a way it is in contrast to what is 'not man-made' – to nature. However, the distinction between 'nature' and 'culture' is not so simple and clear, after all, as it immediately could seem to be. Firstly, the mere distinction between culture and nature is in itself culturally determined. In many cultures, in Arctic Inuit culture, for instance, or in native American cultures, man and nature constitute an integrated whole, and thus man and nature must be accorded the same degree of respect and consideration by each individual. In other cultures, for instance, modern industrial and technological cultures, the separation between nature and culture is more clear-cut. Nature in this culture (e.g. the Danish culture) is perceived as something that is by and large at the disposal of mankind, which people can treat and exploit in the way they find best, based on their own values.

The distinction between culture and nature is thus in itself a product of culture – or a social construct – so to speak.

Secondly, the boundary between what is man-made and what is not man-made is becoming more and more blurred because of new technological advances. When, by means of gene splicing, man, for instance, is able to create new plant and animal species, are these new plants or animals then part of nature, or are they rather examples of material products of culture? And when the climate – to a certain extent – can be influenced and manipulated by man, is the climate then part of culture, or is it still part of nature? Not to speak of man's own impact on the nature of man himself – through pharmaceutical technology and genetic manipulation.

The boundary between what is nature and what is culture is in no way unequivocal, and it is not always independent of culture. In spite of this, I will at an abstract level, maintain a distinction between what is man-made and what is not man-made; between culture and nature in order to focus more clearly on the concept of culture.

To me, the concept of culture can be understood by means of three different dimensions at an abstract and meaningful level: the horizontal culture dimension; the vertical culture dimension and a culture dimension in time. I will briefly outline these three dimensions below and the relationships between them.

The horizontal culture dimension and its different segments

Common for all living creatures is that their survival as individuals and species depends on the relationship between their biological needs (need for food, protection against the climate, reproduction and socialisation etc.) and the opportunities that the surrounding nature offers them. Where more than one person is present in nature, man will always seek to fulfil his basic needs in one form of *social co-action* or another. Not necessarily by means of social cooperation because some co-action may very well be characterised by suppression and exploitation. The ways in which people fulfil the basic needs and organise co-action can vary greatly in time and space, from one group of persons to another, or from one culture to another, even with similar natural conditions.

At the same time, we can observe a multitude of different ways to co-exist and ways in which to co-act to fulfil the fundamental needs in cultural contexts, we can also note certain patterns or common features in these ways. These features make up the essential parts, or central segments of culture in human co-action. In connection with my studies of different cultures I have found it purposeful to work with eight such segments of culture; in a kind of *etics culture analysis*, (see Harris, 199) which can be found in any one culture, but which each and in relation to one another can manifest itself in quite different ways. A difference which it only will be possible to analyse and understand by means of an empirical culture analysis, or by means of an *emics culture analysis* (ibid).

The eight segments of culture, which are equally essential in all cultures, and equally important for the understanding of any given culture together make up what I call *the horizontal culture dimension*. Horizontal because the eight segments of culture manifest themselves, so to speak, on the same level of the culture, that is on the 'perceivable' level. The eight segments, each describing different aspects of human co-action, can briefly be characterised in the following figure (see Figure 1).

- The processing segment: or technology.
- The distribution segment: or economic institutions.
- The social segment: or social institutions.
- The management and decision segment: or the political institutions.
- The conveyance segment: or language and communication.
- The integration segment: or reproduction, socialisation, and learning.
- The identity-creating segment: or ideology.
- The security-creating segment: or religious institutions.

Figure 1:   The horizontal culture dimension

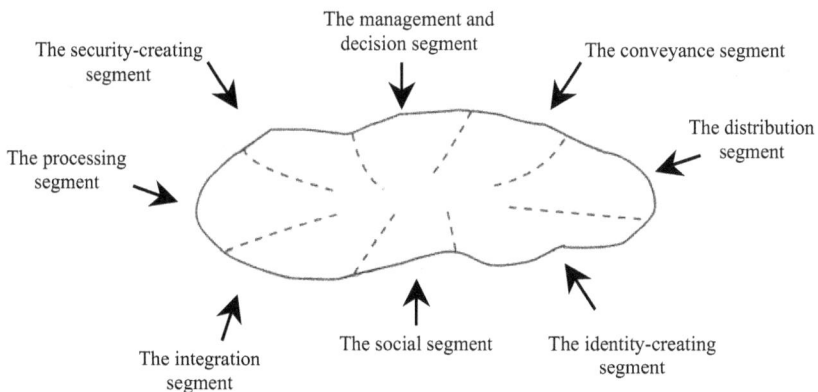

The vertical culture dimension and its different layers

In the encounter with a foreign culture certain perceptions will invariably be more noticeable than others and thereby create a 'first-hand perception' of the observed culture. Actual behaviour, dress code and available products of different kinds will usually provide the foundation for this first-hand image. Soon after the culture actor will also be able to perceive the underlying and difficult-to-perceive social structures, moral norms, and later the social values will begin to materialise before the observer, or the culture actor, (a term I prefer to 'observer'). These materialisations will contribute to a more nuanced image of the immediately perceived culture image.

Therefore, each observation is not equally important for the culture understanding, in-as-far as some – the more immediately perceivable and 'observable' culture features – may only be an expression, or symptom, of a deep culture characteristic, such as attitudes and values. Therefore, it is purposeful to speak of a hierarchy of observations – of a *vertical culture dimension.* The understanding here is that the immediately perceivable dimensions can be grasped through the above symbolising culture layers. The *manifest culture layers* both have significance of understanding, per se, but they also have a symbolising significance for the deeper symbolised culture layers – i.e. *the core culture.*

I have thus found it purposeful to work with six different vertical culture layers, of which the three upper layers belong to the perceivable or *manifest* culture layers with their own as well as a symbolising significance for the understanding of the three lower layers which belong to the hidden layers of the culture.

A. Manifest culture layers – or the symboli*sing* culture layers

1. The immediately perceivable process layer and its resultant outcome
2. The difficult-to-perceive structural layer.
3. The formalised layers of norms and rules

B. Core culture layers – or the symbo*lised* culture layers

4. The non-perceivable existence – or 'that which is without being there'
5. The basic value layer
6. The fundamental world conception

The horizontal and vertical dimensions of culture thus make up a kind of 'skeleton' for the individual cultures, and by adding "flesh" to the skeleton through a culture analysis, through a so-called 'emics analysis', the culture actor can obtain a snapshot, or a *semi-static culture description* of the observed culture. (See Figure 2)

Figure 2: **Culture as a complex entity consisting of culture segments and culture layers.**

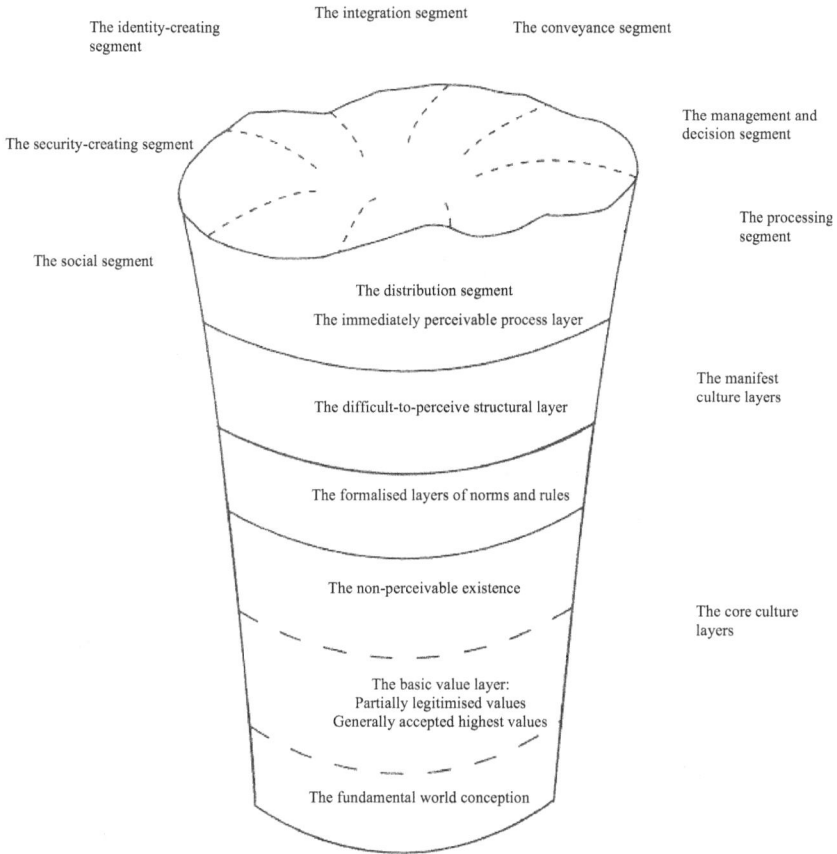

The identity-creating segment

The integration segment

The conveyance segment

The security-creating segment

The management and decision segment

The processing segment

The social segment

The distribution segment

The immediately perceivable process layer

The difficult-to-perceive structural layer

The manifest culture layers

The formalised layers of norms and rules

The non-perceivable existence

The core culture layers

The basic value layer:
Partially legitimised values
Generally accepted highest values

The fundamental world conception

The semi-static model

The culture dimension of time

No culture is however static, hence the term *'semi-static cultural description'*. On the contrary, any given culture is continuously exposed to a perpetual pressure to undergo changes, both from external and internal factors – what I refer to as *change-initiating* factors. These factors are called 'initiating' because they (by means of changes in many different ways) 'push' changes in the observed culture. These pressures may not necessarily lead to changes, though. Whether there really will be a change in the observed culture, and in which direction such a change will move are determined by quite different sets of change factors. I label them *change-determining* factors.

Among the culture-*external change-initiating* factors we can find both conditions in nature, as well as situations in and from other cultures. Nature's constant change means that human co-action, or human culture, which precisely makes possible a group of people's existence under certain natural conditions, is exposed to a perpetual pressure for change. Any one culture therefore has a kind of two-way relationship with nature. On the one hand, culture makes up the total complex of culture segments and culture layers which a group of people have developed over time with the purpose of fulfilling their own and their descendants' fundamental needs under the given social and natural conditions. On the other hand, this culture is, in all respects, changing the very same social and natural environment which makes up an essential part of the conditions of existence for the culture.

Of greatest significance, in most cases, are, however, culture-*external* factors which come from other cultures. This can be seen from the fact that major elements of a given culture usually have been taken from other cultures and have been made part of the existing culture. In such cases it is elements – which consciously or unconsciously – have been assessed and adapted to the observed culture, but which nevertheless are foreign elements that have been taken from other cultures through external *change-initiating* factors. These changes especially happen because of modern communication technology. The resultant changes for the individual cultures may be good or bad.

The culture-*internal change-initiating* factors are factors that have arisen 'within' the observed culture in the shape of new creations, research, political changes in attitude, and other types of creative action.

Whether a given impact of change will actually lead to culture changes will be determined by the *change-determining* factors and the relations between these and the initiating factors of change. In this connection I operate with four different factors in-as-far as I speak of *the degree of integration,* which is an expression of the similarity and uniformity between the different values of a culture; and the *degree of homogeneity,* which is an expression of the breadth and width of the aggregate knowledge and insight of the observed culture; of the *culture-internal power relations,* and the *interplay between the change-initiating factors and the relevant values* of the observed culture.

The degree of integration primarily influences the strength with which the observed culture rejects or accepts a given impact of change, either positively or negatively, depending on the interplay between the content of the integrated values and the value-related content of the change-initiating factors, whereas a disintegrated culture will react more weakly and unpredictably. In a strongly disintegrated culture the culture-internal power relations will thus gain much influence on the actual course of change, in-as-far as the contents of the accepted values of the powerful persons will exert a decisive influence.

The degree of homogeneity will be of immense importance for the direction in which the observed culture will move towards the culture-initiating factors. A very homogenous culture will solely 'relate to' culture changes that are as good as 'tailor made' to a very homogenous knowledge and insight into the culture, whereas a more heterogeneous culture, by means of a broader understanding, will relate to far more diverse culture impacts. Thereby the contents and shape of the change-initiating factors receive far bigger importance in homogenous cultures than in more heterogeneous cultures.

Culture as a dynamic totality and the three dimensions of culture

Pulled together, the three dimensions of culture offer a *dynamic under-standing of a given culture* (See Figure 3). It also produces a picture of the reality that partly determines the actions of people living within the given community. Thereby the culture becomes a central element in the understanding of the way in which a given person, or group of persons, perceive and interpret their surroundings, in-as-far as they perceive 'reality' through their own culture. They 'see' 'reality' through their own "cultural preparedness" or glasses.

The elements of the manifest culture in the different segments of culture help define society's 'undecided' issues, and thus the issues which researchers and politicians 'choose' to deal with, and for which practical solutions are sought. And they are also the ones who have 'a voice in' which solutions are demanded and ultimately accepted. It is, however, on the basis of the deep core culture that the overall formulation and management of the perceived and conscious problems are made, in-as-far as the actually perceived problems in society are clearly rooted and justified in the fundamental world conception and values of the specific cultures.

In the early Middle Ages of Europe, all major problems in society thus took their point of departure in the then prevalent world conception which was that the earth was flat and was the centre of the universe, and that every living creature was created by God and in the form and shape it had at the time. Any intellectual or political issues had to be based on this world conception. Intellectual or developmental work that went beyond this world conception – e.g. theory of heredity, global navigation or astronomy, religious independence from the Catholic Church – had slim chances of being *recognised* and *perceived*, let alone *be implemented*. It was not until an acceptance of the inability of the existing fundamental world conception to explain such issues had gained ground that a basis was created for a new world view and research activities were undertaken to gain new insights that could guide new developmental initiatives. A case in point is the ground-breaking research, conducted by people such as Newton and Darwin, led to new understandings of nature and its creation, thereby paving the way for a change of the existing world conception and the fundamental values. This, in turn, paved the way for new questions about the new world conception which in turn led to new changes. But – and this is crucial to remember – this ongoing process of development, in which we continue to find ourselves, did not change the fact that the prevalent world conception and values (at any given time) *were, are and will remain* the foundations of the issues that are perceived and placed on the political as well as the research agenda. The same holds true for the European cultures of the past and the present.

There is every reason to take interest in common features, if any, in the European cultures, and to assess whether, in this plurality of cultures, it is possible to ascertain any common characteristics and world conceptions which are of crucial importance for the content of the European social debate, and of the way in which problems in Europe *are identified* and *sought solved*.

The Danish Social Debate

In the following I will describe how some common characteristics exert influence on three central phases in the debate in society. I want to illustrate this impact by a brief discussion of Denmark's attitude to some topical issues in society today.

The three central phases in the social debate can be described as follows:

1. The way in which we acknowledge social issues in Europe

    That is the way in which we acknowledge and formulate the issues which will become the conscious product of our observations and experiences

    a. in the individual European cultures
    b. in the relationships between the single European cultures and any other culture inside and outside Europe, and
    c. in the relationship between the single European cultures and the surrounding nature.

2. The determination of the contents of the knowledge and insight we demand and which we consciously seek to generate through research and developmental work.

This content is partly influenced directly by cultural characteristics and common features, partly influenced more indirectly as a result of the acknowledged and formulated issues.

3. The contents of the knowledge and insight that are not demanded, and which we accordingly do not seek to generate through research or developmental work.

Figure 3: A Dynamic Model of Culture

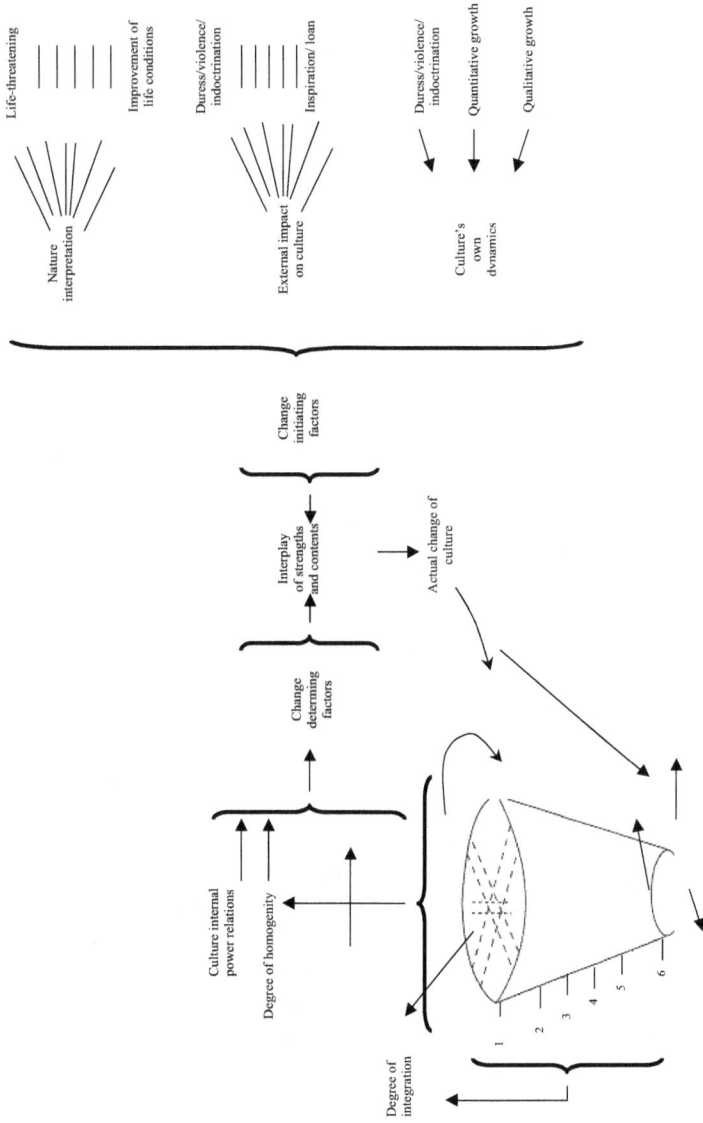

That is the knowledge we do not seek because we fail to acknowledge the issue, but which we could have acknowledged through conscious research and developmental work, which in turn could have contributed to developing alternative solutions to the perceived problems in Europe and the countries outside Europe.

The model of culture I presented above is abstract and theoretical in the way that it operates with a (clearly) delineated culture, which more or less unequivocally can be delineated from other cultures. In practice, in the real world, such a distinction is however very unclear, as the individual cultures will merge with each other and move in different directions. Most individuals find themselves in different contexts and, at different times, form part of **different categories of culture**. These categories may be *national cultures* (e.g. Danish, Swedish, German, Indian, etc.) and *occupational cultures* (e.g. craftsmen, academics, health workers, unskilled workers, etc.) The individual will not only be influenced by his or her national culture, but also by other cultural categories that he or she is part of, albeit with varying degrees of consciousness and force depending on the situation and point of time.

The other dimension is the *'dimension of hierarchy'*, on the basis of which the individual will perceive him – or herself – and others will perceive the individual – as part of the different levels within the different categories of culture he or she is part of. Within the *national category of culture,* a person may in some situations perceive him- or herself – and be perceived by others – as part of *the Danish culture*. In other situations, the case may be that he or she is seen as being part of a wider culture within the national category of culture – e.g. as part of the *Scandinavian culture* or *the Northern European culture* in contrast to *the Southern European culture*. Or perhaps merely as part of *the European culture*. In contrast to this, the individual can also be seen as part of a culture on a lower level of the hierarchy than Danish culture. He or she may, for instance, be seen as part of the culture of the island of Zealand, of the peninsula of Jutland or the culture of the area of Himmerland in Northern Jutland. The culture category and level of the hierarchy of the category in question that will be essential for the cultural understanding depend on the context and point in time the cultural understanding is sought. In this article it would be the *national category* and *the European level of the hierarchy* which would be relevant (see figure 4).

I will now present, in brief, some European common features which I find to have tremendous influence on the three phases mentioned phases above, and which must be presumed to carry similar significance in other European countries as well.

Figure 4: Culture hierarchy

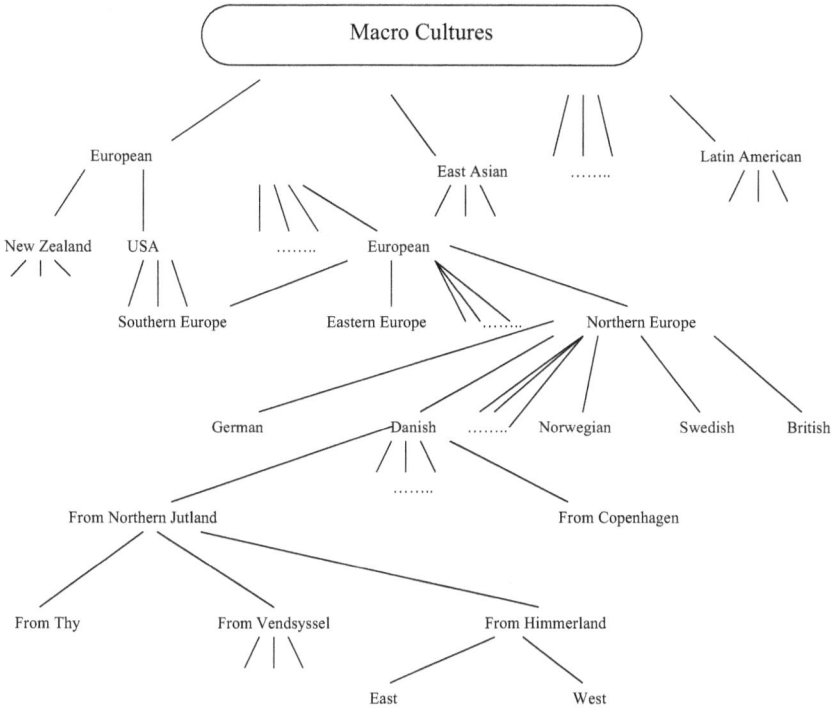

Characteristics of European cultural values and the European world conceptions

The European way of life and the way in which the single European countries have structured their societies offer a diversity which renders it difficult to identify common features in the European core cultures. Yet there seems to be a number of areas in which the European cultures, as well as their 'sister cultures' in Australia, New Zealand, USA, and Canada, mutually deviate from a number of other cultures; for instance, the Arab cultures, the cultures of East Asia, and Polynesian cultures, and the Inuit cultures, and many more. Even though there *is* a diversity of cultures in Europe, this diversity also presents a number of characteristics which makes it meaningful to speak of common cultural features in Europe. High up in the hierarchy, we can speak of a 'European culture'; and further down in the hierarchy we can speak of a 'Southern European culture'; an 'Eastern European culture': and a 'Northern European culture'. This level will be followed by the cultures of the specific countries. At the bottom of the hierarchy we will find a number of cultures of the different regions or areas of the specific

129

countries. Examples include the culture of Western Jutland as opposed to that of Copenhagen, or Bavarian culture in contrast to that of Holstein (see Figure 5). But on top of the hierarchy we find European culture comprising a number of common cultural features.

Naturally, it is difficult to determine what these common features are. Not only because of the diversity of cultures, but also because of the contents of such common features. As has been mentioned already, such observations strongly rely on the eyes of the observer and on the perspective through which the culture actor observes them. It goes without saying that this does not mean that the European cultures in fact change in reality depending on the observer, but it means that the culture actor's own culture – i.e. his or her own *cultural preparedness* will be of decisive importance for which European culture elements he or she is aware of, and in which direction he or she relates these common features of the social debate.

Some culture actors will focus on the Christian faith and consider it as an important common feature of the European cultures, with a Protestant variety in the north and north-west, and a Roman-Catholic variety in the south and south-west, as well as an orthodox variety in the east and south-east of Europe. Other observers will focus on the relationship among the citizens and the state, and emphasize the democratic element of culture, or the welfare state as an essential common feature (bearing in mind, of course, the fascist regimes in the 1930s and 1940s, the communist regimes in Russia and eastern Europe until the end of the 1980s, as well as the present growing influence of powerful multinational corporations and organisations that detract from this common picture).

Thus, we can – and will – look at different perspectives of European culture. In the following I have chosen to present a perspective that is technical, economic, rational and business-oriented, and to use this perspective for my reflections of European common features. I am doing this because of who I am right now: a Danish social science researcher with a background in the theory and practice of business economics, with approximately 35 years of experience in cross-cultural research, education and developmental work. The chosen perspective is in part a foregone conclusion, in part chosen by me, but it is in no way an expression of an 'overall' or 'ultimate' perspective. It is merely an expression of reflections based on actual cultural preparedness. But to revert to the initial question: which European common cultural features can one reasonably observe on the basis of the above-mentioned cultural preparedness?

A money-economic reality perspective

Most European economies are described as being market-driven or money-based. This, in effect, means that the results that can be expected from an actual decision or actions are given a utility value whose size depends on the individual's assessment of what the observed result or utility can be used for (a coat, for instance, can both be used for protection against the climate and to signal some kind of social belongingness), and it depends on the different ways in which the items can be used (does the individual, for instance, already have other coats, or does he only have this one? Is there any doubt about his status, or is it certain, with or without the coat etc.?)

Beside the utility value, it also has a barter value which expresses the value which can be obtained in exchange of the observed utility (is it e.g. possible to get 10 shirts in exchange for the coat or is it only worth 5?). This barter value – usually expressed in the value of money – has gained a crucial importance in assessing single decisions and actions in European culture. Expectations of huge barter values measured in *money-economic* revenue or in *money-economic* savings will usually be more important in the decision processes than the expectations of a less rewarding *money-economic* result if another action is chosen, although the latter action will involve fewer resources in terms of raw materials and time, less pollution and perhaps even less human malaise. That is Europeans prefer an action that, based on a bigger *money*-economic rationality, leads to the same expected utility value rather than an action with less *money-economic* rationality, and, thereby, less barter value, but which would result in a bigger *real economic* rationality achieved through less raw material and time consumption, as well as less pollution. That is rationality measured in terms of consumption of materials and time, pollution and possible human happiness.

With the introduction of interest rates in southern and central Europe around 500-600 years ago, and with the introduction of methods of calculation used in modern managerial economics and accounting according to which any future value or expense is discounted with a given rate of interest to a present value, this *money-economic* mindset has not only detached the interest of the decision maker from the *real economic* considerations, but also from more long-term consequences of a given decision and instead encouraged focus on considerations of short-term consequences or even present consequences.

The implication of the *money-economic* mindset combined with the applied principles of calculation seen in the light of the massive investments in production facilities and public utilities have meant that *many alternative decisions with far-reaching real economic consequences for the utility value are basically determined on the basis of their short-term money-economic barter value!*

Mini social oriented stakeholder considerations bordering on individual considerations

The culture's generally accepted fundamental values exert tremendous influence on which social entities the individual feels most attached to, and therefore is most loyal towards. At one extreme the social entity valued most highly by the individual can consist of just one single person. Often this person is the individual him/herself, but it can also be another person, such as a charismatic leader. At the other extreme, a person may feel attached to, and be fundamentally loyal towards, the collective entity of humanity or towards each single human being on earth. In such case, the individual will be attached to a bigger social entity, such as a nation, a universal political or religious ideology or something similar. Between these two extremes there are other cultures where the individual is mostly oriented towards medium-sized social entities; the family, the tribe, a village or local community.

The loyalty and feelings of the individual will naturally be aimed at the same social entity at any time and situation. Notwithstanding this, however, I find it reasonable to state that in their daily lives, most Europeans carry a loyalty and affinity that is primarily aimed at *relatively small social entities,* such as the close nuclear family and circle of friends – or a certain company or organisation.

The mini social oriented consideration bordering on an individual stake-holder consideration is, however, in certain situations met with a sort of contrast, because in other contexts strong national feelings approaching nationalism can be observed. This nationalism does not necessarily follow formal state borders; rather, they often transgress these, and in different contexts they may have a significant influence on everyday life, which – for one – can be seen in the former Yugoslavia. It is, however, my opinion that it is only in special and extreme situations that nationalism replaces *the mini social oriented* group loyalty.

That this is the case can clearly be seen from the way in which Europeans perceive, both consciously and unconsciously, some types of economic crime against the broader society or international organisations such as the EU. Tax evasion bordering on tax fraud as well as fraud in connection with subsidies and similar creative economic transactions receive far more lenient punishment than similar, or far less serious economic crimes, towards individuals, such as shop lifting or plain burglary. Indeed, in many social contexts, economic crimes against the general public, or such similar crimes are perceived as almost clever and heroic acts. An example is the former Danish Member of Parliament Mogens Glistrup's comparisons of tax evad-ers with freedom fighters under the Second World War.

This *mini social orientation bordering to an individual orientation* together with the other common European features constitute a strong contributing factor in the failure to recognise many issues relevant for big social entities or mankind as a whole. Even when such recognition takes place, for in-stance, in connection with aid to support third-world-country exports, it is after all often downplayed in such a way that it only features on the political agenda to a lesser degree. This can be seen when Europe wants to protect its own companies against imports of goods from the same third world count-ries to which they have just donated production and export aid through development assistance.

The value of curiosity and growth philosophy

Since the Age of Enlightenment a characteristic feature of European culture has been a perpetual attempt to satisfy an insatiable and permanent curiosity, which cannot even be fulfilled with the most comprehensive or omniscient knowledge. As is the case with other characteristics, it goes without saying that curiosity is not only found in Europe, but regardless of this *the existence of a perpetual curiosity of which the satisfaction is perceived as a pervasive legitimating value* is a typical European culture feature. Much insight and knowledge have been generated in European culture because of curiosity, and today mankind admittedly is able to do a lot of things it would have been unable to do had it not been for this European curiosity.

This perpetual curiosity combined with the impact from other European common features, such as the more individually oriented values, and the *money-economic* rationality perception, have – however – also led to knowledge and insight in other areas that would not at all be in demand if other value foundations were applied. Especially not prior to the knowledge and insight which we lack today in a number of significant areas within the development of society. An extreme example is the research and developmental activities that were undertaken by politically passive researchers during WW II in Germany for the sole purpose of finding rational techniques to kill the greatest possible number of people in the most efficient way in the Nazi concentration camps.

The value of curiosity understood as '*the wish to satisfy a perpetual curiosity as a legitimating value for the use of any amount and type of activity and resources*' has been a dominant feature of European culture ever since the Christian dogmatism and fundamentalism let go of their grip around the beginning of the 16th century. The curiosity-oriented philosophy combined with the money-economic rationality, as we have in the European culture to produce the *growth philosophy* which for good and bad characterises European culture. That which 'can be found out' *has to* be found out, and that which *can* be produced *has to* be produced, that is, if it is rational in a *money-economic* perspective. Of this there seems to be no doubt in the European culture.

The unknown, anonymous human being as an instrumental object

In connection with many decisions and acts in European culture man – or rather *the unknown, anonymous human being* – is perceived as an object or instrument which does not, in itself, have an independent intrinsic value as a living individual. This 'objectification' is most clearly seen in national wars and civil wars in which the anonymous individual largely is perceived as a necessary instrument for the battling parties whose fate the decision makers rarely accord much significance. On the other hand, the consideration of the individual, unknown, anonymous human being is given some importance in cases where his or her fate can be seen as having a certain utility value in relation to one or more of the dominating values in the actual situation. An example can be that the propaganda machine can present the fate of an otherwise anonymous individual as a suffering victim of terror acts of identified groups. But even in such a case the unknown, anonymous person is actually merely perceived as an object.

This trend of objectification is, however, not only seen in extreme situations; it is also seen in everyday life where the consideration for the single individual very often takes second place to other values than his or her own as a living human being. An example of this is that in situations where *money-economic* profitability is accorded so much importance that even if statistical evidence demonstrates that a number of casualties will occur at workplaces and in traffic within a certain period of time, this evidence will not lead to decisions that may save the lives of the many anonymous people. But the most obvious example of man's instrumental status is his role in the production process and as consumer. I will elaborate on this aspect in the section on technology.

The situation is changed radically if the unknown, anonymous individual is made 'personal' in the way that he is given a name and a face. When this happens – e.g. by media publicity, political accounts, most considerations are put aside to 'save' this, by now, personalised individual. The political debate is rife with such examples, cases where people suffering from severe or widely debated diseases or illnesses, or who have experienced serious accidents. In such situations there is hardly any limit of the size of means which are made available to save these now personalised individual cases. But usually these means are given without consideration that fewer resources spent in another way could have helped a far bigger number of people.

This tendency of objectifying anonymous people in European culture linked with the individually-oriented attitudes have the effect that the majority of mankind, including 'other Europeans', in the mindset of the Europeans is largely perceived as individuals – or objects – without any intrinsic value. They are perceived as *'things'* which by and large can be equated to instruments in the ordinary production process or as consumer entities of the finished products of this production process.

Nature as an objectified object

Nature is also perceived as an object or merely as a 'thing' by most Europeans, the same way that anonymous people are 'instrumentalised'. Nature is both seen as an (almost) inexhaustible resource of all kinds of raw materials, and as an (almost) endless garbage site for all kinds of garbage. Thus, in itself, nature amounts to nothing. Not even the living components of nature – the animals and plants – are accorded any value *in their own right*. Living nature is merely perceived as objects and things whose only raison d'être is to be useful to man, and in the European culture especially useful to the Europeans.

In recent decades, an increasing number of Europeans have become more environmentally conscious. This is positive seen in the light of many considerations. But this change is hardly a basic change in the perception of nature itself; for instance, towards attributing a value to living nature or a raison d'être *in itself*. Rather, it is a realisation that if human beings do not 'treat nature decently' mankind will ultimately pay the price – they will be worse off. After all, don't we all maintain our car to make it last longer without thinking of it as anything but 'a thing'?

The attention that whales attracted in Europe some years back can hardly be seen as an example of a radical change in the European perception of nature as anything than an object, in as far as this attention has not been directed towards smaller species of animals that are equally in danger of becoming extinct, such as the wolf and warthog. Perhaps the reason is that these animals have not become "humanised" to the same extent as the whale. We normally speak of the songs of the whales and the play of the dolphins, but not the songs and plays of the wolves; they merely howl and roam about.

Therefore, the heightened consciousness of nature hardly changes the situation that today living nature is only perceived as an object or *'thing'* by Europeans; things that man can exploit as he pleases, and as best serves the individual human being's consideration. Whether the heightened consciousness about nature will change this situation in a long-term perspective only future generations will show. Perhaps we are in the middle of a radical transition, perhaps we are only experiencing a ripple on the surface!

Partial perception of reality and orientation towards action

The last common feature of European culture I find relevant to stress is the tendency of letting many activities be guided by a limited – or partial – perception of the surrounding world. Many activities have been pursued based solely on the wish to optimise an actual activity without being aware of possible negative side effects in other areas. For example: the gain of many staff rationalisations in the public and private sectors in terms of the *money-economic* calculations may turn out to be less than the costs that are added to other 'sectors', such as the public sector within the social and health sector and the private economies of the 'redundant workers'. From an overall view, many situations can be registered where a skilful rationalisation has been made of partial elements of the totality, but at the same time the totality has become far less efficient than prior to the rationalisation. Just think of the many automatic answering machines and their 'offers to press for extensions to receive service'. These are no doubt highly cost-reducing for the organisation in question but at the same time highly time-consuming for those who make the calls, and therefore they add to the costs for the individuals.

This tendency of partial perceptions especially characterises decisions and actions in the public sector, but also, and perhaps especially, the relations *between* the public and private sectors. Several of the former governments in Denmark especially focused on the number of employees in the public sector, and accordingly they tried to reduce *that number*, as if the actual number of employees in the public sector in itself was of significance. From an overall view it is far more important to contemplate *which social tasks* should be carried out, and *in which sector* these tasks most expediently can be carried out. By a sole partial interest in the *number* of employees in the public sector, without consideration of what they actually do, how efficient they are, or how efficiently these tasks could be undertaken by others the result is most times that public expert employees are laid off. The only purpose is to bring down the number of employees in the public sector but in effect they are subsequently often re-hired – but now as private consultants, and with a higher pay. Partial optimisation, yes – but at a cost for the entire society!

The partial optimisation is a culture feature which has produced many excellent results within European technology and science. But the mere research, development and administration are and have been concentrated on optimisation of single elements of the whole of society. Unfortunately, this development has also produced many side effects in the terms of man-made environmental destructions and reduced quality of human life in the form of stress and marginalisation of minority groups who have been made superfluous.

Some Implications of the observed common features in European cultures

The individual European countries naturally have many different themes in their political debates, but in my mind there are also a number of recurrent themes in most of the European countries. It goes without saying that the relative weight of these themes will vary, and in one country one theme may dominate the debate whereas it will hardly be debated in some of the other countries. On the basis of my general outline of the European political debate and my own technical economic rationality perspective I will venture to state that the following political themes carry a certain weight in all the European countries:

- Technological development and the effects of technology
- The growing inequality among different groups of populations
- The problems of refugees and immigration
- The European Union – EU
- The relations with third world countries
- The relations between employees in the public and private sector.

I will only highlight three of these themes in the succeeding sections of the chapter by the use of examples, knowing very well that they overlap and may not necessarily be perceived as the most important ones in all European countries.

Technological development and the effects of technology

A discussion of European technology development and its effect go straight to one of the manifest culture segments, namely the segment that was called *the processing segment* in section 2.

Prior to a discussion of how the recognised issues of this culture segment are influenced by the European common features a brief discussion of the concept of technology is relevant.

Seen from a social angle the concept of technology can expediently be divided into six elements, of which three make up the narrow and static concept of technology. They are *'technique' (T), 'organisation' (O) and 'knowledge and skills' (KS)* (see Figure 5). I take technique (T) to mean the material and physical elements of technology and their associated processes – i.e. the applied raw materials and the methods by means of which these are changed and composed. By *organisation (O),* I mean the man-made ways in which the single processes are organised prior, during and after the actual material processing. Finally, I take *knowledge and skills (KS)* to mean the necessary insight, experience and specific knowledge that are necessary and fundamental to master the observed technology. As an analytical tool to understand the technological culture segment of European culture, the narrow concept of technology is, however, inadequate. It must be seen in a broader perspective – i.e. the results or products that will be the output of a certain technology process, and the underlying values and attitudes which are built into any technological process seen from the culture model's perspective. Therefore we need to expand the concept to a broader and more dynamic concept of technology.

These new elements are *result (R), values on people's relations to other people* (VPP) and *values on people's relations to nature* (VPN). This offers us a broader and more dynamic concept of technology making it possible to penetrate deeper into the underlying core culture of the observed technology segment.

The *result (R)* of technology is the material and immaterial output in the manifest layer of the culture, which are the result of the technical treatment of the input. The result is an essential element in the technological process for the following reasons. *Firstly,* because the output or the product is often decisive for the other technological elements, as the output is usually the goal for the technology process itself. *Secondly,* because the product is decisive in the sense that both the material products which are not directly consumed or used, and the immaterial products such as knowledge and skills acquired through the technological processes will form part of the subsequent technological processes.

Figure 5: The expanded technology concept

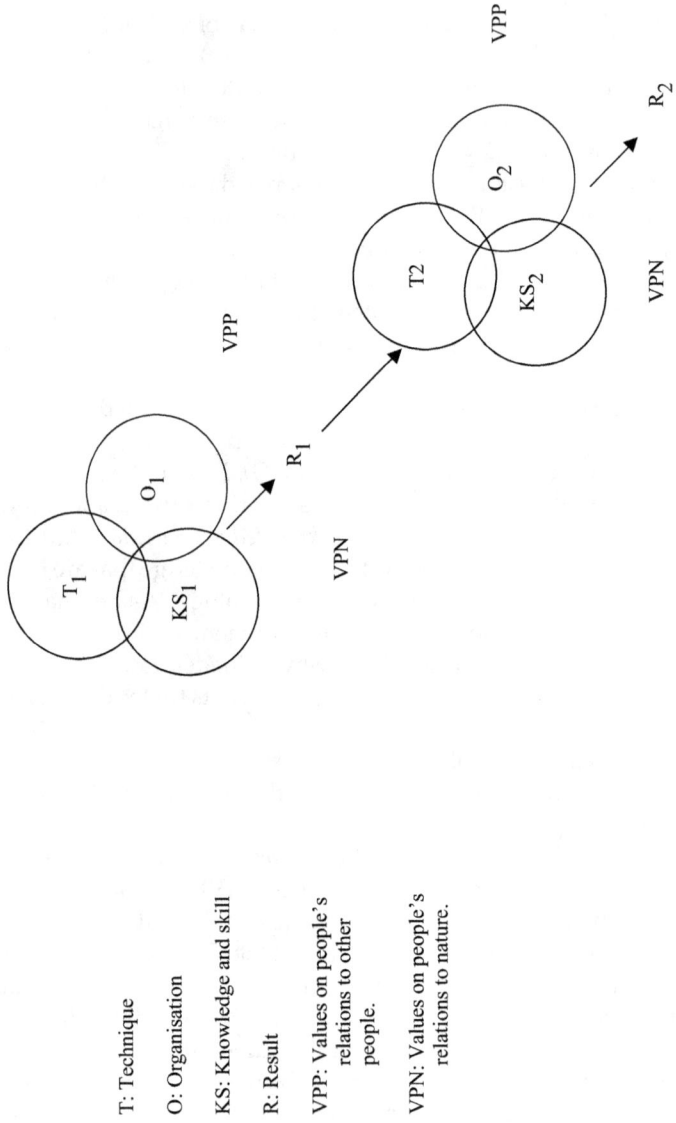

T: Technique

O: Organisation

KS: Knowledge and skill

R: Result

VPP: Values on people's
relations to other
people.

VPN: Values on people's
relations to nature.

Values on people's relations to other people (VPP) are about how individuals and groups of individuals relate to one another in the technology process itself, and in their capacity as consumers of the output of the process. Concepts such as competition, cooperation, selling of labour, power, product quality, therefore, become central concepts in connection with this element.

Values on people's relations to nature (VPN values) deal with the issues of how human beings regard and treat nature. To which extent, for instance, is nature viewed as a bottomless dustbin for the refuse of the technology process? Or the other way round, to what extent is technology viewed as part of nature's cycle? In the latter case nature becomes, at one and the same time, a needed resource and a limiting factor for the design of technology. Questions of chemical additives and their long-term effect on the human body and nature's cycle and issues of any wrong exploitation of the raw materials will here be some of the essential points in an analysis. Having included the last two technology elements the processing segments have been taken all the way down to the central layers of the core culture.

T: Technique
O: Organisation
KS: Knowledge and skill
R: Result
VPP: Values on people's relations to other people.
VPN: Values on people's relations to nature.

If we now return to the European common features we can immediately see that in different ways they influence the essential *'values on people's relations to other people'* (VPP) and *'values on people's relations to nature* (VPN) in European technology in the same way that they exert influence on the design of the four other technology elements. But on top of that they will, at the same time, express or be the results of the actual design of these VPP and VPN and the contents of the other four technology elements. There is a reciprocal feedback process and interdependence between *the common characteristics of the European cultures* and *the European technology*.

I will subsequently elaborate on this interdependence in relation to three phases in the public debate; 1) the way the technological issues are acknowledged and formulated; 2) the contents of the demanded technological knowledge and insight; and 3) contemplations of the contents of the technological knowledge and insight which are *not* demanded.

That man on the whole is viewed only as an instrument beyond the contexts of the close family or friends can be seen from the way the individual person is part of the technological processes. In these processes labour, the person that is, participates on an equal footing with the other factors of production which means that on an equal footing with land, machines and other capital goods. Naturally, this objectification of man in the process of production does not necessarily mean that employees in European industries are badly treated. On the contrary, for one could be tempted to say, after all, that machines are treated properly in terms of maintenance; otherwise they would become too costly to use.

But there is one important aspect: the decisions of pay and working conditions are made on the basis of the same type of decisions that lay down that certain machines are set up in special rooms with certain temperatures and humidity content, whereas others are oiled and checked at regular intervals. What matters is to get the factors of production to work as efficiently as possible on the basis of *money economic* profitability estimates. The same way that the machine does not enjoy any rights or any raison d'être in technology in its own right, people's rights and raison d'être in technology are only judged in the light of the individual's *money economic* value in the production process, and not in the light of the person's intrinsic value as a human being. A closer study of managerial economics and practice will fully support the above views.

Naturally, I am fully aware that people in the production process can organise themselves (and this is not the case for the machines). Through organisation they can gain power and exert influence on the decision-making processes in the technological development. This, however, does not alter the fact that the cultural common characteristics, by and large, lay down the technological agenda in terms of acknowledgement of problems and decisions about which type of knowledge and insight that are wanted. Let us not forget that in this context the employees are, after all, also part of the European culture, and thus they are themselves subjected to – and creators of – the common cultural features, both positively and negatively.

Techniques which involve great risks for the people in the production process, for instance, in terms of physical or mental wear and tear or stress, can easily be justified on the basis of several of these cultural common characteristics. One is society's wish for growth and a high money economic rationality and competitiveness. Real life also shows that for a good part of the way both business leaders and employees and their organisations accept such justification.

The techniques which were used in Denmark until some time in the 1980's[3] in manufacturing asbestos are products for the construction industry or the techniques that are still used in different processes of chemical surface treatment of different subjects are all examples of highly health detrimental techniques whose application especially has been justified by production efficiency. The strongly *'mini social oriented'* values, furthermore, have the effect that production conditions which would not have been accepted in the European countries seemingly are used and supported by European companies in many third world countries without provoking anxiety or ethical concerns. Examples of this can be found in the many chemical factories in India and ship de-construction yards in Bangladesh and India.

Frequently, though, the application of health detrimental techniques is also due to insufficient knowledge of other and less health detrimental techniques. The lack of needed knowledge and insight, however real this knowledge may be perceived presently, will, however, be a result of the common cultural characteristics. In this case, it is especially a result of the *money economic* profitability values and a general wish for growth. Only the general *'curiosity values'* could possibly encourage research and developmental activities with the purpose to find more healthy and human friendly products, and production techniques. But there are limits for this general curiosity value – limits that are also caused by *money economic* considerations. For instance, the need for new knowledge on how an alternative and more health-friendly techniques to manufacture healthier products compared to the hitherto known asbestos products for the construction industry was not *acknowledged, demanded* or *produced* until after the demand for them from employees and their trade organisations became so massive that they no longer could be ignored. So there is valid indication that the needed knowledge and insight for production of new technology could have been procured earlier, provided the *money economic* profitability considerations had not had such crucial importance. And I wonder which profitability considerations lie behind the Danish government's present demand for *'a shorter time lapse from research result to invoice'*. Could it be *money economic* profitability considerations?

Parallel examples and analyses could be presented in connection with the common cultural characteristics' impact on technology's VPN (values on people's relation to nature), and thus technology's relation to nature. Although there has been an indisputable change towards a far more sympathetic view of technology's impact on the environment and nature, the debate seems to indicate, as mentioned earlier, that this changed view has not come about out of concern for nature itself. Rather it has been triggered by the consideration for man's own means of survival in the somewhat longer term. And even if, as mentioned, these changes *may* express a future change of attitude, nature continues to be perceived as a *'thing'* in the European cultures, a thing without *raison d'être* and, therefore, can solely be understood in the light of considerations for man. Evident examples of this are industrialised agriculture's treatment of battery hens, porkers and confined sows.

The growing inequalities among different groups of population

The growing inequality is one of the most overshadowing social problems in most of the European countries. It is a problem which naturally is a painful experience for those groups of the population who, for some reason, are marginalised or isolated from the labour market or mainstream society. This is especially the case for the young people who experience – or fear that they will experience – such isolation. This is the case although many European countries have experienced a declining rate of unemployment, partly due to negative population growth, partly due to the development in society great parts of Europe have witnessed until today. That is a development in society where the basis of common cultural characteristics continuously have endeavoured to achieve new technical and organisational methods to manufacture increasingly more products with an increasingly lower number of people. This development has been based on a partial *money economic* rationality consideration. Other cause of marginalisation and isolation include the increasingly higher educational requirements for the labour market (which not everyone can honour), and partly cultural (or even racial) differences.

Although such a development will lead to increasingly cheaper products and consequently increased standards of living (just think of the importance of the development within the electronic industries), this development will also lead to an increasing decline in demand for labour and consequently increased marginalisation and isolation from the labour market. Unemployment will continue to rise as long as *the labour made redundant is not demanded for other and new tasks,* and as long as culturally determined stereotypes such as *the length of work* are restricted to the current – and in reality quite arbitrary – *number of work hours a day or week,* and the present *distinction is maintained between what is considered 'actual' or 'real' work, and what is considered 'free-time activities'.* I submit that the European "mental" marginalisation and increased social inequality is partly a consequence of the common cultural characteristics, and partly a consequence of the current European perception of the concept of work.

If the concept of work were given another content than it is today, and if unemployment, instead of being perceived as a huge social problem, would be perceived as an extremely opportune situation where much back-breaking and unhealthy work that no one wants to take on, was made superfluous, a number of other issues would be placed on the political agendas of the whole of Europe. New knowledge and insight would be demanded and generated. If that were the case, we would no doubt realise that unemployment is not the only alternative for those made redundant, and that we would face a new situation full of unimaginable possibilities for the future.

More and more people realise that traditional production will not offer more workplaces. Therefore it is less expedient to discuss *how increasing number of traditional jobs* can be created; instead the focus should be an active discussion of the following:

1. The *concept of work:* How can the concept of work reasonably be redefined so that we get rid of peculiar perceptions of what work is. For instance, a school teacher educating future citizens and a sales person of unimportant knick-knacks are considered to perform equally important work. Whereas a football coach for young boys, or a scout master for young children, a visitor's friend of old and lonely people

or a young person who has been job activated by the local authorities are not perceived as having real jobs.

2. Need-*driven division of labour:* How can we restructure our companies and organisation in such a way that they can function and keep up their current level of efficiency and at the same time allow for greater work flexibility than today? An introduction of flexibility in working hours and labour will allow for an increased of part-time jobs of varying lengths and different types of full-time and part-time leave of absence at different times. Flexibility can allow for a greater provision of welfare needs in our societies – e.g. care of children or elderly persons. In short, how is non-standardised labour best organised based on the demands of society and companies?

3. *Work Perception and Management:* How can we improve the organization of the current state of things whereby we constantly have a lot of people 'on holiday' receiving a reasonable amount of 'holiday allowance' and at the same time generally maintain our living standard? How can we reach a point where those who are 'on holiday' do not have to be 'on holiday' all the time, a situation which makes most of them feel marginalised and isolated, and on the other hand those who are not constantly 'on holiday' do not feel stressed and worn out? How can the perception of work be changed in a way that allows for the distribution of 'holiday opportunities' to be changed for the better?

4. *Reconsideration of our labour policies* Why are unemployed people actually prevented from performing any sensible and socially beneficial activities during the day simply because our labour laws require them to place their services at the disposal of the labour market even if there are no paid jobs immediately available to them?

It goes without saying that there are many economic, political and human problems involved in solving these complex issues. Finding the useful and realistic solutions to these problems is not easy. But, nevertheless, I believe that the mere fact that society and individual decision makers let go of some of these European cultural characteristics, and for one, more specifically, change their attitude of what the concept of labour constitutes, and the issues of marginalisation and isolation so that instead of trying to procure more traditional jobs a new attitude would also encompass launching new and relevant research and development activities. In that case, it would lead to new knowledge and insight which in turn possibly would contribute to a more constructive way of solving the increasing social inequalities in Europe.

The refugee and immigration issue

The refugee and immigration problems of today's Europe must be said to be of a smaller magnitude compared to those that Europe experienced during and immediately after WW II, and far lesser than in many other countries in the world today. Yet the refugee and immigration debate has left quite a significant mark on the political debate throughout Europe. The reasons for this may be many and they may be difficult to ascertain. However, there is no doubt that they are rooted in common European cultural characteristics.

The persistent and growing economic distortion of the distribution of advantages and disadvantages of the technological development across the world, and the many sins of the colonial past contribute to the biased debate. The borders between many third world countries today were artificially created during the colonial era. These borders were made without any ethnic and/or historical considerations. In this way, many ethnic groups were placed in several states. This implies that hard-to-reconcile ethnic groups found themselves together in the same state. These circumstances all underlie today's refugee problems, although they fail to be a substantial issue in the European refugee debate.

In similar ways, the *money economic rationality values* have had a strong influence on the refugee debate, especially in the context of different unemployment situations, and in the different models of the welfare state. Another aspect that characterises the debate is the *objectification of the anonymous person*. Even in Denmark, where in 2003 the celebration of the 60th year anniversary since the rescue of Danish Jewish refugees ferried to Sweden during the Second World War was observed, many Danes seemed to find an obvious contradiction easy. Namely, to live *both* with pride and joy of belonging to a peoples that rescued the majority of its own Jewish population from the Nazi extermination camps, while at the same time legitimising derogative and negative attitude towards refugees that have come to Denmark from other countries in recent years. Such attitudes are, for instance, demonstrated towards many refugees from the former Yugoslavia or from different countries in the Middle East, e.g. Iraq and Iran, who some Danes consider to be refugees of convenience whose only preoccupation is to exploit the welfare system. Even if there are only a few Danes who voice such attitude, the number is sufficient to make a strong mark on the current refugee debate – especially because of the present political situation of the nationalist/xenophobic Danish People's Party. [4]

The cause of a substantial part of the world's refugee problems – although in no way all of them – can, reasonably, be attributed to Europe. The actions of the colonial countries in the centuries leading up to the 1960's and 1970's, and Europe's present lack of understanding of its own trade policies towards many third world countries are contributing factors to a major part of the world's present refugee problems. But the European refugee debate suffers by and large from a lack of recognition of responsibility. Thus the debate predominantly centres on the economic and practical problems in a short-term view. The flow of refugees to the European countries *is* of course both a practical and economic problem. Possibly *there will,* at some point in time, also be a limit as to *how many* refugees the individual countries can receive. That is essential – even though the current number of refugees to Europe is far below such a possible limit, both in Denmark and in other European countries, in the light of the fact that many European countries are experiencing a declining population growth.

However, the flow of refugees to Europe is more than mere economic and practical problems.

The flow of refugees can also be seen as a positive contribution to the European countries and European culture in general. There is abundant historical evidence to prove this. As noted in the introduction to this chapter, Europe and European culture had not been the Europe with the European culture we know today had it not continually been exposed to refugees, immigrants and other permanent or temporary settlers. And many Europeans count one or more immigrants and/or refugees among their ancestors if we go back just three or four generations.

The positive side of the flow of refugees in the form of new ideas and thoughts quickly materialises in cultural areas, such as the theatre, literature and art in general. This also translates in the way most big European cities are getting more and more so-called ethnic restaurants and diverse foodstuff shops. This supply adds excitement and inspiration to life in these cities.

In the long term, and in situations where refugees and immigrants return to their original countries, Denmark and other European countries, if they were to have a well-planned and different refugee policy than the one practised today, would then have a large number of voluntary ambassadors of Danish products, Danish companies, and not the least Danish culture and lifestyle in general.

The European refugee and immigration debate is an apt example of how the whole issue and definition of what constitutes the knowledge in demand is based on the common cultural characteristics. Other examples could be given to illustrate how European culture has a marked influence on which social problems receive attention or are ignored.

Getting rid of the negative implications of the common cultural features in the European cultures

On the basis of the theoretical reflections presented above, there seems to be much support for the proposition that a number of common cultural characteristics, which I have termed European culture, are not only crucial in determining which issues are placed on the social agendas of Europe but also for the way in which these issues are acknowledged, formulated and made concrete in terms of contents. In the actual contents of the political debate, the cultural common characteristics become decisive for the selection of which research and developmental activities are launched in the different countries. This, in turn, will be significant for the current knowledge production and the knowledge and insight that will be available to the populations and the formal decision makers both in the public and private sectors. This is naturally how things are. But for this exact reason there is perhaps all the more reason to be conscious about these things. However, I am not saying that Europe will be able to eliminate all of its social problems just by reflecting over its cultural characteristics. But I do believe (and the examples above support this assertion) that Europe has hitherto partly **overlooked** a number of important alternatives views of 'reality'; partly, in consequence thereof, have **limited** the European knowledge production. A number of essential scopes of actions and solutions are, therefore, not brought forth, and they will not become part of the social debate. To put it in crude terms: we are going in a given direction – in a culturally determined direction of development.

If we want to seek new ways to solve social problems we would need to remove our current cultural blinkers so that we could view the whole spectrum of issues confronting us. It may well be that *the way we progress* will be different from what we off-hand had imagined, and it may contain more digressions. But the crucial point must be, after all, that, at the end of the day, the chosen path will prove to be the most optimal one judged on the basis of a given set of fundamental values. This will help us, to the extent it is possible, to find alternative and acceptable solutions to global as well as local social problems of today and in the near future.

On a tangible level, I will suggest that we launch some projects which first and foremost *aim at alternatives ways to produce knowledge* in Denmark. By easing the heavy blinkers we currently use, alternative and untraditional suggestions will be able to enter the social and political debate and guide our decision makers in how to address the challenges that confront us. This observation has encouraged me to put forward the following three proposals.

Proposal 1: An interdisciplinary *Social Development Council (SDC)* is established to replace or supplement the existing Danish Economic Council. The proposal is presented because the majority of social problems can be perceived from a variety of dimensions, the economic dimension being only one of them. It is, therefore, only expedient to analyse and assess these in a far broader perspective than the economic one. The members SDC should be independent economists and independent experts from a wide number of fields such as philosophy, biology, ecology, anthropology, sociology, law, political science, architecture, engineering, history and health. The appointed members must have expert knowledge in their own fields and interdisciplinary interests, which will enable them to place their expertise into a wider perspective. The council should be permanent but the individual members must be changed at regular intervals. SDC's task should be to advise the government and parliament on social issues. It should also (on its own initiative) undertake analyses and assessments and subsequently present the results thereof for public debate.

Proposal 2: A number of *smaller standing committees* must be established to supplement and partially replace the traditional commissions and committees who mainly have representatives from different industrial organisations and interest groups. These committees are to consist of members who do not have organizational affiliations. Such independence will enable them to focus more on untraditional solutions. Members of such committees could be people with relevant professional expertise as well as varied cultural backgrounds and experience. Analyses and reviews from such committees must be seen to be at par with traditional commission reports and make more nuanced and creative contributions to the political debate decision-making process.

Proposal 3: A new research institute, *The Institute for Current Re-Analysis of History (ICRH)* must be set up at a Danish university. The purpose of ICRH is to establish interdisciplinary research free of cultural and historical limitations of modern European culture. ICRH is an attempt to establish a research tradition in which modern natural scientists, historians, and anthropologists (possibly from different cultures), embark on common projects to highlight observations from former historical periods that have so far seemed incomprehensible. An example of this could be how the Incas were able to fit huge slabs of stone so neatly as they actually did without modern technology, or how the populations of India (about 1500 years ago) were able to create an iron column of such a high iron content as is the case in a temple about 80 kilometres outside New Delhi – without the use of our modern technology. Did they have other kinds of knowledge or technology which have passed into oblivion? If this is the case, could such a technology be combined with modern technical know-how to create quite a new social development through untraditional paths of development?

ICRH is to base its research on the recognition that in former historical eras in other cultures than that of Europe knowledge and insight have most likely existed. This knowledge and insight have been forgotten today or have not be recognised as having existed, but in combination with modern knowledge and insight it could provide the key to issues that remain unsolved.

Concluding remarks

I have outlined some common characteristics in the European culture and their significance to the social debate in Europe and Denmark. In doing so, I do not mean to postulate that all the common characteristics I have discussed are unique for the European culture, and that they are not found anywhere else in the world. Rather, I have attempted to demonstrate that by taking point of departure in a more precisely defined cultural perception, one can focus on certain common characteristics of the European culture. Through their contents, the common characteristics possess strong guidelines as to how we in Europe are made aware of and acknowledge the social issues that appear on the political agendas and engage the attention of researchers. Furthermore, I have demonstrated that the accepted cultural guidelines also impose some limitation on the possible solutions we seek for our problems. Therefore, the result is that in many instances alternative solutions do not even enter the political agenda, and need not attract our knowledge seeking efforts. I have also made three suggestions for reducing the limitations inherent in our current common cultural characteristics and to broaden the social debate in Denmark and the rest of Europe.

Notes

[1]   A few of the more essential contributions include the works of such scholars as Edgar Morin (1998): *Europæisk Kultur [European Culture]*; Anne Knudsen (1989): *Identiteter i Europa [Identities in Europe]*; Søren Mørch (1991-1992): *Det Europæiske Hus 1-6 [The European House]*: Ole Feldbæk (ed) (1991): *Dansk Identitetshistorie 1-IV [The History of Danish Identity]*; Uffe Østergaard (1992): *Europas Ansigter [The Faces of Europe]*; Anne Knudsen og Lisanne Wilken (1993): *Kulturelle Verdener – Kultur og kulturkonflikter I Europa [Cultural worlds – culture and culture conflicts in Europe]*; Thorkild Borum Jensen (ed): *Danskernes Identitetshisorie – en antologi [The History of Danish identity – an anthology]*; Uffe Østergaard (1998): *Europa – Identitet og identitetspolitik [Identity and Policies of Identity]*; and Nils Hybel (2003): *Danmark I Europa 750-1300 [Denmark in Europe 150-1300]*.

[2]   Note that I will observe European cultures in the way they can be perceived with a cultural background such as mine, because it is my clear understanding that 'reality' will always be perceived and understood through a person's own culture, – i.e. through one's own cultural preparedness. 'Reality' – or a substantial part thereof – is thus constructed on the basis of one's own culture background and experience. Detailed discussions of my perspectives on culture are contained in my latest book on the subject – Gullestrup, Hans (2006) *Cultural analysis – towards cross-cultural understanding* (Aalborg University Press and CBS Press).

[3]   Sussi Handberg (1990). *Asbest: det kriminelle tidsrum?* [Asbestoses: the criminal lapse of time]. Aalborg: Cementarbejdernes Fagforening, 248 p.

[4]   And the former Danish prime minister's justification for the former Danish government's repatriation of Jewish refugees to Nazi Germany in the years preceding the Second World War is thought provoking in-as-much as same the prime minister's own government today repatriate

refugees to Iraq and/or Iran, and in some instances certain imprisonment or torture awaits these people.

References

Gullestrup, Hans (2006) *Cultural analysis – towards cross-cultural understanding* (Aalborg, Aalborg University Press and CBS Press)

Handberg, Sussi (1990) *Asbest: det kriminelle tidsrum*? [Asbestoses: the criminal lapse of time]. (Aalborg: Cementarbejdernes Fagforening).

Harris, Marvin (1999) *Theories of Culture in Postmodern Times* London: Sage Publications.

Chapter 8

WEAVING THE MORAL FABRIC: EMERGENCE, TRANSMISSION AND CHANGE OF MORAL VALUES

Verner C. Petersen

Verily, men have given unto themselves all their good and bad. Verily, they took it not, they found it not, it came not unto them as a voice from heaven.
…
Change of values – that is, change of the creating ones. Always doth he destroy who hath to be a creator.

Friedrich Nietzsche (Thus spake Zarathustra)

Perhaps We Only See It When We Don't

What I am talking about is the moral fabric of society. It may be difficult to see what it is, because it is so much part of our daily lives that we usually do not see it or think about it. Only when it is torn, leaving unexpected gaps, or holes or perhaps when we run into a fabric of a different hue than ours, do we think of such things.

That we only see it when we don't may be characteristic of many of our social habits, conventions and norms. Here is a beastly illustration in an excerpt from an interview made by Swedish television with a former doctor and SS-Untersturmführer, Hans Münch, who once belonged to the Auschwitz camp personnel.[1]

Swedish Television: Did you see the crematories yourself?

Münch: Yes, of course. It wasn't part of my daily routine, but it was impossible to avoid it, even if I hadn't known what it was. Everybody active in the SS in Auschwitz knew of course what the crematories were, and it was impossible not to notice the smoke and the chimneys and feel the smell. In the SS the use of gas was discussed quite openly.

ST: Were doctors present at the gassings?

M: They had to be present. According to strict regulations they had to be present, as in civilized states at every normal individual execution for legal reasons. In the same way there was a military order that at least one doctor had to be present at exterminations by gas in Auschwitz, for two reasons.

Firstly, the whole thing had to be under medical supervision. And the gas wasn't thrown in by the regular camp personnel, but by the camp doctors' medical orderlies.

ST: What objections did your colleagues have who were for it?

M: "Is it necessary to do this in the middle of the war? There will be time for it later." "One should try to get as big a work force as possible. It would be better if the people were fed better." That was one view. Then there was the opposite view. "It has to be done at once. If we wait any longer there will be objections, and there are those who are against it."

ST: From a purely technical point of view, people were against it? And economically?

M: That was the main problem.

ST: But ideologically?

M: Ideologically...

ST: The majority was for it?

M: The majority of the doctors were against it from a purely technical point of view, and also because of economic reasons.

ST: But ideologically in favour?

M: Ideologically nobody differed.

The striking thing about Hans Münch's statement is that it is nothing special. What he describes was some everyday, humdrum activity that had to be carried out. There is a strange sense of almost normalcy about the whole description – the orderly way to exterminate people, the necessity of legal reasons, the medical supervision, "this is the way it must be done, you see," the economic and technical arguments against the extermination. There is disturbing reasonableness of reasons, as if not having done what one did would have been odd, like not having the right table manners. At the time the activities of Dr Münch were almost normal daily activities. Camp personnel presumably drove on the right side of the road, greeted or rather saluted each other in a courteous way, made promises, kept promises, took deliverance of Zyklon B.

Now perhaps we see it, because we do not see it in Dr Münch's explanation – the moral fabric that we take for granted. The reasonableness of his arguments may scare us: we may see them as pseudo-scientific, pseudo-legal and pseudo-economic and not the least moral. This must surely represent the views of a man lacking the most basic moral sense mustn't it? He cannot have been like you and me? Or – can he? Is that the really scary part about this story?

Listening to the NATO spokesman Jamie Shea a few years ago during the bombing of Serbia, Montenegro and Kosovo, we were treated to another kind of strange normalcy: numbers, maps, counts of destruction, surgical strikes, estimates of collateral damage and pictures of destructive precision made from aircraft 15,000 feet above sea level, or perhaps even from the noses of the smart bombs. We are punishing the veiled enemy at no danger to ourselves. This is just a technical description of our competence, expressed in a tone of destructive normalcy, almost like the one we saw in Dr Münch's statement.

Or think of the video apparently showing the view from an Apache AH-64 helicopter over Iraq[2], shooting people who do not seem threatening, at least, in the moment, with 30 mm grenades, vaporising at least three persons; that can only be seen as small white figures, due to the thermal images. The scary thing is that it looks like a bad computer game, with the gunner in the player's position. Bad, because the quality of the game and the view of the dead are not as good as they would be in an average computer game. One wonders if some of the young soldiers are continuing their shoot-them-up arcade games from their homes, just having to accept to work with lower quality pictures and no sound.

But wait a minute, these are just wars, moral wars, fought for humanitarian reasons, not, for instance, for territorial gains or to exterminate a race. This at least is what those responsible for it are declaring very loudly, although one may wonder about constitutional problems, legal grounds, the role of the UN and other slight irrelevancies.

Still, these descriptions of precision destruction and the normalcy of it may make us slightly uneasy, even after performing the implicit cost-benefit analysis that shows that they had to do all this in order to save someone else.

Being suddenly confronted with a tear in the moral fabric, we may become aware of the importance of this fabric, and perhaps start wondering about its nature. How solid and dependable are the values we believe we hold today? Are they robust enough to guard against the sort of tear that Dr Hans Münch and others represent?

What may have been the process that created the fabric we believe in? What are the basic strands of the weave, its pattern and its texture? How do values get transmitted and inculcated from generation to generation? And in what way do we contribute to the reweaving of parts of the fabric, when wear and tear is discovered, or when there is a need to weave additions, changing the pattern, texture and colour of the fabric to fit changes in society?[3]

A Fabric Weaving Itself?

In Hofstadter's book Gödel, Escher, Bach we find a fascinating story called the Ant Fugue (Hofstadter, 1987). The story is illustrated with a picture of a colony of ants building a living bridge with their own bodies. Does that mean that the ants practise a kind of cooperation as we understand it, or that they have knowledge of what they are doing?

According to Hofstadter and others[4] the answer is a resounding "no!" From what we know it would seem that the co-operative behaviour of ants does not really represent cooperation in the sense we usually talk about. As human beings we may at least believe that we have some sense of purpose and that our behaviour stems from "mind-full" activity.

To understand the "mindlessness" of the ant level one may think of an experiment in which a couple of robots, looking remarkably like ants, are milling around on a level playing field surrounded by an immovable barrier. A round cylinder is placed on its side somewhere on this playing field. The robot ants are programmed to move forward, unless they meet an immovable barrier, in which case, they wait for a while and then back off to continue their aimless activity in a random direction. Two robots hitting the rolling surface of the cylinder at right angles within the same short time interval and from the same direction will be able to move the cylinder. Often one hits the cylinder, often more than one from different directions, but the cylinder does not budge. Now waiting for some time we may see that by chance two robots happen to hit the cylinder from the same direction at right angles, and it moves. Because it moves, the robots continue to push. Now imagine that an outside observer comes along. To this observer it may look as if the two robot ants are cooperating in rolling the cylinder along.

What we have is a kind of statistical cooperation coupled with a simple programmed response. Perhaps this is the cooperation we find with ants too. And perhaps this is also a characteristic of some of our human efforts; for instance, in situations where we have no idea of how to solve a problem that we do not really understand. More sophisticated simulation projects involving a similar kind of reasoning can be found at MIT's Starlogo site.[5]

In some cases it would seem that spontaneous coordination is possible to achieve even with large numbers of individuals involved. Some of you will have seen football games and maybe even have taken part in one of those giant "la Ola" waves sweeping around a stadium, made up of spectators alternately rising from their seats and sitting down.

Now let us shift to another thought experiment with human players. An experiment involving two men, with no knowledge of rowing boats or rowing. They are placed side by side in a small rowing boat and given an oar each. They are then asked to row across a small lake to a point on the other side of the lake. In the beginning it may look as if they would never get anywhere; their unsynchronised moves make the boat move erratically this way and that. Then by some tacit process the rowers by and by fall into sync and when they have synchronised their movements the boat moves along in the intended direction. Slower or faster, as strength, wind and water permits, or according to the urgency they feel, but at least with less erratic gyrations.

Hume (1740) apparently had the idea that the utility of cooperation in such a case could be felt directly, instead of being a result of deliberations and conscious reflection. "Two men who pull the oars of a boat do it by agreement or convention, though they have never given promises to each other" (Hume quoted in Copleston, 1994, p. 344). They can feel, for want of a better word, the advantages of cooperation directly. This again leads us back to the idea of the two robot ants happening to push in the same direction at the same time.

No compact was expressed for general discussion and mutual consent. Instead, a tacit cooperation on concrete problems, like oar-pulling, showed itself to be advantageous, and this made it become more frequent, until its frequency gradually produced a habitual, voluntary and, therefore, precarious acquiesce in the people. In the oar-pulling process the cooperation may become better and better every time one has to row together with others. In other forms of cooperation, stable patterns more important to morality may have emerged, in reciprocal exchange of favours, in trade arrangements and so on. Slowly this may have led to changes in expectations with regard to other individuals, and in emerging dependence on each other.

In other words, certain forms of behaviour may have coagulated in conventions, habits or norms, that, by and by, may have lost their close ties to the problems that brought them about. The result simply leaving generalized impressions in the tacit strands of an invisible moral fabric.

Jumping to a conclusion we may get the idea that the habitual responses produced, what Hume called additional force, ability and security of men acting together in society,[6] and the first embryonic forms of a moral fabric.

What we get from these examples is the idea of a slow progression from what might be seen as spontaneous communities to highly structured societies, with explicit regulation of behaviour and institutionalisation of responsibility.[7]

Other very popular attempts to explain the evolution of cooperation and social order are based on game theory and simulations based on this theory. In some of Axelrod's game simulations (Axelrod 1984; Axelrod 1986), cooperation results from the interplay of very simple and single-minded individual players consisting of nothing more than small programs representing different behaviours, running through a number of iterations or repeated games. Axelrod builds a whole theory of cooperation on these simulations, although it would seem that the end results are very sensitive to the initial parameters of the players and the game. Much more comprehensive and convincing is Sugden's attempt (Sugden 1986) to account for the emergence of rights, cooperation and welfare, through a game theoretical analysis. Or Elster's theories of social order in "The Cement of Society" (Elster 1989).

What is happening has to be a kind of spontaneous self-regulation, or self-production. Forms of coordination and cooperation apparently emerge without a conscious conductor as it were. This may be due neither to some property of the individuals making up the group or society, nor something in the environment, but perhaps something that "lies neither in the organism nor in the environment, but at some emergent level between the two" (Bates 1984, p. 189). Emergence referring to "The arising of novel and coherent structures, patterns, and properties during the process of self-organization in complex systems. Emergent phenomena are conceptualized as occurring on the macro level, in contrast to the micro-level components and processes out of which they arise" (Goldstein 1999, p. 49).

The examples and experiments recounted here may indicate that given certain rather primitive conditions. Virtual societies can be created that foster cooperation and a certain group coherence. Admittedly, other experiments show that the actions of individuals acting in their own interest may not result in cooperation and the emergence of social norms, but instead in prisoner's dilemmas, and commons dilemmas, or tragedies as in the so-called "Nuts game" (Edney 1979).

Perhaps the experiments demonstrate the delicate interplay between the emergence of social norms and self-interested action.[8]

The Basic Strands of Morality

Traditional approaches to the problem of social order would focus on the social contract. Here one might refer to the answers presented by Hobbes, Locke, Hume or Rousseau. We shall use a somewhat different approach, beginning with an attempt to find some of the basic strands of the moral fabric.

De Waal (1996) makes an attempt to find the origins of right and wrong in a study of the behaviour of primates. He attempts to find out whether animals show behaviour "that parallels the benevolence as well as the rules and regulations of human moral conduct" (de Waal 1996, p. 3). He wants to make an attempt to understand what may motivate such behaviour, whether animals realise in some way how their behaviour affects others.

Now why would animals like primates need something like moral strands? The answer sounds simple. Animals living in groups need each other to find and get at food; they may live in constant conflict with other animals and need the group for defence. To hold the group together internal strife and conflict has to be contained. De Waal talks of conditions for the evolution of morality. Some of these reasons for the evolution of morality may also be found with Darwin. And one may also be reminded of Hobbes' brutish war of all against all.

Using his own and other studies he finds evidence of emerging strands of moral behaviour. He notes how groups of primates may show cooperation in getting food, and in the sharing of food. He also finds a kind of reciprocity between males and females, in food for sex exchanges, for instance. Although of course this kind of reciprocity might be seen as sexual harassment in our societies. He even finds evidence of a kind of moralistic aggression, of punitive actions against cheaters; for instance, evidently comparing this to the moral indignation and the demands for retribution that we find in our societies whenever tacit or explicit behavioural norms are transgressed or broken. Some form of moral aggression seems to be necessary to preserve the arrangements of reciprocity, sharing and so on. This also seems to be the case in human interaction (Sigmund, *et al.*, 2002).

Other studies show reconciliation between former combatants, and also forms of conciliation or peace-making within the group through intermediaries. To de Waal, this is a sign that "In so far as the interests of different individuals overlap, community concern is a collective matter" (de Waal 1996, p. 205).

It might be possible to explain this seemingly moral behaviour of primates as having come about without an inkling of a conscious intention. While milling around doing this and that, they are suddenly reinforced in a certain kind of behaviour, because it helps them achieve goals programmed into their genes.[9] We saw how this might work when playing with our imaginary robot ants.

It might be problematic to assume that human morality is just an outgrowth of the morality strands we find in the behaviour of primates. After all, we are doing the analysing and we are judging the behaviour of the primates; it is not the other way round.

Deacon seems to agree. He does not think that our moral stance "is directly rooted in the 'simpler' social behaviors of other species. Sophisticated predispositions for cooperative behaviour or for caring for other individuals have evolved in many social species, and need not depend on symbolic reflection to anticipate the social consequences of one's actions" (Deacon 1997, p. 431).

The one really important ability of human beings that made possible the evolution of language and a moral stance is the ability to perform symbolic reflection and manipulation. What we need is a kind of symbolic jump from the abilities of the primates to the human ability to form mental representations. Representations with no immediate reference to physical stimuli and events.

It is the ability to put oneself into the shoes of another person, of holding other views in one's mind, of thinking: what if? It is the ability to anticipate, and much much more. Bruner talks of the ability to understand the minds of others, "whether through language, gesture, or other means" (Bruner 1996, p. 20). Through language, symbolic reflections may be shared between two or more individuals, making possible a shared collective experience.

"Ethical considerations are something in addition to the complex set of socio-emotional responses we have inherited. The symbolic constructions of others' plausible emotional states, and their likely emotional responses to our future actions, are analogous to a whole new sensory modality feeding into our ancient social-emotional response systems" (Deacon 1997, p. 431). This virtual representation of the emotional state of others and their reactions "makes us the only species where there can be a genuine conflict of simultaneous emotional states."

This is a human quandary, and absolutely necessary for landing in an ethical dilemma.

The Faded Patterns

Durkheim had the idea that in order to understand and explain social phenomena at any given moment, whether religion, moral behaviour, social contracts or economic relations, one had to begin by studying the most primitive and simple forms.

From his study of what might be termed historical social facts, he derives, perhaps not unsurprisingly, the function of morality. He argues that the interests of the individual are not those of the group of which he is a member. There may exist a real antagonism between the interests of the individual and the interests of the group. What is significant is that the interests of the group, as a group, may only be perceived dimly by the individual, if at all. In a way, the interests of the group are the interests of no one. "It seems, then, that there should be some system which brings them to mind, which obliges him to respect them, and this system can be no other than a moral discipline" (Durkheim 1957, p. 14).

Durkheim points to the way the guild might help a member who has fallen into misfortune, or to the rules governing the activities of the members of a guild. Other kinds of regulation were aimed at preventing deception and cheating. "The butchers were forbidden to inflate the meat, to mix tallow with lard, to sell dog's flesh, and so on" (Durkheim 1957, p. 23). In 1623 the statutes of the butcher's guild in Copenhagen "forbids all butchers strictly and seriously to sell any kind of fresh meat from animals having died from disease, on punishment of loss of honour and right to be a butcher" (Laugsforordning for slagtere 1623). Today, the deceptions and tricks disclosed in recent food scandals may be somewhat more sophisticated, but one gets the idea.

Durkheim believes that he can find evidence to show that in primitive organisations and societies, the binding collective framework of religion and morality was defined in a concrete manner. This meant that duties were very concrete and did not leave much to the deliberation and initiative of the individual.

Reflecting a little upon this we may see that old societies were dependent on family, clans and guilds, or rather on goods and services provided by concrete persons, meaning that people were more or less directly dependent on each other.

An individual in a modern society is no longer dependent on concrete people, the extensive exchange of goods and services that an individual finds necessary is provided more or less anonymously through exchange mechanism like the market or by depersonalised institutions paid for through taxes.

With the evolution of more primitive societies, duties became more abstract, losing their tight relation to certain given practices, thereby also becoming more difficult to explain. What had once been very concrete and explicit evolved into abstract tacit norms and practices, which would influence concrete behaviour in a very circumspect way, so circumspect in fact that it would become impossible to unravel afterwards. Almost like the grammaticization that Bybee (1998) is talking about in relation to the evolution of a language grammar, where repetition leads to habituation, automatization and emancipation, by which the original concrete instrumental aspects take on an abstract symbolic function.

What might once have governed behaviour in a very strict way, allowing little individual latitude, became less of a strait-jacket on individual behaviour, thereby paving the way for individualism. "And if the collective type or ideal becomes that of humanity in general, it is so abstract and general that there is plenty of room for the development of the individual personality. The area of personal freedom tends to grow as society becomes more advanced" (Coppleston 1994, p. 124). This was seen by Durkheim as important for the development of modern individualistic societies and the idea of the sovereign individual.

By living and participating in society, and by using a common language learned by mimicking others, every individual member of society comes to share in this whole "system of categories, beliefs and value-judgements." Such a system may have become part of the collective unconscious, that is upheld in the minds of every one of us, without anyone being aware of it. This may be part of the invisible moral fabric that we are looking for.

The unconscious part may consist of "everything of which I know, but of which I am not at the moment thinking; everything of which I was once conscious but have now forgotten; everything perceived by my senses, but not noted by my conscious mind; everything which, involuntarily and without paying attention to it, I feel, think, remember, want, and do; all the future things that are taking shape in me and will sometime come to consciousness: all this is the content of the unconscious" (Jung 1978, p.185).

We want to emphasise the collective part of the unconscious, the part that is shared across individuals, and the part that owes its existence not to the single individual, but like a linguistic grammar is shared collectively.

The important point here is that these wholes are not a result of deliberate concerted actions by the individuals, guided by rational intentions and grand plans. It is instead a spontaneous order generated as a result of the individual actions. Actions guided by the limited views of individuals. The results in the shape of the social phenomena we are talking about emerge so to speak behind their backs.

"Phenomena like language or the market, money or morals, are not real artefacts, products of deliberate creation. Not only have they not been designed by any mind, but they are also preserved by, and depend for their functioning on the actions of people who are not guided by the desire to keep them in existence" (Hayek 1955, p. 84).

The individual is not free to do whatever he pleases. Self love is tempered by something outside the individual. We have to see collectives in the shape of social institutions as very real, reified entities that must influence the activities of each and every individual, somewhat in the way an existing anthill society influences the individual ant. In a similar way man shapes social institutions and is in turn shaped by these, albeit in a way that is immeasurably more complicated and complex than the anthill.

Still, we are not just passive reflections of past practices and moral norms; we have the ability to act on our own. With changing material and social circumstances this may slowly change the tacit collective consciousness.

Durkheim asserted that the increasing division of work and the modern economic system would have to lead to changes in the collective consciousness. As long as this has not happened, we live in a state of anomie, which we interpret as kind of mismatch between the material conditions of life and the collective consciousness transmitted from the past.

More recent attempts to explain social order may be found, for instance, in the works of Talcott Parsons (1951), Rawls (1971), Elster (1989) and others. Talcott Parsons seemed to find that the society he lived in was structured in an almost Panglossian way as "the best of all worlds" with morality being important for upholding this world. Anything that would tend to disturb the equilibrium would have to be regarded as dysfunctional by Parsons, and so we get a moral fabric, containing values and attitudes that were seen as supportive of the existing social and economic structure. This view has been, to my mind, rightly criticised for being too harmonious. Gouldner (1971) and Dahrendorf (1959) also criticise Parsons for not seeing that the existing order may not be the best of all worlds to all members of society.

We may be overstating our case a little, but it would seem that such a functionalist colouring is present in all the attempts to give an explanation of the moral fabric that we have encountered. This leads to the idea that the attempts to explain the creation, pattern and texture of the moral fabric can be seen as interpretations and justification for our actual behaviour. This can also be seen as the reflections on and of behaviour that we practise under the tacit influence of an otherwise invisible moral fabric. In this sense, the theories are reflections of the existing values, attitudes and practices of the societies they were written for. They are seen through the moral fabric they are trying to explain, delivering the collective self-con-organization we need for what we are doing.

Absolute or Relative – The Layers of the Fabric

Until now our discussion left open a serious question: can the moral fabric be seen as relativistic – as something that could take many different forms?

We shall argue that there are some universal and absolute strands in our moral fabric, even when seen through the moral fabric of our time and place. These basic and very general strands may represent attachment, succour, emotional contagiousness, conciliatory behaviour, the ability to put oneself into the place of another and so on. Like the strong supporting strands holding the surface tufts of a carpet together, they are the most basic strands that are necessary to hold groups of human beings together.

These strands, which are the most abstract,and least connected to concrete practices, represent the most tacit part of the collective consciousness. This is where we find the part of the moral fabric that to all intents and purposes can be regarded as absolute and universal.

In the faded patterns of the fabric, we may find abstract values that carry notions of universalism, but are interpreted in certain contexts. Perhaps such a notion would be the notion of justice or fairness. Justice is neither fully relative or it would lose its meaning, nor is it absolute and universal. It is at this intermediate level that we locate most of the collective self-con-organization we need for what we are doing; the contract theories, the Protestant ethic, the Panglossian views of Talcott Parsons.

In contrast to this, the individual coloured tufts on the surface of the fabric seem to be more relative. Here it is possible to weave many different colours on the same substratum of basic moral strands. This is the only place where we believe that one can find a relevant place for what has today been called the many morals, or moral pluralism (Moon 1994).

Interestingly Hayek (1962) and Elster (1989) seem to have held similar notions, albeit in a slightly different context. Hayek wrote of the need for "deep rules" to be located in a kind of "supraconscious" that we would never be able to make explicit. Elster stated that social norms are to a large extent "blind, compulsive, mechanical or even unconscious" (Elster 1989, p. 100).

This might mean that the moral fabric would have to be seen as consisting of layers, as illustrated in Table 1. In our version the moral fabric has a substratum of universal strands of morality, and an intermediate level which connects the basic level and the multicoloured surface. Although this analogy would allow for many different versions of morality on the surface, there is a limit to the diversity, and these limits are given by the deeper layers. If the surface tufts lose the connection to the deeper strands of morality we can no longer talk of morality. The weave would become loose and disintegrated; it would certainly no longer be a fabric, just lumps of isolated norms.

Table 1:   Layers of the Moral Fabric

Surface Time and culture specific moral codes	Explicit ethical codes Group specific morals
Intermediate level Context sensitive general notions of morality	General social norms like the notion of justice or fairness, mechanisms for conflict resolution etc.
Deep level Tacit, basic, and universal strands of morality	Some conditions belonging to every system of morality: Sympathy and mutual aid Reciprocity Getting along Symbolic reflection

Perhaps it is the deep unconscious connection to tacitly held moral values that makes us aware that something is frightfully wrong with the views of Dr Hans Münch. There is no doubt that something resembling a strong moral code could be found in Nazi Germany, like the absurd idea of preserving a certain legality in amidst it all. This strange Nazi moral code must have been imposed upon the existing fabric, tearing holes in it, and loosening the surface layers from the basic layers, thereby making possible the kind of insane moral logic found in Dr Münch's statements.

Even if we still cannot see the moral fabric clearly, and ultimately I suppose that this will prove to be impossible, we may at least have a notion of its structure, some of its more basic elements and of its function in society. Now we need to understand how this collective consciousness may be upheld and transmitted from generation to generation.

The Inculcation of Basic Human Values

By studying the behaviour of small children in a family setting, Dunn has attempted to show the beginnings of social understanding and moral behaviour. Children very early on have an idea of harm to others, as shown by the case of a two-year old child, retold by Dunn (1988, p. 27/28):

> Child accidentally knocks baby sibling (Thomas), who cries.
> Mother enters room.
> Child: Poor Thomas.
> Mother: What happened?
> Child: I banged him.
> Mother: Well, you'd better kiss him better.

To Dunn, this can be seen as evidence that children have an early idea of agency, of seeing that they are the cause of something else; in this case of causing pain. Perhaps what we see here is that children show some of the abilities that belong to the basic structure of morality[10].

In a series of small observations, Dunn attempts to demonstrate that children develop an early understanding of some of the basic conditions for morality we touched on in earlier sections. The notion of responsibility, coupled with the idea of agency and the ability to see who is to blame, enters early into the minds of children.

In relation to the mother, to other siblings and to family members Dunn believes that one can see how children develop an early understanding of the view of other persons together with notions of helping, of justice and fairness, of claims, of feeling perception and inner states, of self and self-interest, and a host of other notions. Four features of this understanding stand out: understanding others' feelings, understanding others' goals, understanding social norms and understanding others' minds. This would seem to be closely related to our idea about the conditions for morality, such as the ability to put oneself into the shoes of another, or even indications of the ability to do symbolic reflection. This reflection must necessarily include the ability to compare, to calculate, to assign weight with regard to relevance, seriousness and so on. It would seem that without these abilities it would be impossible to get to a sense of justice, for instance, when deciding what a fair share would be.

The driving force is found in the self-concern of the child, not in the self-interest which is opposed to everyone else's, but in the notion of developing a sense of oneself as cause and agent. This includes helping others and vying for the approval of others. "Children's interest in the realm of what is approved and disapproved by others is wide and persistent by their third year" (Dunn 1988, p. 178).

Children show an early interest in social comparisons, in getting what the adult would term a fair share in comparisons with other children; for instance, when sharing a cake.[11] This self-interest and efficacy in social matters is important for the development of a growing self-awareness.

The child is not just told what to do and what not to do. It actively seeks the limits, vague and unstated though they might be, and it makes its own interpretation and mental representation. It is not just passively imprinted with the stamp of an explicit moral fabric. This might turn out to be really important in relation to our ideas about the nature of the moral fabric. It would mean that it is in the interplay between the child and the world surrounding it that a sense of the moral fabric is developed.

Interaction takes place not only with the mother or the rest of the immediate family. It involves other children as well. Children learn from other children; from their peers, from mimicking certain behaviour, from socialisation in groups of children.

Perhaps certain behaviours, values and attitudes are only kept alive by children, by children being taught by children – cohort by cohort as it were. If a new generation of children grew up only with their parents and other adults, they might never be able to learn this behaviour and these values.

What we get from this discussion on the development of strands of a moral fabric in children are some important tentative conclusions, hunches and ideas.

We see that parents do not have to have any clear conception of the moral fabric themselves. Still, through their interaction with their children they seem to contribute to the development of a moral fabric in the children. Apparently they do not have to talk about morality; they just have to express their sense of morality in their actions, and in their behaviour *vis-à-vis* each other and *vis-à-vis* the children.

Values are revealed by and by, for instance, through the questions and arguments of the children in their interaction with the parents and other children. The parents do not have an explicit set of ethical codes to impress on the child. They release their views of the moral fabric in bits and pieces, not in any comprehensive model of explicit codes. They do it by acting and reacting in day-to-day situations, by tacitly using and expressing in their behaviour the collective and personal values, often in an unconscious way. Cahn once summarised the process: "They [the children] learn group standards from the tone their parents use to say 'liar' or 'thief' and the excited whispers their playmates receive for gutter-talk about obscene occupations and supposedly shameful natural functions. They are taught impressively when wrong conduct is followed by some group gesture of rejection" (Cahn 1955, p. 23). Elster asserts that "social norms have a *grip on* the mind that is due to the strong emotions their violations can trigger" (Elster 1989, p. 100).

Now we may perhaps have the first inkling of how the most basic strands of an invisible moral fabric with accompanying values, attitudes and behaviour may be transmitted from generation to generation, without ever being stated in explicit rules and algorithms on how to behave.

Turning now from an attempt to understand the silent mechanism of transmission of basic moral values, from generation to generation, to an attempt to understand how values and attitudes spread within a society or an organisation, we shall see whether this is also a silent process.

Mimicry and Situated Learning

We have already seen how the most basic and tacit strands of the moral fabric may be transmitted to and developed in children, without their parents and peers needing to have much idea of what these moral strands are. It seems to be an interactive process, with an important role played by an active and "trying" child, with its own hidden agenda.

Perhaps this may indicate where we have to look in order to understand how we all become inculcated with values and norms, while doing everything else but learning about ethics. We believe it may happen through a process similar to the one by means of which children internalise basic moral strands. They do not learn them by heart or rote from textbooks, or via formal education, isolated from a concrete context. They learn indirectly in a situated context.

During a stay at the Harvard Business School some years ago, I had the opportunity to observe MBA classes using case oriented teaching methods. It happened to be during the period when MBA students took the required module on business ethics, and they had been given a series of very well developed cases. It struck me that while many students were very active during the discussion of the cases, they were also very good at seeing all possible angles of the dilemmas and possible solutions, they only needed a little prompting from the teacher to make their analysis seem very sophisticated.

Strange as it may seem, it may be relevant to ask whether the values talked about in the ethics classes mean less than the values tacitly acquired in classes on finance, economics, human resources management, negotiation and mediation, to mention but a few. When being taught finance or HRM, students are not only taught finance or HRM, but also certain values and norms, although neither teacher nor student may be aware of this. Implicitly and tacitly values and attitudes of a much more fundamental character, perhaps related to individualism self-interest and self-reliance, are inculcated, while at the same time the values of empathy, cooperation and mutual reliance are tacitly weeded out.

Miller notes: "The experience of taking a course in microeconomics actually altered student's conceptions of the appropriateness of acting in a self-interested manner, not merely their definition of self-interest" (Miller 1999, p. 1055). This indicates that the canonical assumptions of economics in turn influence the views of its practitioners. Being taught the assumptions of neoclassical economics one might become prone to expect others to act in a self-interested way.

Like a chameleon, we may take on the moral colour of our surroundings. This emphasises once more the importance of the moral environment. To consideration of the idea of situated learning or legitimate peripheral participation. Brown et al. assert that knowing "is inextricably *situated* in the physical and social context of its acquisition and use. It cannot be extracted from these without being irretrievably transformed" (Brown Collins and Duguid 1988, p. 1). In language, we often use what are termed indexical word: this, here, there, above, since and so on; words that only have meaning in a context. Here is an example showing the shift in meaning depending on the context: "*This* is where I want to be;" "Now *this* book;" "*This* is not what I mean."

Perhaps situatedness is important also for ethical proficiency. Reber talks of the need for immersion in the subject matter. He finds that "maximal learning takes place when there is some direction provided at the outset about the underlying nature of the environment. However, this explicit element has little or no educational effect without the extended immersion ... We do not learn about the underlying structure of complex environments by explicit instruction; we must experience the patterns of covariation for ourselves" (Bruner 1996, p. 4).

This would indicate that the environment must have some structure or coherence, or there would be nothing to internalise. It is also tantamount to saying that moral integration tends to perpetuate itself. A chaotic or multi-structured environment may presumably make it impossible to get a coherent sense of the moral fabric. Somewhat flippantly, one may say that it would be equivalent to using many different objects to imprint on at the same time in one of Konrad Lorenz's experiments with imprinting.

Observing and imitating may not be enough; one might not really be able to mimic the actions. If it was that easy to extract what a master does, then knowledge engineers would have an easier time. To Lave and Wenger apprenticeship involves *"participation* as a way of learning – of both absorbing and being absorbed in – the 'culture of practice' ... From a broadly peripheral perspective, apprentices gradually assemble a general idea of what constitutes the practice of the community" (Lave and Wenger 1991, p. 95).

What we notice here is the indirectness and interactiveness of the process of learning, the telling without telling, the slow indirect communication involving more than words. This indirectness may also be very important for the development of individual morality. If one is taught to follow a very precise and strict set of moral rules, demanding only a modicum of knowledge and thought, then by acting according to those rules and prescriptions one may act as if one possessed a morality. However, this would be a kind of exterior or imposed morality, a morality that could be changed by any rule-giving authority, not a morality that was anchored inside the individual, sustained by deep seated feelings, making one want to avoid embarrassment, guilt, shame and dishonour.

The indirect form makes for ambiguity and openness, an ambiguity and openness the apprentice has to cope with. In such a learning environment, the learner must not only find the concrete solution to his or her problems through an effort involving analogies and so on, but must also be able to generalise from the examples, thereby constructing what will become general moral strands anchored in his or her own mind. In some ways, this means that everyone must perform some kind of hermeneutic effort in order to act on concrete problems and in order to evolve the kind of generalisation that manifests itself in certain coherent inclinations and attitudes. Knowledge is most useful to the learner "when it is 'discovered' through the learner's own cognitive efforts, for it is then related to and used in reference to what one has known before" (Bruner 1996, p. xii).[12]

When I see what an example means, this may be a result of interaction with others, and furthermore this hermeneutic effort may take place tacitly, somewhat analogous to the "learning" of an artificial neural network. "The other respect in which these norms are social is that other people are important for enforcing them, by expressing their approval and, especially, disapproval. These sanctions can be very strong" (Elster 1989, p. 99).

Through the transmission processes discussed here we actively become inculcated with strands of the moral fabric. This is the indirect and tacit process that imperceptibly transmits and upholds values, norms and behavioural habits from one generation to another.

Changing Values

Several years ago, a funny South African movie called *The Gods Must be Crazy* showed how behaviour and values may rather suddenly get out of sync and create a potential for change. In the movie an empty coke bottle is thrown out of an aircraft and found by members of what is presumably a merry band of bushmen. To this band of bushmen, the idea of individual possessions had hitherto been unknown. The coke bottle is seen as a gift of the Gods. Everyone wants to touch and keep this magic thing. They become selfish, and fights develop between individual members of the band of bushmen.

To our hero, the gift becomes something that destroys the band – and the most basic values – and he realises that it may represent the wrath of the Gods. He gets hold of the bottle and steals away with it, apparently believing that if he can just give it back to the Gods the problems of the band will be solved. He throws the bottle high into the air in order to give it back to the Gods, but has to realise that this does not work, as it keeps coming back. Other attempts turn out to be just as futile. Not giving up he travels far and wide in order to get rid of the bottle.

The story shows how an external event, the coke bottle falling out of the sky, may influence the behaviour of a band of bushmen and lead to changes in behaviour, which clashes with some of the most centrally held values of this band.

New scientific and technological developments lead to new modes of behaviour, resulting in conflicts with existing ethical norms. New problems created by such development may be handled in a more or less *ad hoc* way within existing values, but that may not solve the problem. Often the *ad hoc* suggestions for solving the dilemmas vary wildly, from condoning the new modes of behaviour to total rejection, where one attempts to cling to old modes of behaviour; for instance, by attempting to throw the proverbial bottle up into the air. This may lead to an increased awareness of something being wrong and contribute to a feeling of a latent need for change. Attempts to solve this conflict may lead to a series of changes or amendments to the more superficial rules and values, accompanied by changes in behaviour. This may not be enough; the *ad hoc* changes may sooner or later lead to clashes with deeply held values and beliefs.

167

Over time, far-reaching changes in behaviour and in the more superficial value layers may accumulate and lead to an erosion of some of the traditional norms and values, belonging to the deeper layers. This may be a slow process, with no change apparent on the surface. At some point in time, the steady trickling down of changes in more superficial ethical rules and norms may cause fundamental changes in deeply rooted values and inclinations. These changes may accumulate like the tension in regions prone to earthquakes, resulting most of the time in only small tremors on the more superficial level; these, at times, can lead to large-scale changes, big quakes, which might represent times of social upheaval.

Time and time again we land ourselves in a kind of value quagmire, out of which we somehow have to pull ourselves by our own hair – or is it the bootstraps – repeating one of von Münchhausen's more improbable feats, readjusting our own behaviour and beliefs in ways that neither of us could have foreseen.

In order to understand how these processes may actually lead to changes in our tacitly held, self-evident values, we have to look for an explanation of such changes. Elsewhere I have tried to create a general model that might help us understand the process of change (Petersen 1985; Petersen 1998). The model operates with a series of stages coupled with what might be visualised as a kind of spiral repeated again and again through time. These steps are:

1. gap between expectations and experiences, latent conflict;
2. catalysis, voice and open value crisis;
3. instability with rivalling attempts to explain and create solutions;
4. convergence around new solutions;
5. new stability, characterised by stereotyped behaviour.

Gap between expectations and experiences, latent conflict. The model asserts that there might be long periods and subject areas with no big value problems. Existing values are taken for granted, as tacit habits, not to be thought about and discussed too much.

Then a coke bottle drops out of the blue sky and suddenly we experience clashes between what we tacitly believe in and the results we experience. New possibilities are opened, new conflicts arise and it is as if the existing moral weave is torn up in places. In a study of social organisation and change it is argued that the equilibrium of a social organisation is disturbed "when processes of disorganisation can no longer be checked by any attempts to reinforce existing rules" (Thomas 1966, p. 5).

Suddenly we realise that there is a gap between our deeply held values and, for instance, the physical and biological possibilities we now face. In a sense, a gap opens up between our collective expectations, based on deeply held values, and the behaviour we witness, which does not fit the expectations any more. This may not matter much as long as only a few isolated individuals feel the discrepancy. Only if there is a general feeling that something is wrong will there be a potential for change.

Individually, they may not feel able to do anything about it; it may just be something that leads to frustration and a vague uneasiness. They may not even know what this uneasiness is caused by. Remember, for instance, the uneasiness one may have felt reading the transcript of the interview of Dr Hans Münch, our concentration camp doctor. He himself may have felt an uneasiness, but perhaps also felt that it was an uneasiness only he could feel. This uneasiness means that the value clashes may exist only in a latent form.

Catalysis, voice and open value crisis. What is needed to go from a latent to an open crisis is discovering that others have the same feeling. Until then it is merely a personal affair.

What is needed is a catalyst in the shape of a voice, which makes the latent and individually felt value clashes explicit, and makes everyone suddenly realise that many others have felt the same way. In other words, voicing the problem, whether verbally, or in other ways, seems to be necessary for individually felt latent value clashes to coalesce into a collective expression of a value crisis.

Someone voicing only his or her own individual misgivings will not lead to any sense of value crisis if there is no widespread latency already. Such voices will yell into an empty void if the timing is not right or if they are the only ones to see a problem. Presumably there will be many cases where there is no latency and the voice will be lost in the cacophony of voices heard all the time.

Voicing may in itself depend on someone having the independence of mind and courage to dare voice their suspicions. It may mean that individuals or groups put their jobs, their reputation and even their sanity at stake, without being sure of having any effect whatsoever. Perhaps they are the whistle-blowers, not only of faulty O-rings, of corruption in the EU Commission, Enron business practices, or the abuse of prisoners in the Abu Ghraib Prison, but of more widespread problems in organisations and societies. Like the first grassroots movements waging battle against the dominating opinions and existing laws for the sake of something bigger, the environment or the future of humanity.

Instability with rivalling attempts to explain and create solutions. Realising that there is a crisis many may initiate trial-and-error attempts to solve it.

A period with many different trial-and-error attempts will be a confusing period, where awareness is raised, explanations and suggestions abound and solutions are sought in many different directions. Inspired by divergent value systems, by comparisons with others and presumably also by a process like the one through which our robot ants happened to stumble upon what outside observers may see as a solution. Many attempts may turn out to be erroneous, like throwing the bottle into the air.

One may well ask whether change could be a result of a majority decision, based on careful consideration and a free discussion, or whether change is a result of actions carried out by determined individuals or very motivated, small, coherent groups. Some views favour the careful consideration and free discussion approach, like the discourse ethics and the notions of ethics as defined by consensus, but they run counter to the layer model that we have established. And in this view, the discourse models are in a way self-defeating because in order to carry out a discourse we already have to share fundamental notions, knowledge and cultural skills. This means that a discourse on a certain concept demands at least a prior, partial agreement upon the use of the concept.

Convergence around new solutions. How is "the right solution" then chosen? And what is a right solution? Does it happen according to some Spencerian "survival of the fittest principle," according to which the behaviour and norms we adopt will be the ones that fit the problem best? Or does the selection of changed behaviour and norms involve a rational choice?

Again the layers model may be invoked. The suggestion being that in order to become accepted new rules and norms must fulfil a few conditions related to these layers of our minds.

First and foremost, the suggested solutions have to be seen as an answer to a latent conflict.

Secondly, the new solutions must in some way connect to the corpus of deeper norms and values that prevail in our minds, in ways that we cannot fully explain. This is presumably a condition that will only be fulfilled after several trial-and-error attempts. We cannot see all the connections between the old and the new before we attempt to practise the solutions, and then they may have to be revised again and again.

Finally, some of the responses may seem to solve the problem, and the solutions converge around these responses. Perhaps we may compare this convergence process with the circular Woozle hunt of Winnie the Pooh. The first time round Winnie follows his own footsteps, the next time the number of footsteps has doubled and next time there are even more. Perhaps we con-organization ourselves in our beliefs by running the same circle again and again, seeing from the number of footsteps that more and more people are apparently doing the same, thereby con-organizationing us in the values we believe in.

No one would be able to design the new values in advance, using existing knowledge. The solution emerges as a result of the process. Changes are not brought about by design or as a result of long deliberations. Several rivalling alternative solutions may be spreading at the same time with their own accompanying bandwagon effects. Through the bandwagon effects the bigger and faster alternatives get even bigger and even faster, and the smaller and slower alternative processes get smaller and slower.

This may explain how new solutions, consisting of changed behaviour, and new norms select themselves. The process does not demand that there is a lot of pondering and discussion, it does not demand a long process of deliberation and some rational consideration involving everybody. It does not demand a pronounced discourse about ineffable things. What it does demand is someone speaking up and someone with a will to attempt to change the existing order.

New stability, characterised by stereotyped behaviour. After a while, awareness of changes may wane. The changed values and changed behaviour may have become generally accepted and adopted. They may become codified in the form of a law or, more commonly perhaps, just a new habit, like the grammaticization mentioned earlier. A habit whose origin is soon to be forgotten, but also a habit that may influence us and through the learning process also the next generation, on a far deeper level than we shall ever be able to understand or explain. That means the circle is closed and we are again responding to value problems in a fairly stereotyped fashion, without ever thinking about decisions as representing value problems.

Reflections of a Collective Conscience

Even if one accepts the attempt to explain the way we reweave and add to the moral fabric, one might still ask whether the new values and the behaviour we adopt may not actually lead us down an incline, into a spiral of increasingly bad behaviour, while still seemingly keeping the values consistent. What is to assure us that the values we adopt are better in any way than the old? There seems to be an abundance of historical examples showing that changes are not always for the best. Just recall Dr Hans Münch's arguments. Perhaps we are living with a precarious balance between up and downwards spirals?

The somewhat evasive answer may be that there is no one else but us to judge whether the new values are better or worse than some alternative values. In that sense, like Nietzsche asserted, all values are human made: "Verily, men have given unto themselves all their good and bad. Verily, they took it not, they found it not, it came not unto them as a voice from heaven."

Taken at face value this view may lead us into a kind of relativism in which strange things might be valued or robbed of all value. Would that not be an argument for a kind of Nazi ideology, robbing certain people of all their human value, degrading them to "Untermenschen", like the view found in the interview with Dr Hans Münch?

From this discussion it ought to be evident that I believe such an argument would be wrong. Here some of the most important reasons are restated.

First of all, when we looked for the emergence of the moral fabric, we discovered what might be termed universal conditions for morality, universal conditions that may be presumed to be important for the survival of not least the human species.

Secondly, we must remember the discussion showing that our most basic values may only be seen when we don't see them, meaning that they are out of reach of everyone. They are to be found in what we (Petersen 2002;

Petersen 2003) elsewhere have called Großvater's Zopf, the collective experience and the collective unconscious generated through all human history, and preserved as inclinations and deep values that are transmitted through generations. We will have difficulty in substituting these inclinations and values with some arbitrary ones freshly made.

Finally, these basic values act as an anchor on attempts to move values beyond certain limits. They are the basic values that new values and behaviours have to fit onto, more or less consistently, like new sentences to existing grammar. The basic values give rise to the uneasiness, the bad conscience, the somatic reactions and so on and it would be difficult to outrun these collectively.

To conclude, there may, perhaps, be a very solid, but invisible foundation, enabling us to judge that Dr Hans Münch and many others with him, even today, have lost that anchor.

Notes

[1] Swedish Television interview made in 1981 with Hans Münch, a former doctor and SS-Untersturmführer in the Auschwitz camp. The excerpts are taken from Internet pages found at: http://www.nizkor.org/ hweb/people/m/muench-hans/swedish-television-interview.html

Another example can be found in the transcripts of the Nuremberg trials, for instance, the statements by the former camp commander at Auschwitz, Rudolf Franz Ferdinand Höss, or in some of the German laws of that period, for instance, the law against mixed marriages (Aryans and Jews): Gesetz zum Schutze des deutschen Blutes und der deutschen Ehre. Gesetz vom 15 September 1935 (Reichsgesetzblatt I S. 1146)

[2] The story was found at http://www.journalism.co.uk/news/story795. shtml.

[3] The discussion is based on my book *Beyond Rules in Society and Business* (Petersen, 2002/2003).

[4] See for instance Bonabeau, E., Dorigo, M., & Theraulaz, G. (1999).

[5] http://education.mit.edu/starlogo/ See for instance simulations experiments involving ant like creatures searching for food or sorting material into heaps.

[6] Hume said it like this: "By the conjunction of forces our power is augmented: By the partition of employments, our ability encreases: And by mutual succour we are less expos'd to fortune and accidents. 'Tis by this

additional *force, ability* and *security*, that society becomes advantageous" Hume (1740/1969, p. 537).

[7]   See also the discussion in Turner (1969/1982).

[8]   "Without deep seated value and morality we would have no society, and with no attempts to maximise and gain an individual advantage we would not have experienced the phenomenal economic and material development seen in Western societies. It stands to reason though that certain values and norms must be more basic than others if we are to uphold a society, and that these values must somehow curb the REMM-like [Resourceful, Evaluative, Maximising Models] behaviour presumed by economic models." (Petersen 2005, p. 6).

[9]   Perhaps this might fit the approach found in evolutionary psychology. See for instance Wright, (1994).

[10] See also Harris (1998).

[11] See also results form experiments involving the so-called Ultimatum games, for instance in Sigmund Fehr and Nowak (2002).

[12] Perhaps this might involve a kind of casuistry, or case based reasoning, as argued by Jonsen, and Toulmin (1988).

References

Axelrod, R. (1984). *The Evolution of Cooperation*. New York: Basic Books.

Axelrod, R. (1986). An Evolutionary Approach to Norms. *American Political Science Review, 80*(4), 1095-1111.

Bates, E. (1984). Biograms and the Innateness Hypothesis. *The Behavioral and Brain Sciences, 7*(2), 189.

Bonabeau, E., Dorigo, M., & Theraulaz, G. (1999). *Swarm Intelligence: From Natural to Artificial Systems*. NY: Oxford University Press, Santa Fe Institute Studies in the Sciences of Complexity.

Brown, J. S., Collins, A. & Duguid, P. (1988). *Situated Cognition and the Culture of Learning*. Palo Alto: Institute for Research on Learning, 2550 Hanover Street, Palo Alto, CA 94304.

Bruner, J. (1996). *The Culture of Education*. Cambridge, MA.: Harvard University Press.

Bybee, J. (1998). *The Evolution of Grammar*. Paper presented at the Symposium "Darwinian perspectives on the origins of language" AAAS, Philadelphia, February 1998.

Cahn, E. (1955). *The Moral Decision: Right or Wrong in the Light of American Law*. Bloomington, Indiana: Indiana University Press.

Copleston, F. (1994). *A History of Philosophy vol. v*. New York: Doubleday.

Dahrendorf, R. (1959). Class and Class Conflict in Industrial Society. London: Routledge.

Deacon, T. W. (1997). The Symbolic Species – The co-evolution of language and the brain. New York: W.W. Norton.

Dunn, J. (1988). *The Beginnings of Social Understanding*. Cambridge: Blackwell.

Durkheim, E. (1957). *Professional Ethics and Civic Morals*. London: Routledge & Kegan Paul.

Edney, J. (1979). The Nuts game: A Concise Commons Dilemma Analog. *Environmental Psychology and Nonverbal Behavior, 3*, 252-254.

Elster, J. (1989). *The Cement of Society – A Study of Social Order*. Cambridge: Cambridge University Press.

Goldstein, J. (1999). Emergence as a Construct: History and Issues. *Emergence*, 1, p. 49.

Gouldner, A. (1971). *The Coming Crises in Western Sociology*. London: Heinemann.

Harris, J. R. (1998) The Nurture Assumption: why children turn out the way they do. London: Bloomsburry.

Hayek, F. A. von. (1955), *The Counter-Revolution of Science: Studies on the Abuse of Reason*. London: The Free Press Collier-Macmillan.

Hayek, F. A. v. (1962). Rules, perception, and intelligibility. *Proceedings of the British Academy, 48*, 321-344.

Hofstadter, D. R. (1987). *Gödel, Escher, Bach: An Eternal Golden Braid*. Harmondsworth: Penguin.

Hume, D. (1740). *A Treatise of Human Nature* (1969 ed.). Harmondsworth: Penguin.

Jonsen, A., & Toulmin, S. (1988). *The Abuse of Casuistry: A History of Moral Reasoning*. Berkeley: University of California Press.

Jung, C. G. (1953/78), *The Structure and Dynamics of the Psyche, Collected Works* 8. Princeton, NJ: Princeton University Press.

Laugsforordning for slagtere 1623, Kjøbenhavns Diplomatarium.

Lave, J. & Wenger, E. (1991). *Situated Learning – Legitimate Peripheral Participation* (1996 ed.). Cambridge: Cambridge University Press.

Miller, D. T. (1999). The Norm of Self-Interest. *American Psychologist, 54*(12), 1053-1060.

Moon, D. J. (1994). Constructing Community – Moral Pluralism and Tragic Conflicts. Princeton University Press.

Parsons, T. (1951). *The Social System*. Glencoe: The Free Press.

Petersen, V. C. (1985). *Planlægning og Samfundsudvikling – fra 30'erne til idag* Stockholm:Nordplan, Nordiska Institutet för Samhällsplanering.

Petersen, V. C. (1998). *Tacit ethics – creation and change*. Aarhus: CREDO working Paper, Department of Organization and Management, The Aarhus School of Business.

Petersen, V. C. (2002). *Judging with our guts – the importance of an ineffable social grammar*. Working paper. Aarhus: CREDO/ The Aarhus School of Business.

Petersen, V. C. (2002/2003). *Beyond Rules in Society and Business*. Cheltenham, UK • Northampton, MA, USA: Edward Elgar.

Petersen, V. C. (2005). *The otherworldly view of economics – and its consequences*: CREDO working paper, The Department of Management and International Business, The Aarhus School of Business.

Rawls, J. (1971*). A Theory of Justice*. Cambridge, Massachusetts: Belknap.

Sigmund, Karl, Ernst Fehr and Martin A. Nowak, 2002. The economics of fair play. *Scientific American* 286(1) (Jan.): 81-85.

Stone, C. (1987). Earth and other Ethics: The Case for Moral Pluralism. Harper & Row.

Sugden, R. (1986). The Economics of Rights, Co-operation and Welfare. Oxford: Blackwell.

Thomas, W. I. (1966). *On Social Organization and Social Personality*. Chicago: University of Chicago Press.

Turner, V. W. (1969/1982). The Ritual Process – structure and anti-structure. New York: Aldine.

Waal, F. d. (1996). Good Natured – The origins of right and wrong in humans and other animals. Cambridge MA.: Harvard University Press.

Wright, Robert. 1994. The Moral Animal: The new science of evolutionary psychology. NY.: Vintage.

Chapter 9

CULTURAL FACTORS IN THE ECONOMIC
DEVELOPMENT OF CHINA AND EGYPT

Sven Burmester

Introduction

Why is China doing so much better than Egypt in its economic development? That question obviously has complicated answers, but my research in
the countries themselves supports the idea that cultural factors play a decisive role. This article is an attempt to support this view.

Over the last 25 years, economic growth rates in China and Egypt have
been significantly different. In the case of China, the average has been about
10%, while Egypt has experienced a growth rate of about 5%. At the same
time population growth has continued to decline in China, while despite
some decline it has remained high in Egypt. That has left China with average per capita economic growth rate of 9% and Egypt with 3% or less. Despite the global economic crisis, there is good reason to believe that this
situation will continue for decades, leading China to developed country
status in the near future, while Egypt at best will be a middle income country.

I have been responsible for World Bank development efforts in both
China and Egypt. I was in charge of the Bank's education projects in China
from 1983 to 1987, and I was the Bank's representative in Egypt from 1992 to
1995. I also led the UN Population Fund in China and North Korea from
1997 to 2001. At present, I still spend time in both China and Egypt every
year as guest professor at Sichuan's Population Institute in Chengdu and as
external scholar at the library in Alexandria.

What are the major differences between the Chinese and Egyptian development experience? My main point is that traditional World Bank analysis is
not sufficient to explain what is readily observed as a gap in development
capacity and ability between China and Egypt.

I cannot consider my efforts in this area of culture and development as
academic, in the sense of dealing with hypothesis and proof. But I do believe
that my experience over several decades in both Egypt and China lends
some credibility to my conclusions. Many economists are nervous about
dealing with a factor like culture, because culture by its very nature cannot
be quantified. Economists want numbers. Even though statistics in the social
sciences are notoriously unreliable, economists often choose bad numbers

over no numbers at all. I believe that common sense often outweighs unreliable numbers.

The World Bank mainly looks at development as caused by three fundamental factors: macroeconomic stability, good governance and investment in human resources.

Macroeconomic stability

Macroecomic stability basically consists of keeping inflation low, the exchange rate stable and the interest rates low. That will ensure both domestic and foreign investment. Growth should follow. Over the years, China has done better than Egypt, but not significantly so.

Good governance

Laws and regulations are not very different in the two countries, but the extent to which they are observed by the population is better in China than in Egypt as witnessed by Transparency International. Most effects in this area are very hard to quantify. Corruption is high in both countries, but tends to be qualitatively different. In China, corruption essentially consists of buying influence. To be able to do so, money is obviously necessary, and money is most easily acquired in the market. Thus productive behaviour is necessary before influence can be bought. In the Egyptian case, the corrupt individual seeks power, and when power is obtained, money is extorted. Production levels remain the same.

Transparency International makes an index of corruption in most of the world's countries. Not surprisingly, Egypt and China are not among the most honest of countries, ranking 105 and 72 respectively. Noteworthy though, that China is faring better than Egypt.

Investment in human resources

This area mostly deals with investments in health and education. The amounts invested per capita in Egypt and China tend to be larger in Egypt than in China. Statistics in these areas are notoriously unreliable, particularly as far as private investments in health and education are concerned. But Egypt, by and large, has invested more than China, but with lower results.

In health, Egypt has focused too much on investment in hospitals, whereas China has concentrated on public health and primary health care. Investment in hospital care is expensive and tends to disproportionally benefit the better off. Primary health care with focus on water, sanitation and healthier life style gives a much larger bang for the buck.

In education, Egypt has spent too much on higher education, neglecting the fundamental importance of teaching every child to read and write.

China has done the opposite. The quality of education at all levels is dismal in Egypt with poorly qualified teachers and too few textbooks of acceptable quality. Often teachers do not show up for classes but rely on private tutoring for their income. The situation is vastly different in China where teachers still are well educated and revered by students and parents. Textbooks are available to all.

So the results in the two countries are vastly different. This is only marginally seen in indicators like life expectancy and levels of education, but is obvious in the quality of human resources.

The importance of cultural factors

One is forced to conclude, that the traditional World Bank explanatory factors are not sufficient to explain the difference in development outcome between China and Egypt. Cultural factors are not sufficient to explain the entire difference either. Climate, geography, and natural resources clearly also play a role. My contention is that culture is also important and at times decisive.

I will look at three cultural factors and describe their influence on economic development. They are: language, history and values.

Language

Chinese and Arabic are both complicated languages. The first question is, therefore, whether a complicated language, per se, is an impediment or an incentive for development. It takes a Chinese child five hours a day, six days a week for nine years to learn the mother tongue to an adequate level of proficiency. This is more than twice what it takes a Danish or an American child to reach the same level in their languages. The much harder effort by the Chinese child is likely to lead to higher levels of stamina, ability to memorize and self discipline than for the Danish or American child.

One could, of course, argue that an easier language, such as Danish or English, might lead to an ability to deal with instructions and to easier comprehension. I cannot exclude this possibility. But more interesting is the question of why Chinese should be helpful for development, when the equally difficult Arabic does not have the same influence?

The harsh answer is that Arabic is not a living language. If you ask an Egyptian what is his mother tongue, he will answer Arabic. You will get the same answer from a Moroccan. But they cannot understand each other. What they are speaking are, in fact, two different languages, Egyptian and Moroccan. However, they are not written languages. Written Standard Arabic is a modernised version of the Koranic language and is not a mother tongue for anyone or widely spoken. When educated Arabs get together they tend to speak either English or French. Basically the situation is similar to the Middle Ages in Europe, when Latin was the equivalent of Standard

Arabic and Italian, Spanish and French corresponded to what the Arabs themselves call dialects. The difference is that Italian, Spanish and French today are written languages. Egyptian and Moroccan are not. It stands to reason that not having a colloquial written language could be hindering development.

History

History in itself would influence development. Egypt has had a harsher colonial experience than China and for many Egyptians this is a standard excuse for the lack of development. The metaphor for colonialism is used for Israel's behavior in the Middle East and equally considered a major factor in the slow development.

But the major influence of history is the way it makes individuals look at development. The West basically has an optimistic outlook, most strongly in the United States where any presidential State of the Union message will conclude that America is doing well and will be doing even better tomorrow – although president Obama may be a little more hesitant on that score. It is likely that such an attitude will lead to optimism, vision and self-confidence, which then will influence development positively.

The Muslim view is pessimistic and backward looking. The hope among Islamic fundamentalists is to return to the state of affairs at the time of the Prophet in the 7th century. The advent of Islam led to impressive development during the caliphates of Damascus and Baghdad, followed by the Safavid, Moghul and Ottoman empires. Decline, however, set in in the 16th century and it has been downhill ever since. It is very unlikely that this backward looking view of history will have anything but a negative influence on development.

History dominates Chinese thinking. This was clearly evident at the opening ceremony of the Olympics in Beijing where 5000 years of Chinese history and achievements were celebrated. There have been tremendous ups and downs in Chinese history, with dynasties coming and going. Eventually, however, the Chinese people has always prevailed and reached new cultural and material heights. This has inspired patience and self confidence in the Chinese population, attitudes which are clearly helpful for development.

Values

Muslim values are based on three sources, the Koran, Hadith (traditions around the Prophet) and the Sharia (Islamic law). Islam is not only a religion but a political ideology, which pretends to have answers as to appropriate action and behavior under all circumstances. This leads to rigidity, to what one could call an "either-or" attitude, which is not beneficial for development.

There is also in the Muslim value system very little interest in material development. The world will end at Doomsday and the most important fact for any Muslim is to prepare for this event where judgment will be metered out to all the believers, based on how well one in this life has followed the five columns of Islam: citing the creed, praying five times a day, giving alms to the poor, fasting during the month of Ramadan, and performing the pilgrimage to Mecca. These endeavours may be good for the soul and eternal life, but are nor helpful for material development.

Chinese values also have three sources: Confucianism, Daoism and Buddhism. Confucianism inspires the individual to learn and to improve himself throughout life. It also insists on discipline and authority, obedience towards the ruler, the father, the husband, the older brother and the older friend, but the ruler at the same time has an obligation to be helpful toward his subjects.

Obedience towards authority implies that the authority knows better than the subject. If that is not the case, the subject has the right to overthrow the ruler. In Confucian language, the emperor loses the Mandate of Heaven. Also important is the concept of lifelong learning and personal responsibility. This in combination with the Yin-Yang concept, which is a complimentary rather than a conflict creating idea, creates an ability to hold opposite views in the same individual and at the same time. One could call this a "both-and" attitude which gives the necessary flexibility for the continuous change of modern life.

Daoism is in many ways the opposite of Confucianism, insisting on enjoyment of life, the pleasures of love, wine and food, or just sitting by the river writing poetry. The Chinese can, with their "both-and" attitude, be Confucianists and Daoists at the same time. Contrary to the Muslim rigidity, this gives almost total flexibility. In China, you can be a capitalist and a communist at the same time; you can be a plumber and a baker; so if there is a need for more plumbers, the bakers will start working as such, without interference from labour unions. All this is essentially based on the Yin-Yang concept.

Buddhism has had less influence in modern times, being basically a pessimistic ideology, that considers life as suffering. In the present extraordinary progress in China, such an ideology recedes in the background. It was not mentioned at all in the spectacular show at the Beijing Olympics where both Confucianism and Daoism played a central role.

The influence of the Chinese and Egyptian models

China is an example for the developing world. Everyone wants to copy the 10% growth rate, that China has experienced over the last 25 years. Vietnam is on its way to doing so.

The question is whether the Chinese model in fact is replicable. I doubt that will be the case, outside what one could consider Greater China –

China, Korea, Japan, Vietnam and Burma – where the Confucian ideology prevails. The Chinese experience is embedded in Chinese culture and that is unlikely to be copied outside this Greater China area where it already exists. It should be noted, however, that China is now showing its "soft power" by establishing Confucian institutes in all the major capitals of the world where Chinese language and culture is taught.

In many ways, the Chinese themselves consider their experience unique. They do not share the missionary zeal of the West with its insistence on human rights and democracy, nor of Islam with its truth, based on the concept of one almighty God.

No-one would be eager to copy the Egyptian experience. In development terms, it is a failure. This is most directly seen in the low economic growth rate, but perhaps more significantly in the attitude of the Egyptian people. Pew Research Centre examines attitudes of ordinary people around the world. The Chinese consistently rank very high in happiness with their lives; Egyptians, on the other hand, are dissatisfied with a majority of young men wanting to leave their home country, given the chance.

The next 50 years

China is set to continue at its very rapid pace and reach developed country status within a few decades. Egypt will stumble along with inadequate policies and will only truly develop if Islam in its present form is reformed, particularly with respect to its attitude towards women.

Might there not be impediments to Chinese type growth? The most obvious would be resource scarcity caused by climate and environmental change to such an extent that economic growth is halted. I assume that the present crisis, although harsh, will only have a temporary effect.

Climate change is influenced by three factors: the technology used in production (the cleaner the technology, the less the harm done to the environment), the size of consumption (the higher, the more damage) and population (the more we are, the more we will pollute).

There are great gains to be made in using appropriate technology. Science and research continues to make progress in this area. But there are limits as to how much we can do with improved technology. Whatever we come up with, there will still be an influence on the environment, and there will still be a limit to how far we can grow.

There will always be differences about the time-frame. Are we talking about the near future before reaching the limit, or is it a matter of hundreds of years? Nobody knows the answer to that question, but it would be prudent to assume that fairly rapid damage could take place. The situation is similar to buying fire insurance in one's house. Fire is unlikely, but if it occurs, it is good to have the insurance.

The insurance in this case would come from limits on consumption and population. It is very unlikely that consumption can be voluntarily limited.

The governments of the world, even in the richest countries, still deal with ensuring economic growth as the most important element for staying in power. Most recently, this has been evident in the election in the United States. Yes, there is a recession with negative growth, but the government still considers long term growth its ultimate goal.

So we are left with population as the key factor in controlling environmental damage. The fewer we are, the less we pollute. And we are becoming fewer in two major areas of the world, Europe and Japan on the one hand, and China on the other.

I lament the fact, that in Europe and Japan at least, we complain about the population decline which is already taking place. To my mind this is a God's send; we should praise the couples that decide to have no children, rather than punishing them over the tax bill and supporting the couples who have three or more children.

China has the right attitude towards population. With present fertility rates, China's population will peak in a couple of decades, and then fairly rapidly decline to about 800 million Chinese a hundred years from now. China has used harsh policies to control its population. But preventing half a billion Chinese from being born is clearly the most important step in world history towards protecting the environment. China deserves praise and not blame for its handling of the population issue.

Conclusion

Egypt and China are vastly different. Egypt can only be seen as a negative model. The incompetent government, the discrimination against women, and the horrible quality of education, all pointed out by the Arab Human Development Report in 2002, prevent Egypt from attaining per capita income levels that will give ordinary people a reasonable standard of living. Reform is required. And that may very well include religious reform, because Islam, to some extent, is responsible for the three problems pointed out by the report.

On the other hand, China is the shining example for the rest of the developing world. With appropriate policies, good governance, and intense investment in human resources and science and technology, China is well on its way to joining the rich world.

ABOUT THE AUTHORS

Magdalena Andrałojć is Assistant Professor at the Labour and Social Policy Department, Poznan University of Economics, Poland. Her research interest focus on international human resource management and culture differences – mainly in the field of compensation and reward system. She has participated in many international research projects including *The socio-economic determinants of citizens' work life attitudes, preferences and perceptions, using data from the continuous web-based European Wage Indicator Survey (WOLIWEB)*, VI Framework Programme of EU. E-mail: m.Andrałojć@ue.poznan.pl

Sven Burmester is cand.scient. in organic chemistry from the University of Copenhagen and has a Master's degree in economic development from Princeton University. He has been the representative of the World Bank in Egypt and of the United Nations Population Fund in China and North Korea. He is currently a guest professor at Sichuan Population Institute, a visiting scholar at the Library of Alexandria and an adjunct professor at Aalborg University. Email svenburmester@hotmail.com

Malene Gram is Associate Professor at Aalborg University, Denmark. She is the head of the Cross-Cultural Programme at the University. Her research focus is on cross-cultural communication and market communication from both business-to-consumer and business-to-business perspectives. She has published in journals such as the *Journal of Marketing Communications, Journal of Consumer Culture* and *Young Consumers*. Email: gram@ihis.aau.dk

Hans Gullestrup is Professor Emeritus at Aalborg University. His research work is in mainly on intercultural understanding between and within organizations operating in different parts of the world. He has extensive research and consultancy experiences and has worked in different countries including Greenland, Polynesia (especially Samoa), India and China. Email: gulle@business.aau.dk

John Kuada holds Grundfos Chair Professorship in International Business and Intercultural Management at Aalborg University, Department of Business Studies. He has an extensive experience as a business consultant and training advisor in areas of management, marketing and cross-border inter-firm relations in Europe and Africa. He is author and/or editor of some 10 books on management and internationalization of firms and has written over 100 articles in refereed scholarly and professional journals on a wide range of international business issues including international marketing, intercultural management, leadership and strategy. He was the founder and former editor of *African Journal of Business and Economic Research* and founder and current editor of *African Journal of Economic and Management Studies* (published by Emerald) **Email:** kuada@business.aau.dk

Verner C. Petersen is Docent (Senior Associate Professor) at the Department of Management, Aarhus School of Business, University of Aarhus. He is the leader of CREDO (Centre for Research in Ethics and Decision-making in Organisations). His research focus is on value-based leadership and self-organisation. His latest book is on *Errings of the Welfare State* (Vildveje i velfærdsstaten Denmark; Informations Forlag 2008). Email: vcp@asb.dk

Dorthe Serles is Director of Brazbiz, and international consultancy company which specialises in advising Brazilian companies on entering and operating in European markets. She holds MSc degree in international business economics from Aalborg University. Her research interests include operating in distant markets and organizational energy. Email: dorthe.serles@brazbiz.dk

Olav Jull Sørensen is a professor of International Business at the Centre of International Business (CIB), Department of Business Studies, Aalborg University. He initiated the establishment of the centre in 1984, including an MSc. programme in International Business. The Centre is globally connected with university partners in both develop, developing and transition econo-mies. Professor Sørensen's major research interests include *the internationali-zation process of companies; the global industrial dynamics and the global value chain,* and *government-business relations.* Email: ojs@business.aau.dk

INDEX